Celebrate

the

DIVINE FEMININE

*Reclaiming Your Power with
Ancient Goddess Wisdom*

EARTH
The Body of the Goddess

JOY F. REICHARD, M.A., C.C.H.T.

Endorsements for
Celebrate the Divine Feminine:
Reclaim Your Power with
Ancient Goddess Wisdom
Earth: the Body of the Goddess

SEE WHAT OTHER powerful women are saying *about Celebrate the Divine Feminine: Reclaim Your Power with Ancient Goddess Wisdom—Earth: the Body of the Goddess.*

"Joy has compiled a powerful & fascinating treaty to the Divine Feminine. A herstorical breakdown of the ancient Goddess wisdom that unfolds the secrets we hold within us. Puzzle pieces that connect contemporary women to the roots of Mother Earth. Insight, guided visualizations and powerful rituals enable us to experience the Sacred Feminine, and translate the yearning into being, the unknown longing into personal transformation."
~Jennifer Duchene, Author of *Le Chic Cocoon, 7 Steps to Creating Your Selfish Space.* www.ChicCocoon.com

"Joy Reichard has created a feast for women (and men) who are hungry for true spiritual nourishment from the Divine Feminine. Her book is filled with a rich array of critical information, spiritual teachings, and guidance for reconstructing and renewing a vital new/old religious form that the world truly needs today. Hers is part of the next generation of wonderful work propelling women's spirituality forward."
~Marguerite Rigoglioso, Ph.D., Author, *The Cult of Divine Birth in Ancient Greece* and *Virgin Mother Goddesses of Antiquity,* http://cultofdivinebirth.com

"Because of her own intense personal journey from patriarchy to the Divine Feminine, Joy Reichard understands the need for women's rituals. Here, she offers rituals in honor of the goddesses of earth, together with supporting myths and cultural information. A useful resource!"
~Patricia Monaghan, Author of *The Encyclopedia of Goddesses and Heroines,* Editor of *Goddesses in World Culture*

"In my own search for self discovery, I found this book to be an extremely insightful, thoughtful and well-written expose on the 'Her-story' of the

Goddess. Joy offers inspiration and tools for gathering women and wisdom to Celebrate In Her Name. Through the reading of the myths of the seven goddesses, one receives daily direction and support. *Reclaiming your Power with the Ancient Power of the Goddess* will expand your awareness of the Divine and broaden your spirituality. Joy's inspirational tools will empower women to create their own circles to gather and Celebrate In Her Name."

~Ana Maria Sanchez, M.S. Empowerment Counselor and Bestselling Author *Girl From The Hood Gone Good*

"In a time where female leadership is needed the most, this book can offer a new and expanded version of walking into our ancient Goddess Wisdom to revolutionize our communities, families as well as ourselves. Tailored for women seeking a way back to re-connecting with a new version of Feminine Power. Creatively weaving the past with the future, Joy Reichard masterfully shares an engaging journey that allows you to explore the meaning of Goddess Wisdom and learn ways to integrate this powerful energy into your life."

~Stephanie Marie Beeby, M.S., Intuitive Business Consultant, Ping! Intuitive Communications, http://www.ThePowerofPing.com

"Blending ancient myths of feminine archetypes and deities with practices and rituals for today, Joy Reichard guides us to discover and celebrate the wisdom energies of the divine feminine. This is a time that has long been in the making, begging us all to reintegrate both feminine and masculine energies, and to embody and honor the Divine Feminine. This book offers a rich offering with personal rituals and practices to help do just that."

~Tambra Harck, Transformational Mentor, Author, Speaker, TambraHarck.com: Spiritual Mentor for Visionary Leaders, EmergentWomen.com: Women in Transition

"Joy has offered a wonderful combination of both Goddess reverence, ceremony and research. Through her personal journey to the Goddess, she now shares the knowledge she has received from her practice with the rest of us. What a blessing to have this wisdom available to the community."

~Leilani Birely, Teacher, Author, High Priestess, http://www.daughtersofthegoddess.com

CELEBRATE THE DIVINE FEMININE

Reclaiming Your Power with Ancient Goddess Wisdom

Earth - The Body of the Goddess

JOY F. REICHARD, M.A., C.C.H.T.

Published by Bush Street Press
237 Kearny Street, #174
San Francisco, CA 94108
415-413-0785

Printed in the United States of America

Table of Contents

Acknowledgements

IT IS INCONCEIVABLE to me how any work of art could be produced without numerous people in the wings offering support, guidance, suggestions, and advice—solicited or not—along the way. This has certainly been true for me. My first acknowledgement goes to the Divine Feminine herself who has guided me at every step. I credit her with leading me to the amazing work of Marija Gimbutas and whetting my desire to enter the Women's Spirituality program at New College in San Francisco. There I was introduced to and inspired by great leaders of the Women's Spirituality movement such as Vicki Noble, Elinor Gadon, and Lucia Chiavola Birnbaum. The co-directors of the program—Dianne Jennett, D'vorah Grenn, and Judy Grahn—instilled in me the importance of being academically grounded in both my research and the work that I present. I owe D'vorah and Dianne an immense debt of gratitude for the many versions of my thesis they tirelessly waded through. It was this tedious learning process that enabled me to formulate and complete this work for publication.

I am indebted to my dear friend and writing mentor, Lillian Barden, who gave me the idea of putting the personas of the Divine Feminine into four different books based on the elements of earth, air, fire, and water. Her suggestion helped me take what seemed like an insurmountable venture and break it down into a manageable project. She has encouraged me during the whole process and volunteered to act as my initial proofreader and editor. I am also grateful to my friend Kirsten Weiss who volunteered to pitch in and help with the editing, as well as make some great suggestions for my website. I have come to appreciate her writing and marketing skills as she has taken over various aspects of promoting my work. I am forever grateful to Karin Lautsch who volunteered hours of her time to read, proof, process, and offer valuable feedback on this manuscript. Her suggestions led to additional, but much needed, revisions—making this a more engaging and less academic piece of work. I also want to thank Shirley Brim and Dasha Bogdanova; they too spent time reading my manuscript and offering their encouragement and feedback.

Words fail me in expressing my thanks to Shannon Dawn who has helped me produce the In Her Name Circles since August 2008. Not only has she supported me in setting up and taking down the circles, but she has actively participated in all aspects of their creation. She has contributed to both the planning of the rituals and guided visualizations, and has helped me work through areas in which I felt blocked, or simply had run out of insight and creative ideas.

How can I thank Kristal Jensen enough for her artistic contributions to my book, CD covers, and the graphics for my website? She took my suggestions and created an imaginative presentation far beyond my expectations. I also want to thank the San Mateo Unitarian Universalist Congregation for hosting my In Her Name Circles since February 2008. Many of the members have either participated in the circles, or have offered words of encouragement and support. I feel deep gratitude for this wonderful community.

I can't forget several dear friends who have offered words of encouragement and support along the way. They include Elizabeth Barton, Marguerite Rigoglioso, Dasha Bogdanova, Claudia Harkte and, of course, Shannon Dawn.

I am extremely grateful to Lydia Ruyle, artist, author, and scholar emeritus on the Visual Arts faculty of the University of Northern Colorado in Greeley, Colorado where the Lydia Ruyle Room of Women's Art was dedicated in 2010. Lydia came to my aid when I needed images for the Neolithic Goddess section. She graciously allowed me to use her sketches of the Venus of Willendorf, the Venus of Laussel, the Mother Goddess of Catal Hoyuk, and four of her glorious "Spirit of the Divine Feminine" banners. To include them is especially meaningful to me, as I traveled through Turkey with Lydia and her banners. We visited Ephesus, the Neolithic site of Catal Hoyuk, and many other fascinating goddess sites. Please visit her website at www.lydiaruyle.com to view her entire collection.

How to Use this Book

CELEBRATE THE DIVINE Feminine: Reclaim Your Power with Ancient Goddess Wisdom - Earth: the Body of the Goddess may be used in a variety of ways. You may read it purely for the information, or it can be used as a facilitator's guide if you want to gather women to honor the Sacred Feminine. This book is rich in material; anyone who desires to learn more about the goddess and how to celebrate and honor the Divine Feminine in all her manifestations will find it to be a great resource.

Part I focuses on just who is the Divine Feminine, why she matters, and her history or "herstory," which dates back to the Neolithic Era, when our ancestors viewed the earth as the mother. There are also many contemporary images of the Divine Feminine, including Mother Mary, Mary Magdalene, Saint Bridget, and Our Lady of Guadalupe (who is featured in this book). To date I have researched twenty-four different Divine Feminine personas. They have been divided into the elemental categories (earth, air, fire, water) that I feel are most appropriate for their characteristics, based on their mythology and the research I have conducted. Of course, many of the goddesses may fall into more than one elemental category, and I acknowledge that this is my personal point of view.

Part II is a facilitator's guide for those interested in leading their own circles. It contains information gathered from my personal experience with the In Her Name Circles that I developed and began leading in 2008. Though the book was conceived to help others facilitate their own circles, it is absolutely possible for each section to be explored individually. For individual work I suggest getting a journal or notebook, as allowing yourself time to process and write down your thoughts will help you integrate the material and thereby receive maximum benefit from it.

Preparation for leading sacred circles, I quickly came to realize, begins weeks, if not months, in advance. I offer many tips and suggestions gleaned from my personal experience. Setting up an altar for each circle helps members focus their intentions on the Sacred Feminine persona being honored, as well as setting the right intention for each event. Suggestions for constructing altars and a Table of Correspondences are found in the section on "Creating Altars." One additional suggestion would be to encourage participants to bring something to place on the altar as this will help them connect even more deeply with the process. Instructions for casting the circle to create sacred space can be found in the section on "Circle Format."

Part III contains a variety of information on seven Divine Feminine personas. It may be read for enjoyment, or used to create a circle of your own. This first book focuses on the female deities that I feel resonate most closely with the element Earth: the Neolithic Goddess, Grandmother Spider, Demeter and Persephone, Hecate, Lakshmi, and Our Lady of Guadalupe. Some of the information is presented from a feminist point of view and may vary from the "established" version. Since history is usually written from the dominant perspective, which in our Western culture is the patriarchal viewpoint, the female story was often submerged or considered insignificant. As this book celebrates the Divine Feminine, I feel it is valuable and appropriate to point out when the information has been filtered through the male or patriarchal lens and, therefore, may not be the full story. Hence I prefer to use the more feminized term "Herstory."

Each section on a Divine Feminine manifestation includes:

❖ Invocation poem

❖ Information on the "herstory" and mythology of the Divine Feminine persona featured

❖ Guided visualization

❖ Ritual or experiential piece

❖ Music suggestions for the ritual and guided visualization

❖ Integration activities

❖ A Table of Correspondences on the colors, foods, and relationships or items that are special to each Goddess

❖ Recommended circle agenda

The presentation on each goddess may be read, paraphrased, summarized, or simply used as background information. A ritual for each circle is provided that focuses on a specific theme such as release, transformation, compassion, self-acceptance, abundance, etc. These rituals can be used within the circle or performed independently for other sacred events (see the section on rituals for a more thorough explanation). Recommendations are also made for activities or journaling to facilitate integrating and processing the material.

Connecting with the Divine Feminine is a personal experience and often elicits deep inner stirrings of memories, thoughts, and insights. To encourage these personal connections I have included a guided visualization with each section. Digital recordings of the guided visualizations are available for a nominal fee on my website (www.celebratedivinefeminine.com). Each visualization is from 15 to 20 minutes in length and gives you an opportunity to have your own unique experience with the different Divine Feminine archetypes. I have included the text, so feel free to make your own recordings as well. It is also possible to have one member read the visualization while others journey inward.

Please enjoy the information and insights on the Divine Feminine which I have provided. The creation of each circle, and subsequently this book and the three to follow, has truly been a labor of love. It is my hope that this book will be both a guide and an inspiration to encourage you to create your own circles to celebrate In Her Name.

PART I

Who is

THE DIVINE FEMININE

and Why She Matters

1. Reclaiming the Divine Feminine

IN CULTURES WHERE the masculine is considered divine, women tend to be perceived as "other." For example, despite all the efforts over the past 50 years to balance out inequalities, women still earn less than men. This is still true even though US women, according to the A.T. Kearney research firm, control some 80 percent of all household spending decisions. Growing up, I observed the same dynamics within my own family. My father, a Methodist minister, was the dominating authority. My mother was sweet, nurturing, and...submissive. What she modeled of womanhood was not always useful as I tried to negotiate through two turbulent marriages. Nor was it helpful when I tried to navigate in the business world. I remember almost resenting being a girl. Oh, I liked being female—I just wanted more power.

According to Gerda Lerner, a pioneer in women's history and author of *The Creation of Patriarchy*, patriarchy is a creation of history. In a patriarchal society such as our Western culture, masculine ideals of competitiveness, assertiveness, objectivity, and logic are more highly valued than feminine traits such as subjectivity, nurturing, and being in touch with feelings and emotions. Lerner states that patriarchy is a new cultural system, when we take into account the entire evolution of humankind. She suggests that originally social systems were matrifocal (focused or centered on the mother) and matrilineal (succession follows the mother's line). She focused her research on ancient Mesopotamia, in contemporary Iraq, since it was the civilization which provided the earliest written historical records. What Lerner reports is a gradual transition from an older and more matriarchal society to one that was more patriarchal, including a shift from a matrilineal to a patrilineal kinship organization. There was also a shift in their creation myths, the religious stories of how the world was created. As the myths of the male gods and their prestige increased in importance, those of the female goddesses decreased. Over time women's rights and prestige also declined (p 7). Some of the earliest recorded laws written (the Code of Hammurabi c. 1780 BCE) include laws that regulated the rights of women. In contemporary Iraq women still have far fewer rights, and less freedom and mobility, than we have in the West. The residual effects of this great cultural shift that occurred thousands of years ago are still being felt today.

Part of my own healing and growth involved my search on how to be a strong woman in a patriarchal society. I was fortunate to study and work with Jungian therapists who introduced the idea that we are each both male and female.

Karl Jung was a product of his time, which means that his theories were developed through the prevailing patriarchal lens of his time. Recent credible arguments exist which hypothesize that gender is more a designation of power and status in our society than a sexual designation. Other credible theories debate whether sexual traits and behaviors are the result of nurture versus nature, or social conditioning versus our human genetics. These discussions are interesting and of great importance, but I would like to table them for my second book. For this discussion Jung's theories, which hold that every human possesses both female and male qualities, enable us to open up a dialog on gender and gender traits.

Our Western culture categorizes certain behaviors and traits as being either feminine or masculine. Men, according to Jung, possess the anima— their inner feminine—which helps them feel compassion and love; to be reflective, intuitive, and receptive; and even to be understanding of the irrational. Women possess the animus—their inner masculine—which provides courage, determination, and a willingness to face challenges and to venture out into the world. A person is in balance when they have a good relationship with both their masculine and feminine selves. According to the Kabbalah (a study of human ego development from the instinctual body to spiritual awakening), when this balance is achieved internally it results in the Sacred Marriage, or Hieros Gamos.

A healthy balance between the feminine and masculine parts of our selves is necessary in order to operate in today's culture, and here is why this is so. Typically feminine traits in our Western culture are considered more receptive and holding in nature: women receive the seed and create a container—their womb—which is a safe place for the seed to gestate. When new life is born they both nourish and nurture it while it grows. Therefore feminine qualities are: receptivity, compassion, and the inclination to nourish and nurture. Women tend to be relational and are more in tune with and expressive of their emotions, which is supported and encouraged by our culture. Women are fertile with potential. These qualities are considered to be more passive in nature. Masculine traits involve more action and force: doing, competitiveness, assertion, thrusting, and domination. Men are out in the world taking action and doing things. Both feminine and masculine traits are equally important, with neither being more important than the other.

Knowing that as women we also possess the inner masculine we can befriend and learn to work with the positives and shadow aspects of both our feminine and masculine sides. This can help us navigate in our individual worlds, and in the world of business. For example, when I am in session with a client I am in my feminine side as I create a safe container while listening compassionately. I rely on my feminine intuition to facilitate the process. While in the feminine, I am receptive and holding space. When I am doing my finances, however, or when I am working on my business strategy, or negotiating a lease, or working on an advertising campaign, I am in my masculine side: I am doing, I am active, I am out in the world. Being comfortable with both your feminine and masculine sides helps you flow from one aspect to the other more easily and effectively.

Girls who have had good feminine and masculine modeling, i.e. positive parent figures, develop both healthy masculine and feminine sides and are able to navigate more effectively in the world. When there is poor modeling resulting from dysfunction and/or divorce, death, abuse, substance abuse, etc., then children have difficulty cultivating a balance within. Feminine receptivity can devolve into submissiveness, or nurturing qualities can devolve into the co-dependent caretaker. Alternatively, a daughter who views the male as more powerful can over-identify with the masculine and be accused of being abrasive, aggressive, or "the bitch." Or she can try to align herself through marriage or relationships with the masculine as a way to get power rather than developing her own strengths and empowerment. In other words, there are a lot of opportunities for imbalance and internal disharmony which can disrupt our outer lives.

Despite recent advances our society still perpetuates dysfunction; if this weren't true then why are retail bookshelves so full of self-help books? Many women and men need a new myth, a new model of the feminine to whom they can relate. A new model of the masculine may also be important, but that is not within the scope of this work, as my focus is on the Divine Feminine. What are needed are myths, stories, and opportunities that meet women's and men's relational needs for community, ritual, empowerment, and emotional support.

WHY THE DIVINE SHE?

If there were a "Divine She," girls and women alike would have a Sacred Feminine role model they could emulate and identify with. Too often female public figures are vilified by the media: Sarah Palin, Hillary Clinton, Nancy Pelosi, Gloria Steinem—each one is a powerful female role model. Yet someone who is reserved, timid, or shy might be hesitant to emulate someone who is publically attacked and ridiculed on a regular basis. By observing the many manifestations of the Divine Feminine we can study different feminine traits and characteristics. We can safely "try them on," reflect on what it might be like to be assertive like Artemis the Huntress, who is confident and courageous in defense of the vulnerable. For others the Sacred Feminine might take the form of Mother Mary, who embodies compassion, protection, and unconditional maternal love. By identifying with the archetypes of the Divine Feminine and using their myths and legends as teaching stories, opportunities are created for women to identify and connect with a source of divine power, compassion, and protection while cultivating previously untapped inner strengths and resources. By using images of ancient female deities, women can re-discover valuable models to emulate and develop new personal myths that will facilitate healing their feminine selves from wounds caused by our collective patriarchal heritage.

Each woman is unique, and each woman changes as she matures, struggles, heals, and becomes wiser. A Divine Feminine persona exists for all these stages, to which we can gravitate as we need them. Identifying with the Sacred Feminine is a means for a woman to feel the divine within so she can more readily embrace her own qualities of strength, beauty, and power.

The Divine Feminine was key to my own healing; to my own acceptance and love of self as a woman. Part of my work as a hypnotherapist is to help other women heal by achieving greater conscious awareness, self-appreciation, and self-care. For example, recently a woman (let's call her Dianne) came to see me for a "Goddess" guided visualization. She was dangerously overweight and her doctor had recommended Dianne go on a medically formulated but restrictive diet. We worked on many issues together, and she had come a long way, losing about 40 pounds with me. Dianne was quite concerned, however, about her ability to adhere to her doctor's directives. We created an internal Amazon warrior who moved with resolve and determination and would fearlessly battle to win. Dianne left feeling much more confident about her ability to succeed.

For another client, Rachel, who was struggling to improve her life, I often felt called to weave into her guided visualizations Our Lady of Guadalupe, who is compassionate and hears the cries of her people. Our Lady of Guadalupe first appeared when Rachel, a manicurist who aspired to be a hair stylist, was taking her exam. She had failed twice and was nervous about failing a third time. Visualizing Our Lady of Guadalupe as Rachel's protectress and guide, we were able to infuse her with a deep sense of calm and confidence. I also gave Rachel the suggestion that the answer to each problem would effortlessly float to the surface of her mind as she took the test. She passed! Rachel is now on her way to becoming an outstanding hair stylist. In another session in which Rachel was struggling with her beautiful but willful pre-adolescent daughter, I brought in the presence of Our Lady and wrapped them both in a pink mist of healing, compassion, and love. The source of contention faded away and Rachel recently shared with me that her relationship with her daughter continues to deepen and grow.

The image of Kuan Yin, the compassionate and merciful Buddhist Bodhisattva, has brought solace and comfort to many of my clients. One particular client, Deborah, has rheumatoid arthritis. She was wrestling with the meaning of life in general, and the purpose of her own life—a life which was often filled with pain. By introducing Kuan Yin to her I was able to help Deborah find peace in the present moment. Kuan Yin helped her to be more gentle and compassionate with herself, more loving towards the people in her life, and to feel more gratitude for the many simple but wonderful things life has to offer. Deborah bought a statue and created an altar to Kuan Yin, then went on to introduce the Bodhisattva to many of her friends.

There are many myths and images of powerful female deities from all cultures on the globe who can provide female-affirming archetypes for women to emulate. These women-honoring archetypes and symbols make up the composite of what I call the Divine Feminine.

The Divine Feminine, as I interpret and experience her, honors women and all things of Woman. It is the valuing of motherhood, female bodies, emotions, and feminine ways of knowing which include subjective processes and intuition. This does not exclude objective reasoning, but it is beneficial to be open to all ways of knowing and processing information— even men trust their "gut" instincts. Through reclaiming and reconnecting to the body and emotions, women who have been submissive and subordinate can begin to claim, or reclaim, their personal power, their passion for life, and a sense of the erotic. The Sacred Feminine serves as a positive model illustrating feminine strength and power that has a deep and honoring connection to the body. It involves the reclaiming of our voice, which many of us have learned to silence in order to be perceived as good and nice and acceptable, or to be good daughters, or perfect wives and mothers. Reclaiming the Sacred Feminine also involves having the courage to speak our truths. Women's circles, like the In Her Name Circles, are a safe place for women to speak their personal truths. But to speak our truth, we must first discover it! For many it has been buried deep, locked away in our subconscious. To find it may require a descent into the underworld.

DESCENT AS A MODEL FOR RENEWAL AND TRANSFORMATION

For some, embracing the Sacred Feminine may mean confronting Ereshkigal, the Sumerian Queen of the Underworld. Inanna, the ancient Sumerian Queen of Heaven, confronted Ereshkigal in her descent to the "great below," where she journeyed to discover the truth behind all things.

Ereshkigal was an ancient Sumerian goddess who, according to myth, was raped by the gods and exiled to the underworld. She is a metaphor for that part of the feminine that has gone underground. She is also symbolic of all the women who feel compelled by society to endure the wounds of abuse, rape, and incest in silence, shame, and guilt. Ereshkigal is the part of woman that is body, nature, and emotion—the raw, primal feminine energy that is split off from consciousness. She is the woman who has been derided and devalued for her instincts and intuition—a persona of death and decay. A woman meeting Ereshkigal may confront her unexpressed rage, despair, guilt, shame, regrets, or sense of hopelessness. This is where she may confront her lost dreams, her illusions, her cultural assumptions and beliefs, and the glass house she has erected as masking perfection. Confronting Ereshkigal is also a place of transformation and new life as decay becomes fertilizer for potentiality, creativity, and raw feminine power (Murdock, p 104).

Some women's search for the Sacred Feminine takes them deep into their subconscious where they confront their deepest selves—their dark side that feels shameful, violated, and impure. Hecate, the Hellenic Goddess of the Underworld, is a powerful guide for those women who choose to do this deep inner work. This can be a time of deep reflection, a time to examine each belief and assumption about themselves and the roles they play as they sort out that which no longer serves them. They may recognize old patterns and paradigms, dysfunctional behaviors, their complicity in dysfunctional relationships, their unexpressed anger for endured injustices, and their years of silence. Their former activities, friendships, careers, and relationships may no longer be compatible with who they are, or who they now want to be. When a woman is going through this process she frequently begins to assert herself. She may be perceived as being disagreeable, unfriendly, uncooperative; unwilling to serve, placate, or take care of others. For example, I realized I was going through such a deep process of transformation when I no longer wanted to take care of others. For me this was a major shift away from a lifetime of co-dependent behavior.

The Divine Feminine is all that is positive and good about women. It is what is authentic and true, which can look very different from the nice and kind girl, the perfect wife and the good mother image that our culture attempts to impose as the only acceptable experience of being female. A descent that is embraced with courage enables a woman to cut through all the cultural illusions and assumptions she has constructed around herself so she can discover her true self, which is a composite of her likes and dislike, her interests and values, her beliefs and her concept of the Divine.

The Sacred Feminine is the belief that each woman can transform. Just as the lotus grows from the muck and mire at the bottom of the pond, each woman can become the blossoming flower nourished and transformed by the debris and waste of their lives. Sekhmet, a fiery and powerful Egyptian Goddess, can pave the way for transformation. She is a woman warrior considered so mighty that her image was carried into battle by Egyptian kings. As a sun goddess, Sekhmet shines light into the deep crevices of our minds and hearts, bringing illumination and clarity.

HEALING THE WOUNDS OF WOMANHOOD

A woman in need of healing might reach out to Kuan Yin, Mother Mary, or Our Lady of Guadalupe—all Divine Feminine archetypes of compassion and mercy whose consoling presence provides comfort and support during the darkest hours. If in need of courage a woman might call upon Kali, who fearlessly fights demons. If it's wisdom and strategic thinking that's needed a woman might call upon Artemis the Huntress, or Athena, Goddess of Wisdom. If a woman is struggling with her own shadow work she might call upon Hecate or Inanna, both goddesses with extensive experience with the "underworld." If a woman needs inspiration she might reach out to Brigit -- or Saint Bridget, as she came to be called when she was appropriated by the Catholic Church. Brigit is the solar goddess of the Celts, with ties to the ancient faery folk, the Tuatha de Danann. She is the protective mother who provides for her children as well as being the fire of inspiration for poets, bards, and blacksmiths. There are many Divine Feminine archetypes which can alleviate and heal the wounds of womanhood.

One wound that affects the core of all women is that of our devalued and often demonized female sexuality. There are many beautiful, often exotic, and sometimes erotic images of the Sacred Feminine that can help with this healing. There is a part of Woman that is erotic: it is the sensual and sexual part of feminine nature. It is the part of Woman that enables us to feel vibrantly alive and passionate about our interests and the people in our lives. Unfortunately, the sensual part of Woman has been misinterpreted and wounded by our patriarchal heritage. Our passionate feminine nature has been trivialized and cheapened into a marketed commodity. The messages that the media and marketing industry communicate to our young women about themselves and their bodies are beyond regrettable. Young women should know their bodies are sacred and beautiful; to be honored, not objectified. From Aphrodite we learn there is more to the erotic than just sexuality—it is about being alive and passionate about what we are engaged in. In Aphrodite's earliest images she was the Mother Goddess who inspired a zest and vitality for life as well as fertility and sensuality. The persona of Aphrodite and other Divine Feminine archetypes can help to reinforce the message of the sacredness of our bodies.

In my practice I assist women in achieving their full potential by helping them identify and remodel mental blocks which keep them stuck in low self-esteem and/or low achievement. In the monthly circles I lead on the Divine Feminine I am reclaiming the history and mythology of goddesses from around the globe. I find that each woman relates to different Divine Feminine personas, which can change based on what is going on in their lives. By presenting different manifestations of the goddess, it is my hope that each woman will find an image of the Sacred Feminine with whom she resonates.

Using the mythology, legends, and art of the feminine that has come down through history as teaching stories enables women to reclaim pride in their femaleness in all its strength, beauty, and sensuality. A woman can and should have a strong sense of self; be confident, self-assured, and assertive. At times she may draw on her inner masculine for the power, assertiveness, and energy to take action or to move forward. A woman can also be that fierce mother bear when it comes to protecting her young. For example, I recently had a client who was in the midst of a contentious custody suit. We activated her mother bear energy, which helped her stay focused and in her power so she could withstand the brow beating and intimidation by her ex-husband. We also strengthened her connection with her Mother Mary energy so she could appropriately transition into her understanding, compassionate, nurturing self when interacting with her children—especially with her son, who was quite damaged by the custody struggles.

The Sacred Marriage

A word about the masculine as it relates the Divine: the power of the masculine is not to be used to dominate and control, but to protect, to lead, and to be the good steward. The male who is in touch with his Divine Masculine respects and protects the feminine and her young. When he connects with his inner feminine he can also be compassionate, nurturing, and caring, because the awakened male is in balance with his inner feminine. As time goes by I am seeing many more awakened males who actively participate as true partners with their wives in all aspects of their family life. Both my sons are able to connect with their inner feminine when they interact with their children, and it is touching to observe them being nurturing as well as protective. We women do our menfolk a great service when we support and encourage their exploration of their feminine sides.

As we as women open to the Sacred Feminine and learn to come into harmony with our animus, the end result—the reward—is the Sacred Marriage, both within our inner landscape as well as without. To get there we need to first reclaim the Divine Feminine so she can take her rightful place beside the Divine Masculine.

In closing, I hope you will be curious enough about these marvelous and rich mythological female archetypes to develop your own relationship with the Sacred Feminine. Some of you might identify with only one; others—because there are so many and it is hard to choose—may want to begin a relationship with your own pantheon of Divine Feminine personas. As you begin to build a relationship with the Divine Feminine you might notice subtle shifts within yourself as you become more compassionate like Kuan Yin, or more willing to let go of your delusions like Kali. You may also find that, like Sekhmet, you are staying in your power more easily as you fight for a cause, or are becoming more sensual and passionate about life and your lover, like Aphrodite.

As your own feminine nature is being nurtured by the Sacred Feminine—as the divine spark of the Goddess within is ignited and nurtured—an internal healing with your inner masculine, your animus, will begin to occur. With it a positive shift in your relationship to men, and with the men in your life, will take place. It happened for me, and I have seen this remarkable shift and healing of relationships occur in the lives of others. The Divine Feminine fosters love, compassion, and healing. She changes those she touches, and those she touches changes!

To appreciate the importance of the Divine Feminine we need to understand Her story, and the reasons how and why the Great Mother Goddess was eclipsed by God the Father during the rise of patriarchy. In the next section I offer a "herstory" of the goddess.

2. History or "Herstory" of the Goddess

I REMEMBER PLAYING Mother Mary at the crucifixion while performing in a Sacred Dance group in college. I danced to a rowdy audience as Mother Mary receiving Jesus' body as it was taken from the cross. During the sacred dance I transitioned from the grieving mother into the young Mother Mary cradling her infant son while singing a lullaby. As I transitioned back to the horror of my son's death, the rowdy auditorium quieted to a hush; many eyes were wet with tears. At that time I was unaware of the ancient theme locked in our collective memories of the Great Mother and the death and rebirth of the Divine Child. It was not the artistic quality of my performance that caused the hush in the audience. My performance, however, triggered that ancient collective memory linking us all back to our earliest roots; connecting us to our common humanity. In the circle on Mother Mary we explore this connection, the direct link of Mother Mary to the Great Mother Goddess as Queen of Heaven.

Women and men around the world honor the goddess in simple, everyday acts; sometimes consciously and sometimes unconsciously. Every time we recycle we honor the earth, which is the body of the Goddess. When we listen compassionately to a friend, we serve as Kuan Yin or Our Lady of Guadalupe who listens to the worries and cries of the people. When we lovingly tend our gardens, or when we decorate our homes with branches, leaves, nuts, or gourds we are reminded of the abundance of the ancient Great Mother, Gaia. When we regard our own beauty in a mirror we honor Amaterasu, who returned the brilliance of the sun back to the world when she saw her own radiance reflected in the mirror. The knowledge of the Great Mother is ingrained in all of us. Even those who are completely secular respond with understanding when I refer to the Earth as the Mother.

For 5000 years the Divine has been perceived as masculine and our cultures have been patriarchal. This is evidenced by the predominance of references to the Divine as male in the sacred text of all the major religions; i.e. male pronouns and references to God as King, Lord, Shepherd, and Father. However, the Divine was not always considered to be male. Archaeological evidence of Neolithic cultures (ranging from the 7th to the 4th millennium BCE) has revealed evidence of a goddess-worshipping civilization that was widespread throughout Europe, Anatolia, and into western China and northern Africa (Gimbutas, *The Language of the Goddess*, pvii).

Being somewhat a scholar I wanted to know if, why, and how our culture transitioned from a goddess-centered culture to a god-centered one. Because of the religious environment in which I was raised I initially resisted—as many Westerners do—the idea of worshipping the goddess. Yet I continued to question because I also felt the deep wounds that some of you as women, or the women you know, may carry. I have felt guilt and shame about my sexuality. I have been paralyzed by low self-esteem and have shriveled up when faced with confrontation or conflict. I have lashed out with uncontrollable rage when I could no longer suppress my emotions. I have undergone the descent, like Inanna, deep into the underworld of depression, and spent many days and nights suspended on the meat hook reflecting on the source of my despair. Then, when life was at its darkest, the Divine Feminine was revealed to me and I knew there was another way. At first I was uncertain, but as I researched the goddess I was amazed at the wealth of material. Since then I have tried to understand all that I could about the Sacred Feminine. Who was she? What happened to her? Will bringing her back into the world's consciousness heal my wounds, the wounds of the feminine collective, and the wounds of the world? My search led me to the ancient mother, and to the source of the wounding of feminine sexuality.

NEOLITHIC MOTHER GODDESS

In retelling the "herstory" of the Divine Feminine we must go back to the beginning. Judy Grahn, in her book *Blood, Bread and Roses*, traces the development of consciousness and civilization back to menstruation—yes, menstruation! Our ancestors were curious and tried to explain the seeming capriciousness of their environment. Eventually women observed that their menstrual cycles entrained, or followed, the cycles of the moon (women who spend a great deal of time out in nature tend to menstruate during the moon's dark phase; this is called "entraining" with the moon). Carvings of lunar movements have been noted on a bone fragment that dates back 30,000 years; interestingly, these moon notations spiral in a serpentine path (Baring, p 43). Observing that the moon and menstruation were both cyclical in nature led our ancestors to notice other cyclical patterns. The serpent sloughs its skin and hibernates—or appears to die—during the winter, and is "reborn" in the spring. The moon dies and is reborn thirteen times in a calendar year. Women entrain with the moon and slough their blood without a wound. When the cyclical bleeding stops, it often signals that the woman is pregnant and there will be new life. Because women were observed to be the source of new life, the great source of all life became the Great Mother.

During the Neolithic period in Old Europe, Anatolia, North Africa, and the Middle East the goddess was worshiped in her earthly form as the snake goddess. The snake embodied fertility and the cycles of nature: life, death, and renewal. Art depicting snakes as goddesses was a popular theme in Old Europe. A classic image depicts her sitting almost regally in a meditative or yoga pose.

Birds and eggs were plentiful and an important food source during the Neolithic Era, so the ancients also began to venerate the bird as another aspect of the goddess. Bird goddesses and eggs are the most common representation of animals in Neolithic art. Numerous small figurines with the form of a human but with the head of a bird have been recovered (Gimbutas, *The Living Goddesses*, p 14). Migratory birds—like the snake, moon, and menstruation—also follow the cyclical rhythms of nature.

Archaeological evidence indicates agrarian Old European culture was matrilineal and matrifocused. Property and land were passed down through the mother's bloodline from mother to daughter, while young men most likely left their mothers' houses in search of adventure as well as mating opportunities. The communities were built around the temple, which acted as the center for both crafts—such as weaving, pottery, metal work, and baking—and worship. The temple owned the land, and the priestesses and wise women governed the social life of the community. The temple complex also served as the administrative center where records, wealth, and communal resources were stored. The culture was highly ritualized and symbolic, and the people believed all life came from the goddess. Their daily lives were tightly interwoven with their spiritual lives (Gimbutas, *The Living Goddesses*, p 74-75).

The success of the Neolithic community depended on the fertility of their land, their domestic animals, and themselves. The sacred women of the temples, the sacred prostitutes, took their lovers from the community or from travelers. To the people of the ancient world the act of sex was holy, so holy that it took place within the temple. The goddess was the creatrix; she was honored as the patron deity of sexual love. Sexual pleasure and the sexual act celebrated the goddess and her gifts, and the sexual nature of the sacred prostitute was an integral aspect of her spiritual practice. Because these people lived close to nature, their deities were nature deities. Dependent on nature's abundance, they perceived their deities as having the capacity to provide or deny abundance. Desire and sexual responses were seen as both pleasing to, and a blessing from, the goddess. New life resulted from sexual union, so these early people connected erotic passion with potent regenerative energy. Sexual union became a fertility ritual, or fertility magic, which was consecrated within the temple as a sacred and holy act. With praises of thanksgiving and supplications to the goddess the

29

sex act was considered a sacred offering; an act that was honorable, pious, and pleasing to women, men, and the goddess (Qualls-Corbett, p 29-30). Over time the role of sacred prostitute became an honored position within the community, and the earliest laws, such as the Code of Hammurabi, protected her rights and good name (Qualls-Corbett, p 37).

The worship of the Goddess of Love and her sacred prostitutes become an accepted tradition within the goddess communities of Old Europe and the Near and Middle East. A festival called Aphrodisia, which is most likely a remnant of older Neolithic traditions, included a ritual in which the priestesses of Aphrodite freely offered their sexual favors. This festival was celebrated all over Greece well into the first century CE. Similar celebrations occurred in Greece's Near Eastern neighbors and have been documented in Babylon, Syria, Palestine, Cythera, Sicily, Cyprus, and Turkey, as well as in various Phoenician cities such as Carthage and Corinth (Wikipedia).

The Old European culture began to collapse with the influx of semi-nomadic tribes of people called Indo-Europeans who, it is believed, originated somewhere in the eastern steppes of modern-day Russia. The migrations began in the borderlands around 5000 BCE and continued in three great waves for the next 2000 years. It was a slow but steady process of invasion. The Old Europeans had few weapons beyond their hunting implements; they were a gentle, peaceful, earth-loving agrarian people who had no prior need for fortifications. Consequently they were easy prey for the equestrian Indo-Europeans, who were more warlike, patriarchal, and hierarchical. With the collision of these two cultures Old Europe was transformed. What resulted was almost a "marble cake" mixture of Old European and Indo-European culture, mythology, linguistics, and history. Archaeologists today are still trying to piece together the minutiae of puzzle pieces that the earth is offering up (Gimbutas, *Civilization of the Goddess*, p 352).

ANCIENT SUMER AND THE ADVANCE OF PATRIARCHY

According to Gerda Lerner, a gradual transition to a more patriarchal culture began around the fourth millennium BCE. Lerner focused her research on ancient Mesopotamia, the civilization which has provided the earliest written historical records. She found that the establishment of religious and state bureaucracies changed the economic structure and the way kinship was organized. Thus from 3100 to approximately 600 BCE, the Sumerian culture transitioned from the older matrifocal and matrilineal culture to a patriarchal society. There was also a shift in religious observances as the male gods became more dominant (p 7).

In her book, *The Creation of Patriarchy*, Lerner makes several main points about how the status of women diminished during this transition, resulting in a lack of female control and decreased power in women's ability to dictate and run their own lives. I have summarized several of her key arguments here (p 7-10):

❖ Appropriation and control over women's sexual and reproductive capacities by men occurred prior to the development of private property and a class society (p 8).

❖ Domination, hierarchical structures, and slavery originated with men who learned to dominate women in their kinship groups and who enslaved the women of the peoples they conquered.

❖ Some of the earliest law codes institutionalized women's sexual subordination *and were enforced by the government!* (italics added) These laws were enacted in Mesopotamia between the eighteenth to the eighth century BCE.

❖ Even after sexual and economic subordination, some women still occupied important positions, such as priestesses, seers, diviners, and healers.

❖ The dethroning of the powerful goddesses and their replacement by a dominant male god occurred in most Near Eastern societies following the establishment of a strong imperialistic kingship…. the Mother-Goddess was demoted and transformed into the wife/consort of the chief male God.

❖ Hebrew monotheism attacked the widespread cults of various fertility goddesses. Genesis appropriated the Great Mother's role in the creativity and procreativity of all life and assigned it to Yahweh, who was "Lord" or "King." All female sexuality other than for procreative purposes became associated with sin and evil.

❖ The covenanted community established a contract with God. Because it was assumed that females were subordinate, women were excluded from both the metaphysical and earthly covenant. Their only important role became that of mother.

❖ This symbolic devaluing of women in relation to the Divine becomes one of the founding metaphors of Western civilization. The other founding metaphor is supplied by Aristotelian philosophy, which assumes as a given that women are incomplete and damaged human beings of an entirely different order than men. It is in the creation of these two metaphorical constructs, which are built into the very foundation of the symbol systems of

Western civilization, that the subordination of women comes to be seen a 'natural,' hence it becomes invisible.

ENHEDUANNA, HIGH PRIESTESS TO INANNA, QUEEN OF THE HEAVENS

During the 1920s archaeologists recovered what is considered the first text record of religious beliefs. They were written by Enheduanna, High Priestess of Sumer and daughter of Sargon, the ruler of Sumer. She wrote poems and hymns both in adoration and supplication to Inanna, Lady of Largest Heart, the Sumerian Queen of Heaven. Elements of the religious beliefs expressed by Enheduanna have appeared in other Middle Eastern cults such as the Canaanite Asherah (with implications of Eve), and the Phrygian Cybele, which supports the theory that the Mother Goddess religion was widespread throughout the Middle East and Anatolia (Meador, p 155-156).

According to Betty De Shong Meador—Jungian analyst, teacher, and author of *Inanna, Lady of Largest Heart: Poems of the Sumerian High Priestess Enheduanna*—Enheduanna describes four aspects of Inanna in rich detail: warrior, priestess, androgyne, and lover. As the Warrior, Inanna is the destructive force of nature, the horror and brutality of war and violence, and the courage to face challenges and difficulties in life. As the High Priestess, Inanna incorporates all aspects of earthly life, from the earthbound to the celestial. She promotes the paradox that life contains all that is positive and life-enhancing, as well as its many challenges which can be life threatening. Individuals must meet their fate and attempt to surmount their challenges based on their personal attitudes, skills, and abilities (p 156-157). As the androgyne Inanna has the ability to cross boundaries, to act both like a woman and at other times like a man, as when she goes to battle. As a boundary crosser Inanna has the ability to transform, to move through transitions, such as when she descends into the underworld and comes back with new insight. As the Lover, Inanna is the sexual desire and passion that generates all life force energy necessary for fertility and abundance. She is the energizing force of the entire cosmos. Enheduanna, in fact, celebrates in her poetry her own sexuality as well as the passions of Inanna, which are at times quite erotic.

Due to the importance of the sacred sexual act, many ancient cultures celebrated a public sacred marriage rite: the *Hieros Gamos*. The sacred marriage occurred in the spring with the High Priestess—as surrogate for the goddess—and the King, as a surrogate for her divine consort. The sexual energy produced by this rite was believed to be a potent and powerful fertilizing source for all life for the year. It ensured the success of the crops, human and animal fertility, and overall abundance. This rite also legitimized the right of the king to rule.

Some of the religious ideas and concepts which Enheduanna expressed in her writings, Meador states, have appeared in later religious traditions, such as the Tree of Life which is also found in the Kabbalah, the Jewish Mystical tradition. The cult of the Assyrian Goddess Ishtar refers to a divine power present within each individual which enables them to communicate directly with the Divine, similar to Enheduanna's very personal relationship to Inanna. This concept of the Divine which can be perceived within each individual is similar to the Christian concept of the Holy Spirit, as well as to the Jewish Shekhinah (I have a great affection for the Shekhinah, as it was through her I discovered the feminine face of God; one of the In Her Name Circles is devoted to her). Enheduanna was not only a brilliant poet and thinker, but she was also a female mystic who was inspired to write by her experience with the Divine Feminine manifested as Inanna (p 157-158).

Enheduanna lived during a time of transition -- from approximately 4500 to 2000 BCE—when Europe, the Near East, and south Asia were experiencing waves of Indo-European migrations from the eastern steppes of modern-day Russia. These invaders brought with them their sky-god and their love of war, aggression, and domination. Enheduanna's father Sargon was a powerful ruler and the first to conquer his neighbors and annex them into his growing empire. His actions contributed to the downfall of the goddess and the religious tradition that Enheduanna was attempting to uphold and protect.

As the Sky-God's popularity increased so did the power of the new priesthood. The governing councils of wise women were replaced by kingships that became "necessary" with the frequent intra-city conflicts and the external threats from yet more invading Indo-Europeans. Starhawk (a peace activist, leader in the feminist spirituality and eco-feminist movements, and author of *Truth or Dare: Encounters with Power, Authority, and Mystery*), points out that during this time power became increasingly centralized in the hands of a few, and individual freedoms diminished. This was especially true for women, who became trophies of war or were enslaved to work in the growing textile industry (p 39). War went from blood and gore between men on the battlefield, to rape, capture, and enslavement for women by warring men. Soon power became sexualized as sexuality became linked to violence and domination, especially towards women and children—those who are the most vulnerable and helpless. Male sexuality became identified with aggression and female sexuality with submission (p 203). Then war became self-perpetuating as those in power realized that war insured their continued rule and authority (p 39).

As the patriarchal invaders and their warrior-like sky-gods grew in dominance and power, they set about undermining the goddess, the matrilineal inheritance structure, and sexual freedom. In a matrifocal-matrilineal system property stayed in the motherline and was controlled by women and the temples of the goddess. Thus initially the High Priestesses were probably forced into marriage alliances in order to establish the patriarchal fathers' rights to lands and property in the eyes of the commoners. Then bit by bit the patriarchal leaders gathered more control and power. One example is the anti-sex drive lobbied by the Levite-led Hebrews—a campaign against sex which was in reality politics cloaked in morality. The reason for this was that those in power under the new patriarchal system wanted total control over women, in order to gain control of their property as well as the property of the goddess. They also wanted governing rights over the region and a guarantee that their patrilineal bloodlines were "pure." Remember, it was the Sacred Marriage that legitimized the king's right to rule, and this evolved into marriage which gave the king or husband the right to the property of women. Paternity now became a primary concern, whereas previously under a matrilineal system the father was irrelevant.

JUDEO-CHRISTIAN INFLUENCES

From the time of Moses there has been a taboo against premarital sex among the Israelites, and marital fidelity for women was strictly enforced. The Old Testament chapter of Leviticus states that transgressors were to be punished with death by stoning. The laws were so strict that this applied even in the case of rape. Merlin Stone, author of *When God Was a Woman,* suggests that the sexual customs of the ancient Mother Goddess were denounced as depraved and immoral in order to curtail the sexual activity of women and thus insure the patrilineal line and uphold the patriarchal system. The Levite priests compiled a code of sexual morality and appropriate behavior for women, while at the same time banning intermarriages with anyone outside of Judaism. If the priests believed the power and strength of women were connected to energy channeled during sacred sex, then these laws and restrictions would have been deliberate acts to cut women off from their natural source of power. Interestingly, there were no similar laws or restrictions for men! Other laws and social customs of Old Europe and the Near and Middle East were gradually altered to favor the patriarchal system that was gaining dominance. Eventually the patriarchal fathers went so far as to appropriate the myths of the ancient goddesses (p 156).

The story of the Garden of Eden -- according to John Phillips, author of *Eve: The History of an Idea*—is one example of how the myths of the ancient goddesses were appropriated and altered to reinforce the subordination of women and the suppression of women's sexual activity. In the original creation myth it was the Mother Goddess who lived in the Sacred Garden with the Tree of Life. Her wise familiar was the Serpent (remember the Neolithic snake goddess!). A Near Eastern creation myth which pre-dates Genesis tells how the Great Mother molded the first humans, both female and male, from clay and (supposedly menstrual) blood and then blew the breath of life into them.

The creation story in Genesis is somewhat different and alludes to the "fall" of humanity through the actions of one woman, Eve. In this story the first mother is no longer a goddess but a mortal female named Eve. In this version God creates a man named Adam. Because Adam is lonely, God creates Eve from one of Adam's ribs. This implies that new life came from man, not from woman, which is biologically impossible! It also usurps the natural life-giving powers of the goddess which are present in every woman.

Adam and Eve are permitted to eat any fruit in the garden except the fruit from the Tree of Knowledge. Possibly, Phillips suggests, this part of the myth is a warning to women to forgo participating in the sexual rites and the fermented intoxicating beverages used at the temples of the goddess. Eve is tempted by the snake to eat from the Tree of Knowledge, however, and ignores the warning. She then tempts Adam to eat the fruit. When Yahweh finds out he is very displeased, and both are punished: Eve and Adam are forced to leave the sacred garden. This can be interpreted as a warning, suggests Phillips, to all Israelite men to resist the temptations of women as well as the sexual rites of the goddess.

Eve's punishment for her sin, which all women now share, is the patriarchal marriage. From that time forward all women were supposed to desire only their husbands. Women must leave the garden -- or the homes of their birth—and follow their husbands. This contrasts sharply with the customs of older matrilineal societies in which women stayed with their maternal household. This change was significant because it separated women from the wisdom of their matriarchal elders and the closeness of their female kinship groups. Women were also separated from the women's collective under the goddess, thus depriving many of the ancient knowledge of herbs that controlled conception and eased the pain of childbirth. Under this new order children belonged to the father, and women belonged to their husbands.

As a result of this myth women were disparaged and blamed for centuries as temptresses, and have shouldered the responsibility for the sexual thoughts and fantasies of men. Religious leaders and those in power have continued to embellish on this myth and to appropriate others perpetuating the subordination of women.

Paul, an early leader of the Christian church, glorified virginity and spoke of the evilness of women, the foulness of sexuality and intercourse, and the merit of denying both the flesh and sensual love. He compounded the suppression of women by introducing his obsession with sin and these grievances that dated all the way back to "the original sin" of Eve. By the 4th century CE marriage came under the control of the Church. Divorce was eliminated, self-denial was glorified, and sex within marriage was considered sinful unless performed solely for the purpose of procreation. Deborah Grenn-Scott, author of *Lilith's Fire: Reclaiming Our Sacred Lifeforce*, maintains that women suffer unfairly by an internal split around sexuality that results in fear, shame, guilt, and embarrassment. Unfortunately many have internalized this shame for what was once enjoyed and celebrated in gratitude to the goddess for her gift (p 59-63).

The Midrash (a compilation of Jewish teachings that are in high regard, but not part of the Hebrew Bible) tells of another first woman, Lilith, who was made of the same clay as Adam. She refused to be dominated by Adam, however, and fled to the wastelands. Though threatened and cursed by God she refused to return, preferring loneliness to subservience. Originally Lilith was portrayed as a protecting and beneficent goddess who looked after young mothers and women in childbirth. She also symbolized love, beauty, and the erotic, which links her to Aphrodite and Venus. In her warrior aspect she resembles the Hindu Goddess Kali, and Sekhmet, the Egyptian Lioness Goddess. Lilith was demonized by the Levite Priests because she valued her independence and freedom. She was said to give birth to a hundred demons every night and to snatch young babies from their beds and devour them. It was claimed that Lilith lay in wait to steal the night emissions of men so she could impregnate herself to produce more demons. Grenn-Scott suggests that Lilith was used by patriarchy to label anyone who was headstrong, sexually alive, and independent as being in reality wild and insane, if they refused to conform or submit. Unfortunately this meant Lilith was ultimately demonized by patriarchy, along with saddling Eve with the guilt of everything that is wrong with our world. Lilith is the shadow side of women, claims Grenn-Scott, the part of women that questions authority; that feels anger and fights for justice. She is also the source of our creativity, sensuality, passion, and enjoyment; we need to embrace her and not fear her (p 35).

MEN, WOMEN, AND THE GOOD-BAD DUALITY IN WOMEN

Men are also caught in the split around sexuality, Grenn-Scott points out. Many adopt the perception of the good-bad duality in women. They want "good" women for their progeny, and they want "bad" women for fun, erotic sex, and passion (p 52). This is reminiscent of Classical Greece during the 1st millennium BCE, when the Greek laws and customs became increasingly oppressive for Greek women, until they were almost prisoners in their own homes, with no more legal rights than a minor. They were kept and traded within patriarchal Greek society to solidify family alliances and produce progeny. They frequently had to resign themselves to being ignored by their husbands, who preferred the company of young boys or prostitutes. Consequently a profitable sex industry in courtesans and prostitutes developed in classical Greece. These intelligent, educated, and beautiful women had considerably more freedom and mobility than many wives and virtuous daughters, especially those at the top of the hierarchy (Kimball-Davis, p 123-124).

Many contemporary women are still caught in the duality of wanting to "please" men and do the "good" thing, so they assume the role of perfect wife, thus surrendering their real identities. Many husbands consequently become dissatisfied with the lack of sexual eroticism in their marriage, and many women are disappointed and dissatisfied with the lack of romance—the fairy tales of Prince Charming and "living happily ever after" must be happening to someone else! Our current expectations about our social gender roles, and what to expect from ourselves and others, have set many of us up for disappointment.

The nuclear family is also in trouble. According to Vicki Noble in her book *The Double Goddess: Women Sharing Power*, the contemporary social network of the nuclear family works counter to the female biological response to danger—which, according to a recent study by UCLA, is to gather and collaborate. In American society, however, women are isolated in their homes. They are told what to wear, what to eat, and what to think by television, which has become the greatest hypnotizer of all times. "This self-destructive female passivity," which is seeping through our communities like a paralyzing virus, creates a serious problem for our survival (p 237). Noble also asserts that when women are empowered the sacred and sexual are not splintered and separate as they are now; instead they are joined, as they were during the time of Enheduanna, and earlier. The 1960's slogan to "make love, not war" was a "deeply intuitive grasp of pre-history when the Goddess ruled and women's ecstatic religion was central to every pre-dynastic civilization" (p 11). Women need to find the priestess within in order to invoke the goddess in both her warrior and lover aspect. The goddess is also mother, maiden, and wise women, and women need to wake up and embrace their own power and all that they are. They need to release the guilt and shame of Eve; reclaim their sassy, rebellious, and independent Lilith; and fight for what is right with wrathful indignation like Kali and Sekhmet.

The Goddess isn't dead. She wasn't even lost, for she remains in our collective memories, appearing in dreams and portrayed in art through the ages. She has survived in patriarchal religions as a saint (St Bridget, Our Lady of Guadalupe, or Mother Mary) or as a bodhisattva (Kuan Yin or Tara). It's just that many of us have forgotten about her; forgotten why the Divine Feminine was and is important.

The Great Mother is the source of all life, and is therefore connected to all life. Native American legends speak of Grandmother Spider or Spider Woman who weaves the world into creation. To Native Americans even the elements - rocks, water, air, and fire - are all part of the interconnected web of life. In the next section we will learn how the goddess is connected to the elements, the building blocks for all life on Earth.

SOURCES

Anne Baring and Jules Cashford, *The Myth of the Goddess: Evolution of An Image.*

Jeannine Davis-Kimball, *Warrior Women: An Archaeologist's Search for History's Hidden Heroines,*

Marija Gimbutas, *The Civilization of the Goddess: The World of Old Europe,* 1991.

Marija Gimbutas and Miriam Robbins Dexter, *The Living Goddesses,* 1999

Deborah Grenn-Scott, *Lilith's Fire: Reclaiming Our Sacred Lifeforce.*

Gerda Lerner, *The Creation of Patriarchy.*

Betty De Shong Meador, *Inanna, Lady of Largest Heart: Poems of the Sumerian High Priestess Enheduanna*

Maureen Murdock, *The Heroine's Journey: Woman's Quest for Wholeness*

Vicki Noble, *The Double Goddess: Women Sharing Power.*

John A. Phillips, Eve: The History of an Idea

Nancy Qualls-Corbett, *The Sacred Prostitute: Eternal Aspect of the Feminine.*

Monica Sjoo, and Barbara Mor, *The Great Cosmic Mother: Rediscovering the Religion of the Earth.*

Starhawk, *Truth or Dare: Encounters with Power, Authority, and Mystery*

Merlin Stone, *When God Was a Woman*

Wikipedia, *Aphrodite*, http://en.wikipedia.org/wiki/Aphrodite

3. *The Elements and the Goddess*

ACCORDING TO EMPEDOCLES, a 5th Century B.C. philosopher, scientist and healer, all matter is comprised of four root elements: earth, air, fire and water. He believed these elements not only had physical manifestations or material substances, but also contained a spiritual essence. Today these elements are still believed to contain and express the energy of all life forms and have become important symbols in women's spirituality and other earth-based spiritual traditions. These elements are necessary for human life, have both positive and negative aspects and are interconnected in both enhancing and diminishing ways. For instance the planet earth without water to moisten it, without fire to warm it and without air to surround it would be lifeless and uninhabitable.

Earliest humans perceived the Mother Goddess as the Creatrix, the source of life, death and rebirth. The elements are essential for human life, and the Mother Goddess is associated with each element.

AIR, THE BREATH OF THE GODDESS

The element of air in many mystery traditions is associated with the East, the direction of both sun rise and moon rise. Therefore, the element of air is associated with freshness, newness, and potentiality. The dawning sun sheds new light on the world. It shines through air bringing clarity and illumination. Air is associated with the mind and the intellect. Its symbols are the rising sun; birds and feathers, especially the hawk and the eagle; the sword, and in some traditions the wand; and the incense and censor. Colors associated with air are white, gold, dawn rose, light blue and yellow.

Flashes of insight, awakening, inspiration and mental creativity are associated with air. As are all forms of communication of thought such as ideas, wit, humor, mental connections and associations. Our mental acuity enables us to organize and strategize, to develop plans of action, and to develop laws of justice and fairness, for which the Egyptian Goddess Maat is honored. It is the part of our mental capacity that thinks, analyses, evaluates and plans.

Sound travels through air and the spoken word and music are often times connected with air. Communicating thought via sound is a primary means of human expression. Verbalization, drum beat and other rhythmical instruments and music have been used to attract attention and to express thought and emotions since our earliest days as human beings. Hindu mantras and meditations involving sound are pre-Vedic and have ties to the ancient River Saraswati, which has long since gone "underground." Saraswati is also the Hindu Goddess of music, literature and the arts. Sound is often linked to her.

Birds fly through the air riding the air currents and spying on the activities below. We often hear of the "eagle eye," the expanded ability to see clearly. Therefore birds and bird feathers are often used as symbols of air, and bird feathers are often used to move air. The Greek Goddess Artemis, who hunts with a bow and arrow, uses mental acuity to plan and strategize for the hunt, as we must plan and strategize in order to achieve our goals. Her arrows, with their neat rows of feathers, fly through the air to hit their target, which is reminiscent of our need to identify and focus in order to hit our targets.

The sense of smell is associated with air and the censor and incense are frequently used symbols for the element of air. One of our most powerful primal senses is the sense of smell, and it has the power to trigger subconscious memories and associations. Incense and fragrant herbs, especially sage, are often used to clear space energetically.

The power of air is the power to know, to experience life, to study and to see things through a new perspective, as well as to perceive deep inner revelations - the Ah Ha moments. Air is the realm of consciousness and of the awakening consciousness. Tara, an Indian and Tibetan Buddhist Bodhisattva/Goddess, assists her devotees in achieving enlightenment through conscious awareness. Mary Magdalene, Priestess of Our Age and the Holy Bride, helps believers achieve a Gnostic (a spiritual or mystical) knowing of the divine. The power of air is also the desire to know, to understand, to pursue the quest for understanding, like Inanna's descent into the Underworld to understand the meaning of life and death.

FIRE, THE BRIGHT SPIRIT OF THE GODDESS

The energy of fire is spirit and is associated with the direction of South. Fire is associated with high noon, summer, the summer solstice when the sun is at its highest point, heat, passion and directed will. Its symbols are the roaring lion, the hoof beat of stallions, the volcano and the fire salamanders. The sword is used by some traditions as a fire symbol to cut away that which no longer serves us. Fire's colors are blood red, black, golden orange, yellow, white, and blue white. Like the Goddess Freyja, the energy of fire can be very sensual and sexual. Like Pele, the Volcanic Goddess, fire can be likened to the exotic thrust of pure raw power and force that is indiscriminate in its path of destruction. Fire can also be the force of directed will, the motivation behind an intent that forges an idea into life as with Brigit, the Patron Goddess of Poetry, Inspiration and Blacksmithing.

Fire is the energy that activates and motivates; it prepares us to move. The mind conceives the idea; fire is the active force that brings ideas into form. It is the power to will, to experience through determined action and struggle. To want is to think about something; to will is to wrestle with an obstacle and overcome it. It is the inner energy, the gumption and strength of character that is action. Fire is also courage, loyalty and the will to live. Egyptian Kings carried the fierce Lioness Goddess Sekhmet into battle both for protection and for her ferocious energy.

Fire also represents our intense emotions, ranging from raw passion and sensuality to ecstatic joy, to rage, grief and impassioned love. Like fire, your emotional energy lights up, heats, purifies and destroys. The intensity of fire can scorch, burn and destroy like the volcano, or it can comfort, warm and soothe like the hearth fire. It is a dynamic energy that can lead to adventures, exploration and discoveries. Gaining mastery over fire energy is to gain wisdom, like the Hindu Goddess Kali, to discern when to create and when to destroy in order to make room for the new. For the forces of creation and destruction are part of the eternal cycle of death, life and rebirth. In the mystery tradition of the Tarot, fire energy is the path of spirit that leads to wisdom.

Fire also represents our spirit, our spiritual ways, and the spark of life within each of us which helps us to connect to the Divine Feminine. It is the energy that pulls us deep within to connect with the depth of our soul. It is our intuitive hits of knowing. Fire is the Kundalini energy that shoots up the spine, activating the body's chakras and stimulating neurons in the brain that allow one to experience the bliss of connecting with the Divine. The Shekhinah, the Feminine Face of God, is the holy divine spirit that resides among the people keeping alive the connection to spirit until we are ready to awaken and achieve enlightenment.

WATER, THE LIVING WOMB OF THE GODDESS

As earth is the flesh of the womb of the Great Mother, water is the amniotic fluid within Her womb. Water is the great primordial sea, that rich stew of nutrients supporting and bringing forth new life. In Egypt it is the River Nile, associated with the tears of Isis for her lost Osiris, which in the past annually overflowed its banks transporting new silt to replenish the desert lands and bring forth new crops. In many mystery traditions water is associated with the direction of West, of the setting sun, of dusk and twilight and the rising moon. Its season is Autumn, a time when we pull in our energies from the fullness of summer, drawing inward preparing for winter. Autumn is a time of slowing down, quieting down and cooling off. Water's colors are blue, green, purple and black. Its stones are quartz, crystals and moonstones. Its animals are fish, dolphins, whales, mer-people, and other water creatures, including water snakes and dragons. The chalice is a symbol for the womb and the liquid life force it contains.

Water is yin—female energy. It is dark, cool, fluid, receptive and nourishing. Yemaya, the African Mother Goddess of the Sea, resides in the ocean and is often depicted as a mermaid. Water is silent unless it impacts another element, then it becomes the sound of crashing waves colliding with earth, or the sound of hissing steam when heated by fire.

The depths of the ocean, its secret and hidden ways, remind us of the depths of our emotions. Water's fluidity resembles the flow of feelings. When unbounded water spreads over limitless areas as do the emotions of sentimentality, sympathy, enthusiasm, and compassion. Water desires to reach out, connect and touch just as humans need to reach out to bond, love and build relationships. Water longs for completeness and wholeness as it seeks out the lowest point to collect as one large body. Water can be moody and expressive, as well as patient, persistent and tenacious. The human body is primarily water, and, just as energy flows through water, so emotions flow through the human body. Mother Mary and Kuan Yin are associated with unconditional love, compassion and mercy and are often linked with the sea, lakes or healing waters.

Water is the great balancer; it seeks equilibrium and when balanced can be mundane in a fulfilling way. When out of balance there is chaos and instability, as when emotions are unchecked and give way to outbursts of anger, rage, jealousy or grief. Yet water can also be a great stabilizer with the power to extinguish fire and dissolve stone. As rainclouds water nourishes the earth as milk from a mother's breast nourishes her young; as air-born water crystals, it delights humans with the beauty of a rainbow. Ix Chel, a Mayan Goddess often associated with the element of water, is frequently referred to as Lady Rainbow. In her crone energy Ix Chel pours out rainstorms from her jug bringing floods that cleanse and destroy making room for the new.

Water has the power to dare, to help us face our deepest feelings, to reflect and wrestle with the deep shadows that lurk in the abyss of our emotions. Water also has the power to dissolve, to carry, to link, to adapt, to shape and be shaped, to release and to transform. It is the power of deep emotions that can be transformative: the power of love, compassion and mercy.

EARTH, THE BODY OF THE GODDESS

Earth is the Great Mother. She is the limitless substance from which all physical things are made. Earth's colors are brown, black, russet, and the green of vegetation. She is the physical body of humans, the vessel that holds our forces of intellect, emotions, spirit, and will. She has been called the universal parent. She is Grandmother Spider, the Creatrix and Weaver of Life. According to one American Indian legend, she is the Earth's great yonic hole from which all people and animals emerged. A Siberian legend claims reindeer hunters descended directly from the Great Mother Goddess.

Ancient Roman Philosophers claimed that the Earth Mother was the mysterious power that awakened everything to life. All things came from the earth and everything returned to the earth. Hindu legends speak of Aditi, the indigenous mother goddess who was the creative mother of all mortals and immortals. Her lap was said to be abundant, and she protected those who were in harmony with nature. Niriti was the death aspect of the Great Mother in the Hindu cycle of birth, death and regeneration. The lap of Niriti forewarned of death and was said to receive corpses back into her womb. Hecate in Classical Greek mythology was the Guardian of the Souls who guided souls back and forth to the underworld. The Great Mother has a long and varied history as birth giver, life sustainer and the receiver of death.

In many mystery traditions, the element earth is linked to the North, the most powerful of directions, and a place of darkness, cold and deep mystery. Though associated with darkness it is not foreboding, but is a time of quiet retreat and deep reflection. It is the silence of the pause between the receding world of autumn and the burst of new life in the spring. In the stillness before rebirth, one can find knowledge when time is taken to listen, look inward and feel deeply. Persephone, dragged by Hades into the Underworld, a metaphor for the abyss of the subconscious, became its Queen and grew wise during her time there.

The earth is the Great Mother upon whose solid matter we stand. She helps us feel grounded, connected and stable. From Her solid substances we build structures and forms that provide shelter and protection. From Her soil vegetation grows which is the source of nourishment for ourselves and the animals that walk upon the earth. Our Neolithic Ancestors worshiped a Great Mother Goddess who they believed was the source of all life. Demeter, the ancient Greek Grain Goddess with links to the Neolithic Goddess, once deprived earth of her reproductive powers out of grief over her abducted daughter. The earth is the Great Mother who provides protection and nourishment yet she also has the power to withhold nourishment and withdraw protection. When respected and well treated she can be generous and abundant, as is Lakshmi, the Hindu Goddess who showers her devotees with good luck and prosperity.

Our physical forms are composed of earth's substances and are the vessels that hold and contain life force energy. Life force energy is passed through the physical body from one generation to another. Our physical form enables us to experience the gift of senses: the joy of touch, sensation and sensuality. We also experience her shaking, cracking and splitting. Her tossing and turning serves to crack us open physically so we can peer into the caverns of our minds with introspection and reflection. Earth wisdom is humbling.

The power of the earth is strength, stability, and endurance. Yet earth is acted upon by other elements – air, fire, water – which can move, carry or transform it. We, the children of the Earth, are not stable and enduring, but are continuously acted upon by the elements, forces of nature, relationships and events. We are in a constant state of change and transformation. Mother Earth provides a stable foundation upon which we can rest, derive a sense of security and learn to build our own personal foundation. When in balance earth characteristics include determination, perseverance, patience, reliability, prudence and generosity. When out of balance earth characteristics reflect rigidity, stagnation, inflexibility, materialism and miserliness.

In this book we will focus on seven manifestations of the Divine Feminine who resonate with the qualities of earth to create, hold, contain, support, and provide abundance, mothering and nurture. They also model quiet times of reflection and stillness, while two exhibit qualities as Queen of the Underworld and Guardian of the Souls. The Divine Feminine is the Mother of the Great Wheel that keeps turning: Life, Death and Rebirth.

Neolithic Mother Goddess - The Great Mother

Grandmother Spider – The Creatrix

Demeter and Persephone – Death and Rebirth: The myth of Demeter and Persephone and the Eleusinian Mysteries

Hecate – Queen of the Witches or Wise Crone

Lakshmi - Hindu Goddess of Abundance and Prosperity

Our Lady of Guadalupe – Mother of the People

Before we move on to the section on "Creating Sacred Circle for the Divine Feminine," you may be curious as to why it is important to even hold circles to celebrate In Her Name.

4. The Importance of Women's Circles to Honor the Feminine Divine

I HAVE ALWAYS been drawn to all things spiritual. My father was a Methodist Minister, and I remember when I was a child of nine or ten accompanying my father on Sunday mornings as he made the circuit to two of his three little country churches high in the Catskill Mountains of New York. You might say that I cut my teeth on religion and the Methodist hymnal. A deep connection with the Divine was instilled in me from early on.

Spirit comes from the word to breathe; it's the breath of life that allows us to be more than just a physical body. When spiritually aware we are able to connect more consciously to ourselves, to others, to nature, and to the great mystery that some of us may try to access, knowing even as we try, that we may never be able to quite grasp its magnitude. Envisioning the Divine as feminine, or masculine, or both, helps us to conceptualize and relate to a small part of this great vastness that is the Mystery.

Spirituality is the part of us that wants to make sense of our world. There are so many unanswered questions! Is life full of random purposeless acts? Is everything orchestrated and planned out at our birth? Did we choose our life? Were we conceived and born by chance? What is the purpose of our life on earth? Are we just here? Are there lessons for us to learn? Is there intelligent design? Or are we just part of Darwinian evolution? These are questions that philosophers, theologians (God-centered) and thealogians (Goddess-centered) have been debating for hundreds, maybe thousands, of years. We may never know all these answers, and each person's answers may be different, but embarking on a spiritual journey can help you make sense of your life and the part you play in the greater design of the universe.

Most men and women share similar values and religious ideals, and we have many of the same needs. Women, however, are more relational than men. Women have an innate need to gather and to be in relationship. In times of stress women congregate to share information, to pool resources, and to support one another. Coffee clutches, quilting bees, sewing bees, women's potlucks, mothers' co-op groups, etc., are just a few examples of women's groups. In Jewish cultural history there is an ancient gathering called Rosh Chodesh which is a ritual celebrated by women on the first day of the new moon. It originated from ancient Hebrew seclusion rituals when women menstruated together during the dark phase of the moon.

Some women find it challenging to relate to the Divine in the traditional Westernized version of the masculine God. For many God might resemble my father, the Methodist Minister of my early years. God is a good dad, but he is authoritative, judgmental and demands obedience! This concept of God helped me feel safe, but it wasn't always comforting, nor did it provide guidance on how to be confident and strong in my feminine nature.

Like many Westerners, I grew up envisioning the Divine as masculine. When I was introduced to the Shekhinah, the feminine face of God in the Hebrew tradition, my perception of the Divine unraveled. Suddenly my consciousness was freed to embrace the Divine not only as a compassionate and loving Divine Mother, like Kuan Yin and Mother Mary, but also as a model of how a woman can be strong and independent and stand in her power, as exemplified by female deities such as Artemis, Athena, Kali and Sekhmet. My understanding of spirituality did not so much change as it expanded to include the Divine Feminine.

Circles such as In Her Name Circles provide a safe community for women to seek greater understanding of the Mystery, deeper relationship bonds, and a more fulfilling spiritual connection. Together we create a communal safe haven which honors feminine values, feminine ways of being in the world, and feminine ways of knowing that are more subjective and intuitive. In Circle we learn to honor our feelings, our need for relationships, and our need to share stories and to be heard with a compassionate ear.

Circles with a Divine Feminine or women's spirituality focus, such as In Her Name Circles, include an additional element that is central to our meetings. We gather to honor and celebrate the Divine Feminine, both in the forms of her many manifestations in global history and cultures, as well as to honor the Divine Feminine within each one of us. Our purpose is to gather to reclaim the Divine Feminine both within and without.

You might be curious as to how I came to create In Her Name Circles. In Part II you will be introduced to my story, and I will explain just what a circle is. You will learn how to create your own altar and why ritual is important. Finally you will be given all the necessary tools and information to hold your own circle, if you should choose to do so.

PART II

Creating Sacred Circle to Honor
THE DIVINE FEMININE

5. Introduction to In Her Name Circle

TEN YEARS AGO had someone mentioned the Divine Feminine, I'd have asked, "What's that?" If they had predicted, "You will be devoted to the goddess." I'd have responded, "Ridiculous!" If they predicted I'd be leading circles, classes and workshops on the goddess, I'd have been horrified. Speaking in public filled me with dread: my mouth dry, my stomach churning, and my heart pounding!

But then, ten year ago I was beyond miserable. I was married to a man who was deep in a bi-polar depression. I soon discovered that he was mixing his own cocktails of prescription drugs that drastically changed him physically, mentally and emotionally. Struggling to care for a partner with no interest in caring for himself or in taking the responsibility for his own healing, I found I was entangled in a situation I couldn't control or fix. It left me with debilitating headaches. I was in such intense pain that no amount of pain medication could even touch it, and my performance at work was suffering. I felt burdened, alone and hopeless.

In 1997 my husband reconnected with his Jewish roots, and we began attending a local synagogue. Two years later we traveled to Israel with a group from the synagogue during which I developed a connection with the Rabbi who led the tour. When my husband was deep in his depression, I heard that the Rabbi was to be one of the presenters at a Jewish meditation retreat. Hoping to find some comfort and a shred of inner peace, I decided to attend. What I found was so much more; I discovered the feminine face of God – the Shekhinah! I still remember that sense of utter amazement when I finally realized the Divine could also be feminine. And not only could the Divine be feminine, but there was a documented history of the feminine face of god in the oldest monotheistic religion. I was directed to a book by Lyn Gottlieb: *She Who Dwells Within: A Feminist Vision of Renewed Judaism*, which chronicles a Jewish Rabbi's journey to reclaiming the Divine as feminine.

Guardedly I began reading about the Goddess, still harboring a lot of doubt and confusion. In desperation I sought out a psychic. He shattered any lingering illusions about my being a dedicated wife and mother when he stated that all I was, and all I had ever been, was a drudge and a caretaker. This was all I would ever be, he said, if I didn't make some drastic changes immediately. Unless I changed, he warned, I would miss out on an amazing life in which I would be of great service to others.

My husband's condition worsened and eventually led to a near fatal accident when he overdosed and tumbled down a flight of stairs. Finally I was able to persuade his psychiatrist to institutionalize him in a dual diagnosis facility. From there he went to a second treatment facility for 18 months. I was left with a mortgage I couldn't afford, bills I was struggling to pay, and headaches that gripped my head in a vise of pain. Needless to say my performance at work continued to deteriorate. Life was hell!

My spiritual quest continued as I was drawn to reading about sacred sites. The word 'goddess' kept appearing. Every time I saw that word it seemed as if a gong would reverberate in my head. References to source material began piquing my interest, and I stumbled onto the amazing work of Marija Gimbutas, specifically the *Ancient Goddess Civilization of Old Europe*. At night I remember arguing with the goddess telling her "No! Goddess worship is heresy, blasphemous. God is the Father. He is male. He is the only one!" I felt as if I was struggling for my very soul and was terrified of being confined to hell if I opened to the Divine Feminine.

Finally, I acquiesced. I began to bargain with the goddess. I told her I would follow her path, but she would have to help. I demanded support, including financial support. She would have to help me find friends and community along the way. I couldn't - wouldn't - do this alone. At the time I didn't realize that she would come through with her part of the bargain—with every part of it—support, friends, community, and even financial support! When I finally surrendered to her path, I found peace.

Then synchronicities started to happen. After reading and relating to Jean Shinoda Bolen's book *Crossing to Avalon*, I discovered Bolen was speaking in Marin County. It was a blustery rainy night, the kind of night in which no one wants to be out. Anxiety ridden about driving to an unknown destination on a stormy night with a pounding headache, I still felt compelled to go. I arrived, a bundle of nerves, and found a seat. As Bolen began to talk, I felt the tension ease out of my body. She presented her book, *Close to the Bone*, which is about people with life-threatening illnesses whose only remaining choice may be how to spend their last days. Either they can choose to be embittered and resentful, or they can embrace the time with grace and love. Those who chose the latter are transformed and healed in ways the body can never be healed.

While listening to Bolen speak I realized it was me, ME, who was poisoning my life! I was embittered, angry and resentful. Finally I recognized just how toxic I was. Everything I touched was polluted with my bitterness. At that moment I made a conscious decision to change my attitude. With that decision the suffocating blanket of despair lifted. A warm peace settled on my heart, and I felt calm inside. When I left that night, I was different, "changed utterly!" The confusion and despair dissipated.

Revitalized, I knew that I now had the energy and motivation to get on with my life.

Though rejuvenated I was still perplexed by the phrase "women's spirituality," which kept re-playing in my head like an annoying fragment of a song. Internet searches were unproductive. Finally, exasperated, I mentioned it to my therapist. She paused and said, "Oh, I think there is a master's program on Women's Spirituality at the California Institute of Integral Studies." I was stunned! "But I don't have my BA," I said. "I believe they have a bachelor's completion program at CIIS which is an accelerated program for completing Bachelor degrees," she countered. She was right! Within two months I was accepted into CIIS' bachelor completion week end program. And In August 2002, I began the education which would bring me even closer to the Divine Feminine.

While all this was taking place, I tore the lateral meniscus in my left knee. The pain and swelling made it possible for me to take time off on disability. Amazingly, due to an eventual total knee replacement (which I would not recommend to anyone), I was able to spend most of the next eight months on disability. This gave me the time I desperately needed to heal more than just physically while completing my BA. Truly it was a gift!

I dreaded returning to the work environment where I felt I had failed. After much prayer and meditation I surrendered my fate to the goddess and went back determined to do my best with as much grace as possible. One week after returning the company announced that the new owners were closing us down and everyone would be offered a severance. If I had not gone back I would have missed out! My severance package, combined with stock options, unused vacation pay and a bonus, helped fund my master's program and training in two hypnotherapy programs, as well as providing capital to establish a practice in San Mateo. The goddess came through with her part of the bargain to ease my financial worries.

The Sacred Feminine continued to support and nourish me while I healed from two dysfunctional marriages and subsequent divorces. Other wounds, however, had been inflicted by the prevailing patriarchal system that devalues women; silences women's voices; demeans women's intuition; enables co-dependency, martyrdom, and self-sacrifice; and exploits sexuality. In the Women's Spirituality program I learned to value myself and my experience as a woman, and to acknowledge the wounds that I carried from our patriarchal system. Men are also wounded. Our social system hurts us all.

Exposure to the many archetypes of the Sacred Feminine during the program enabled me to re-learn what it meant to be female. She is the mother who is caring and compassionate like Our Lady of Guadalupe; She is the protectress like Artemis; She is the woman warrior like Athena; She is the guide to the depths of the underworld like Inanna; She is able to change and transform like Sekhmet; She destroys the old to make room for the new like Kali; She is the creatrix like Grandmother Spider; She is our connection to the earth, to renewal, like Gaia; She is passion, love, sensuality, and all that is fertile and creative like Aphrodite. Her many manifestations model what it means to be female. I realized her many ancient myths and legends could be used as teaching stories to illustrate this message. If women could relate to the Divine Feminine on an emotional/psychological/spiritual level, then maybe they could reclaim themselves as both female and divine. I knew this was the message I was to carry into the world.

It took time to find the right circle format that supported an experience conducive to introducing and strengthening the relationship of Western women to the Divine Feminine. Initially, I volunteered to continue a lecture series entitled "Goddess Is Alive," and invited renowned speakers in the Women's Spirituality Movement, such as Vicki Noble, Luisah Teish, and Joan Marler. Soon I began creating my own work and produced a series of lectures on five female deity images (Artemis, Shakti, Spider Woman, the Neolithic Mother Goddess, and Inanna). Though interesting, it was very academic and something was missing.

Then I was invited to co-lead a program at the Unitarian Universalist Congregation of San Mateo called *Rise Up and Call Her Name*, which explores earth-based female deity images from around the globe. From this experience I learned the importance of incorporating into women's circles music, song, images, poems, readings, and ritual. This, I realized, was what was missing—the experiential piece! Women needed the opportunity to gather in circle and not only learn about the Sacred Feminine, but to see images of her, participate in ritual and to develop a personal relationship with her and her many aspects.

In February 2008, I launched my Circles on the Divine Feminine with a celebration of Kuan Yin, She who hears the cries of the world. By July, though I enjoyed putting on the Circles, I was beginning to appreciate the intense level of grunt work and responsibility which priestessing entails. I needed help! Then I remembered a familiar face that kept showing up. As a matter of fact, she had attended almost every one of my goddess events! Shannon stayed to help clean up after one circle, and I asked if she would like to assist me in serving the goddess. I am forever grateful to Shannon Dawn and her devotion to the Divine Feminine. To date, we have produced circles for twenty-four different manifestations of the Divine Feminine together.

Women who come to my Circles appreciate the experience. They tell their friends and come back as often as they can. During each Circle we celebrate a different manifestation of the Divine Feminine. There are easily a thousand or more different female deity images, and it has been hard to choose which ones to feature. I have given care to select female deities from all parts of the globe: Yemaya from Africa and the Caribbean; Inanna and Shekhinah from the Near East; Sekhmet, Isis, and Maat from Egypt; Ix Chel from Latin America; Freyja and Brigit from Northern Europe; Grandmother Spider from the American Indian culture; Kali, Lakshmi, and Sarasvati from India; Kuan Yin and Tara from Asia; and Artemis, Aphrodite, Hecate, and Demeter and Persephone from pre-Hellenic and Classical Greek cultures. I have also included contemporary Divine Feminine archetypes such as Mother Mary, Our Lady of Guadalupe and Mary Magdalene. Each Divine Feminine archetype is unique and has her own history, myth, special traits and characteristics, and represents a different aspect of the Sacred Feminine. Each offers her own unique message. I love putting together the presentations and giving each Divine Feminine persona her own unique spotlight that shows how different she is, yet also how much she has in common with other female deities.

Each presentation of the Divine Feminine has been thoughtfully researched. History, including myths and legends, has been passed down and written by men. The interpretation is filtered through a male lens portraying a patriarchal perspective. I provide a feminist perspective. Because goddess energy is more right brained, reflective and intuitive, I have found that images speak and tell her story more vividly than words. I enjoy gathering images for the accompanying PowerPoint slides to my presentations, and circle participants appreciate seeing them. Some of the art is of artifacts dating back to pre-classical or Classical Greece, to ancient Mesopotamia, to the Neolithic era or even earlier. Also featured are slides of paintings and statues by famous artists both past and contemporary. Fortunately the Divine Feminine has been a popular subject; the creative muse has kept her image alive for us to enjoy today.

Each circle contains a guided visualization designed to facilitate an individual experience with the Divine Feminine. Time is allowed for each individual to delve within to ask questions of her own inner wisdom, as personified by the Goddess, and to hear the support, advice or wisdom that is offered. Time is given for personal processing and group sharing. Because of the care taken to set the energies, invoke the Sacred Feminine, and create safety, many have reported beautiful and transformative experiences. Copies of various guided visualizations may be downloaded online from my shopping cart http://www.shop.joyreichard.com/Celebrate-the-Divine-Feminine-on-Mp3_c3.htm.

The piece I missed when I first developed my goddess talks was the experiential. Therefore ritual has been thoughtfully woven into each circle. Ritual allows the participants to experience and internalize the traits or insights pertaining to the female deity persona we are celebrating. For instance Hecate is the Goddess of the Underworld and, therefore, the subconscious. She helps us process and let go of what we are ready to release. Once we de-clutter our lives, we have space to attract new opportunities. Our ritual for Hecate is, therefore, about letting go. Once we ritually release, we set a new intention and support each other in its manifestation. Aphrodite is about passion and sensuality, so I invite Dasha, my sister-in-the-Goddess and a belly dance instructor, to lead us in dance as we experience the movement and sensuality of our bodies. We know about the Neolithic Goddess because of clay female figurines that survived the millenniums. As a ritual each woman is given the opportunity to make her own clay goddess. Brigit is the Celtic Solar Goddess; one of her attributes is divination. During the ritual we pass out candles so participants can experience the ancient divination tool of scrying while gazing into a candle flame. Going through the motions of a ritual enables each participant to internalize their experience on a deeper more meaningful level. (Instructions for each ritual and suggested supplies are provided in each goddess section.)

Participants have several opportunities to share during the circle. We ritually and energetically clear the meeting space prior to the arrival of circle participants. At the beginning of each circle we call in the directions to create sacred space. By taking care to create a safe environment, participants can relax more fully into their experience and are free to share as they feel called. Many women report that the circles continue to positively impact their lives. Some have made significant changes, worked through troubling issues, or healed relationships due to their experiences during Circle.

A common complaint is that many women want to attend but can't due to time, family demands, lifestyle or distance. Because of these restrictions, and because of my commitment to bring the Divine Feminine to all who seek her, I conceived the idea of putting together this series of four books each featuring one of the four elements: earth, air, fire and water. In Part III of this book you will be introduced to seven female deities that resonate with the element earth: The Neolithic Goddess, Grandmother Spider, Demeter and Persephone, Hecate, Lakshmi and Our Lady of Guadalupe. The remaining chapters in this part will provide you with all the information you need to hold your own circle, from creating altars to circle logistics. My website contains free material that you will find useful, as well as recordings of the guided visualizations for a small fee. Please take advantage of what is offered. I would appreciate your feedback and comments. http://celebratedivinefeminine.com.

It is my hope that many women, like you, will gather in circle to celebrate the Divine Feminine and will replicate many of the circles included in this book. And possibly, if you find that I have not included your favorite Divine Feminine persona, you will find the inspiration to create a circle on your own. If you do, I hope you will let me know for I believe this is part of a larger movement for women to gather in circles around the world to celebrate In Her Name.

6. What is a Circle?

A WOMEN'S CIRCLE is a gathering of women who usually sit in a circle, so everyone can see and be seen. Circle members have agreed to meet on a regular basis to discuss shared concerns and to offer support and encouragement. Circles can be as small as four members and can be as large as feels manageable for the participants. They can meet in members home, or they might find a home in a church or in a public facility, such as a school or hospital. Relationships are important for women, and circles provide a natural way for women to gather and create a safe place to greet old friends and make new ones. In circle women find the confidence to speak freely from the heart and know that they will be heard, if not always agreed with. Group discussions generate opportunities for new ideas to emerge, and facilitates new ways of looking at old concerns. Time devoted to silent process allows for comfortable moments of quiet while participants reflect and sometimes wrestle with personal concerns. Many times lost dreams are remembered, goals are affirmed, issues are resolved or insights are materialized. Circles create a safe place where women can develop close bonds with other women and feel supported.

A sacred circle is a gathering of women who wish to explore, express and deepen their understanding of spirituality. It differs from a support circle in that, while support and personal relationships do develop, the participants don't concentrate their focus on personalities and their personal concerns, but instead focus on broader transpersonal and archetypal themes that affect people's lives and the world. These circles also offer women an opportunity to create sacred space in which to do ritual and ceremony.

In the In Her Name Circle we explore, define and honor the feminine principle while we celebrate the many manifestations of the Divine Feminine. Learning about the Divine Feminine provides us with insights and expanded awareness and appreciation of what it means to be female. This knowledge and insight facilitates our personal growth as we learn to value our own divine natures within. The Divine Feminine teaches us how to have more functional relationships, to be present with our feelings, to honor our bodies and our selves, to be honoring of women's life cycles, to live according to our personal values, and to find the strength and motivation to pursue our dreams and goals. Sharing ritual and ceremony helps us build community and strengthen our sisterhood with those who share a love for the goddess and the sacred.

In Her Name Circles are teaching circles where women come to learn about the different manifestations of the goddess, as well as to share time with their sisters in the goddess. They have an opportunity to experience the Divine Feminine during guided visualizations, and to participate in rituals designed to help members internalize and make sacred their circle experience. The time we share together is gratifying and enjoyable. We would love for you to join our In Her Name Circle.

A central part of holding a circle, or even if you just want to develop a personal relationship to one of the many manifestations of the Divine Feminine, is creating an altar. The next chapter will give you all the information you will need to build an altar of you own.

7. Creating Altars

SINCE THE NEOLITHIC Era spiritual traditions have used altars. Sometimes they are constructed as permanent fixtures, and at times are temporary for specific events. Altars are used both to create a focal point as well as to concentrate mental energy on a specific intention. Some of you may be interested in creating an altar for a specific purpose such as honoring your ancestors, or calling in a romantic partner, or honoring Lakshmi to encourage her gifts of abundance and prosperity. I created an altar to support my writing and other creative projects.

Our minds are powerful. The popularity of books such as *The Secret* and the *Law of Attraction* and the *Power of Intention* stress the unlimited potential of the mind, especially when combined with visualization and positive emotions. Creating an altar with intention for a specific purpose harnesses this same power of the mind. Altars created for In Her Name Circles concentrate our focus on the Divine Feminine persona we are honoring and are integral parts of the evening's ceremony.

You might say that altars are a reflection, or a mirror, of whatever is significant enough to merit your intention and focus. There is no right way to set up an altar. Practitioners of different spiritual traditions will offer numerous and overwhelming variations on altar construction. Though there are some basic structures that are helpful, within this basic framework you are free to do what feels right. Remember, creating an altar is to help you focus your intentions, so following your intuition will serve you best.

ALTAR PLACEMENT - DIRECTIONS AND ELEMENTS

The proper placement of an altar enhances a positive experience, especially when facilitating a group event. Aligning the altar with the directions (north, south, east and west) and paying attention to the corresponding elements is the initial step in creating sacred space. This helps ground the energies so circle participants feel safe and comfortable. It also promotes greater harmony and flow for the emotional and psychological energies generated during ritual ceremonies.

I find a compass is helpful to locate north, south, east, and west. If a compass is not available, then do your best with the information you have available. The goddess will honor the purity of your intention. Because we are honoring the Great Mother, her most auspicious location is in the north or east. My altars are placed in the north east.

Altars are usually set up on a table or a chest and covered with a cloth used for ritual purposes. This both protects the surface from candle wax, spilled liquid or dust from burnt incense and helps to define the altar space and establish the right mood. Altars can also be created outdoors using a cloth on the ground, or string or rope to mark the edges of the altar space.

At each compass point I place an item or symbol that corresponds to each of the directions. (Please see the Tables of Correspondences at the end of this section for suggestions.)

DIVINE FEMININE AND MASCULINE

Though I am devoted to the Divine Feminine, I also honor the Divine Masculine. A balance between the Divine Feminine and Divine Masculine creates unity, conscious awareness and bliss—or the Sacred Marriage. I set the intention for all beings to achieve the Sacred Marriage within and without by including symbols of the Divine Masculine on the altar.

For many traditions the left side of the altar is feminine, so I put symbols representing the feminine on the left. On the right side I put symbols representing the masculine. I use a red candle, a metaformic color and the color of the first chakra, to represent the feminine. Red is the color of blood, menstrual blood, which connects us to the Great Mother Goddess and is the symbol of life. I use a white candle for the masculine, which represents spirit, the white hot of fire, representing the seventh chakra, the masculine consciousness. In Hindu traditions the masculine consciousness can only be awakened when united with the Kundalini energy of the Great Mother Goddess. Though there is duality, one is not supreme over the other. True balance, harmony and bliss are achieved when both are united.

Other colors that can be used to represent the masculine are yellow, gold or purple. Some traditions will use white or green to represent the Great Mother Goddess. Use what feels right to you.

ALTAR ITEMS

If you have crystals, definitely include them on your altar. Everything vibrates with a different frequency. This includes matter, water, light, sound, thoughts and emotions. Crystals resonate at high frequencies and support working with the energies of Spirit and the Divine. I frequently place my amethyst crystal geodes on the right, or masculine side, and citrine crystal geodes on the left, or feminine side. I tend to group my white, pink and clear crystals in the center.

Finally, and what I find to be the most satisfying, is the search for items representing the Divine Feminine. If you do not have a statue or image, it is an easy matter to print an image off the internet, or to copy one onto a disk and take it to a copy center. As you research each female deity you will learn what symbols, animals, or nature items are sacred to her. Goddesses tend to resonate with the attributes of one or several of the elements. For instance, Kuan Yin is the Goddess of Compassion and Mercy. She is strongly associated with water and the ocean. On her altar you might include symbols representing water: a bowl or chalice of water, sea shells, dolphins, or sea turtles. Artemis is the Goddess of the Hunt so you might want to include a bow and arrow, or images of deer, bear, or forest creatures. Hecate is the Goddess of the Underworld. Her altar might contain rocks, bones, a skull, and dogs (the hounds of hell).

With each Divine Feminine persona contained in this workbook I offer suggestions for altar items in the Table of Correspondences found at the end of their section. Don't hesitate, however, to trust your instincts. I often find that as I gather altar items from my list, others will call out to me wanting to be included. I honor these intuitive hits. The goddess is one, yet she has manifests in many forms. I honor all her manifestations. When she calls out, I find it pays to listen!

ALTARS FOR SPECIFIC INTENTIONS

Altars may be used to help you focus your intention on various areas of your life. For instance, if you want to focus your intention on writing, then you may want to include items that represent Air which is the element for inspiration, intellect and communication. Refer to the Table of Correspondences at the end of this chapter under the element Air and select relevant items. Select a candle that represents writing, or the mind, such as a yellow candle. Also include items that represent the act of writing: paper, a pen, a book, etc. Be sure to include a few things from the Fire column on the Table of Correspondences. Fire is the energy to act, to will, to be motivated. The Fire of action will help you manifest your thoughts into form.

If you are creating an altar to call in a romantic partner, then select items from the Fire column: red hearts, red roses, erotic art, and a phallus or yoni symbol. Also include items that represent the kind of partner you desire, such as a collage of ideal images and qualities, or a list of preferences. Be sure to include a few items from the Water column to foster the merging, connection and flow found in loving relationships. Remember, the important thing is to focus on your intention as you gather items!

CREATING YOUR ALTAR WITH INTENTION

Once you have gathered all your altar items, then set aside some quiet time. Play music that has the right "feel" or sets the right ambience. Then reverently and with intention set up your altar. Once you are satisfied with the layout, light the candle, and incense if you have included incense, and then spend 10 to 20 minutes relaxing, or meditating, in front of your altar. This will help you focus your intention.

If you are honoring a specific Divine Feminine image, then spend time meditating on her. Read her myths and reflect on her attributes. Imagine that if she were present, what would she want you to know, or to do? What advice would she give you?

If you are focusing on a specific intention then take a few minutes to visualize your efforts and time paying off. See yourself in the act of achieving or having whatever it is that you are focusing on, whether it is the blessing of the Goddess, or the completion of a project, or a fulfilling relationship. Take time to feel the emotions of what it will feel like to have your intentions manifested. Then trust that the Goddess will provide it or something better, and allow yourself to feel calm and relaxed. Trust that whatever happens will be as it should be.

DAILY PRACTICE

Establish a daily practice of lighting the candle and spending a few minutes focusing, or meditating, in front of your altar. Time spent at your altar amplifies your focus and strengthens the power of your intention. This daily ritual will make it possible for you to partner the power of your mind with the energies of the universe and the goddess enabling you to achieve your goals with greater ease and fewer struggles. I have a beautiful oak tree off my balcony. Every morning I take a handful of nuts or raisins and stand in front of the tree and allow myself to bond with her. I make my offerings and express gratitude for the abundance she showers on me. For me, at this moment of my daily ritual, this tree is the Great Mother. In those few minutes I feel myself held, contained, grounded and loved. I am ready to "walk in beauty" the rest of the day.

DISMANTLING YOUR ALTAR

When you dismantle your altar, whether it be after an evening's event, such as a circle, or after a period of time, be sure to do it with the same reverence with which you set it up. Take a moment to reflect on your original intention for the altar. Acknowledge how placing attention in this manner has aided you. Then give thanks and release the energies.

The following Tables of Correspondences will be helpful as you gather items for your altars.

TABLE OF CORRESPONDENCES

Elements	Earth	Air	Fire	Water
Directions	North	East	South	West
Colors	Green, black, brown	Yellow, light blue	Red, orange, gold, white	Blue, dark blue, green, gray
Seasons	Winter	Spring	Summer	Autumn
Times of day	Midnight	Dawn – sunrise	Noon	Dusk – sunset
Moon Phases	New/dark	Waxing	Full	Waning
Zodiac	Capricorn, Taurus, Virgo	Aquarius, Gemini, Libra	Aries, Leo, Sagittarius	Cancer, Pisces, Scorpio
Personal	The body	The mind	The spirit	The emotions
Animals	Bear, bull, dog, snake, stag, mouse, wolf	All birds, esp. the eagle, hawk, owl, dove	Lion, galloping horses, gull, fox, ram, lizards	All sea life, dolphins, turtles, swans
Trees	Oak, ash, blackthorn	Aspen, apple, beech	Elder, gorse, hawthorn	Willow, alder, birch
Magical Tools	Pentagram, stone	Athame, sword	Wand, spear, staff	Chalice, cauldron
Elementals	Gnomes	Sylphs	Salamanders	Undines

Sandra Kynes, *A Year of Ritual: Sabbats and Esbats for Solitaries & Covens.*

Items from nature, basic attributes, and powers differ somewhat between traditions. These are the attributes that I use for the In Her Name Circles. They come from several sources.

Elements	Earth	Air	Fire	Water
Items from Nature	Stones, rocks, plants, herbs, flowers, fruits, nuts, tissue of the womb	Feathers, pictures of clouds, the sky, sunrise, birds, wind blowing through nature, breathe	Volcanoes, red rose, red hearts, fire in any form, phallus or yoni to designate sexual passion, spicy foods	Shells, sand dollars, waterfalls, water lilies, lakes, rivers, oceans, amniotic fluid in the womb
Powers	To possess strength, stability, endurance	To know	To will	To shape, dissolve, transform, move on, sustain. It is a meandering and flowing power.
Attributes When in Balance	Birth, growth, Foundation, reflection, going inward, determination, endurance, patience, the silence of the pause, reliability, generosity, connection, death	Knowledge, Learning, intelligence, intuition, inspiration, thought, communication, creativity of thought, truth, wit, humor, clarity, awakening, ideas,	Healing, Purification, transformation, protection, personal power, passionate energy, directed will, energizing, motivation, action, passionate emotions (joy, sex, rage, grief, love), act of producing creative works of art – manifesting into form	Linking, Carrying, shaping, creativity of expression, adaptability, primal intuition, human emotions that allow us to flow into or merge in a loving way, mercy compassion, empathy, love, courage, inner wisdom, cleansing, release, receptivity, mystery, dreams
Attributes When Out of Balance	Rigid, stagnant, greed	Cruelty, cunning, misleading speech, gossip, mental cruelty	Violence, rage, destruction,	Co-dependency, enmeshment, clinging
Senses	Touch	Smell	Sight	Taste

SOURCES

Sandra Kynes, *A Year of Ritual: Sabbats and Esbats for Solitaries & Covens.*

Ruth Barrett, *Women's Rites, Women's Mysteries: Intuitive Ritual Creation.*

8. *Why is Ritual Important?*

IT IS 5:45 on Friday afternoon and Shannon and I have just gathered at the Unitarian Universalist Congregation in San Mateo for our monthly In Her Name Circle. We've been putting the Circles on together for over three years so we know the routine. With little need for communication we begin moving furniture, setting up tables, chairs, projection equipment and altars. With my Aries Sun, I am a whirlwind of activity. Thankfully, Shannon's Capricorn Moon helps to slow me down and ground. Usually after her third "Don't you think we should ground?" I finally stop, breathe and give her a sheepish smile. She has caught me in another one of my "Aries" moments.

Shannon and I have developed a pre-circle ritual. With a deep breath I mentally slow down, consciously inhabit my body and connect to the earth. Then I light either sage or incense. We circle the meeting room clearing it of negative energies with the incense and declaring it sacred for our evening's circle. Then we each gently wave the sage or incense over each other as we clear our personal space, our auras, if you will. This simple ritual helps us ground and center. My Aries Sun enables me to be superbly productive, but without these moments of grounding and returning to center I can whirl out of control into a frenzy, or burn out my adrenal glands resulting in exhaustion or illness. After our ritual we meditate and invite the Divine Feminine to be with us and offer guidance as we lead this circle in Her honor. After this we return to our preparations, but now our movements are more measured, thoughtful and reverent.

Many people are unfamiliar with the concept of ritual, especially those who might be new to the Divine Feminine or have limited spiritual or religious experience. Just the word ritual might conjure up unsettling or disturbing images of men and women in lavish or expensive clothes performing stylized performances with numerous lighted candles, and heavy incense. Or they might think of people from indigenous cultures in colorful clothing of feathers and animal skins performing enthusiastic and dramatic dances. Thoughts of ritual might bring feelings of discomfort, especially for those who are more reserved or cautious. For those from monotheistic religious traditions, participating in a ritual honoring the Divine Feminine might create feelings of conflict. I know it did for me when I first began to seek out the Divine Feminine. The warnings and old tapes about "worshipping false gods" can have a disconcerting impact for those who want to branch out to explore and honor the Sacred Feminine.

Yet if you stop and reflect on your daily life you will realize that your day is made up of rituals. What is the first thing you do every morning? Mine is to turn on the teapot. Do you brush your teeth at certain times? Do you comb your hair, bathe, put on your clothes in a certain order? Do you go to work the same way? Our days are filled with little rituals. What if we were to place more value on those rituals by making them sacred? For instance, with my first cup of tea I might pour a bit on the earth in gratitude for all that has been given to me. When I bathe, I might view it as a cleansing ritual, removing the old debris of yesterday and preparing me for the opportunities and experiences I will face today. Marija Gimbutas, the world renowned archaeologist, writer, and founder of archaeomythology, claims our ancient Neolithic ancestors viewed all of life as sacred. Ritual and a sacred respect for life were rolled into their daily activities, as well as into their celebrations of the cycles of the moon and the seasons.

What if we were to consciously create more ritual in our lives? Take the moon, for instance. Most of us are aware that the moon has different phases, but few of us take note of it unless we have an interest in astrology. Yet if we were to note its different phases and to mark them as important, we would then know that the new moon is a sign of new beginnings, of birth, potentialities and new opportunities. The full moon is about our projects coming to fruition, the fulfillment of our intentions. The waning moon is about letting go and releasing. In this way the cycles of the moon can take on a depth of new meaning and have more importance in our lives. If we want to set intentions for an exciting new project we might create a simple ritual like lighting a candle in the new moon phase. If we want to celebrate the completion of a major project, such as signing a contract or landing a major account, then during the full moon we might want to take some nuts or fruit to a spot in nature and leave them for the animals. If we were intent on releasing a relationship we might go for a walk during the waning moon and pick up a stick and break it signifying letting go of the relationship. In this simple way we augment the happenings in our life and come into flow with the flux of nature. There is a cycle to life. By resonating with it, rather than resisting it, we can achieve balance and harmony. With my stubborn Aries Sun that wants everything "now" and "my way," this helps me to slow down and flow with the energies of life.

In *Truth or Dare*, Starhawk says that in ritual we create a symbolic space of protection and safety, in which we break the negativity and censorship of our own mind so we can express freely whatever needs to come forth. Ritual, Starhawk claims, is one of the great tools of the weavers of culture. It is how humans mark and make note of important events. It marks major transitions or rites of passage. Baptisms, Confirmations, Bar Mitzvahs, marriage ceremonies, the rosary, and memorial services are all rituals. Ritual is an opportunity for transformation, because each of these rites of passage commemorates the point at which the individual is transitioning into a new stage in his or her life.

Rituals can be structured and formal like a Catholic mass, or they can be spontaneous and simple like breaking a stick to signify letting go. The rituals included in this book fall somewhere in between. Each ritual evolved as Shannon and I were planning the circle, and they are mostly our own creations. Some we have found in our research and have adapted to meet our needs. We invite you to use our ideas as planned, or to elaborate or simplify them to meet your needs, or the needs of your circle.

Each person has a different level of comfort with ritual; therefore many of our rituals involve silent process. Verbal instructions and cues are given, and there is some movement, but generally each individual is allowed to process their experience internally and silently. Frequently we allot time for participants to integrate their experience by journaling or doing some simple art work following the ritual. Because each individual's experience is unique and rich we allow time for group sharing. We learn from each other and many times what the Goddess has offered one individual is really for all of us. By sharing with the group, we can each take what we need and leave the rest. Ritual provides an opportunity for participants to deepen their individual experiences with the Divine within and without.

Now that you know what a circle is, how to create a circle and why ritual is important, you are ready to learn how to "Call the Circle."

9. Calling the Circle

Circle Energetics

IT IS THE second Friday of the month. Shannon and I have gathered again to lead an In Her Name Circle. The participants have arrived. Shannon is calling in the directions establishing our sacred circle. As she calls in each direction I feel the tingling sensation which lets me know the energies have been called, our space is sanctified and I have transitioned into the role of Priestess who will facilitate tonight's honoring of the Divine Feminine.

Facilitating a circle honoring the Divine Feminine is sacred service. If you are reading this with the intent of leading your own In Her Name Circle, know that when you facilitate a sacred circle you function as a priestess, whether or not you have gone through a training or initiation process. Assuming a sacred role makes it imperative that you serve with clear intentions and reverence. Clarity of intention helps to establish a favorable mood and is central to cultivating a powerful and meaningful experience for participants. The greater the clarity of intention the easier it is to facilitate and maintain harmony and balance within a circle. This information will also be helpful if you are an individual practitioner. Creating sacred space for oneself in which to conduct a ritual can be powerful, rewarding and healing. Using visual, kinesthetic (touch), auditory (sound) and olfactory (smell) stimuli help to create and maintain the appropriate mood, which is a result of the energetics set by your clear intentions.

Quantum physics revealed that everything has a frequency and vibrates at different levels. This includes rocks, blades of grass, trees, all cold and warm blooded creatures, and liquids as well as our thoughts, emotions, light and sound. We live in a sea of energy. Reiki, Healing Touch and other energy workers have been trained to channel energy through their bodies to bring healing to themselves and others. When facilitating a group, energy can be manipulated and directed. Hitler accomplished this with the masses in Germany which resulted in mass destruction of life and property. Billy Graham was able to manipulate energy with the vast crowds who packed his religious services and presentations bringing them closer to the Divine as he envisioned God. Both had charisma which made it all the easier for them to manipulate energy, create moods and sway the masses. When you facilitate a circle you are also in a position to manipulate the energy, so it becomes your responsibility to set the energies early and to be clear and pure with your intentions.

It might help to think of your circle as a journey that has a purpose or destination. For instance, when working with the energies of Persephone the intension is to connect with our deepest emotions so we can better know who we are and learn to trust our intuition. When we work with Lakshmi we release old thoughts of undeservingness so we can make room for more abundance in our lives. We work with the energies of love and compassion when we celebrate Our Lady of Guadalupe. Being clear with your intention and knowing your destination will enable you to set and maintain the mood more easily and effectively.

Preparing for the Circle

Begin preparing for your Circle several weeks prior. Set aside an hour or two to review the material. If you are working with co-facilitators, call a meeting so you can do this as a group. Spend 10 to 20 minutes meditating on the material and the Divine Feminine persona you will be celebrating. Reflect on her myths, cultural history and characteristics. When Shannon and I meet we call in the directions and the Divine Feminine, then we sit in silence while absorbing her energy. We ask for guidance so that we may present what she wants others to know and experience. We begin sending energy to the ritual space preparing it in advance for the Circle. Finally we always ask her to send out a call to all the women who will benefit from the circle inspiring them to attend. Many participants report they simply felt compelled to attend and couldn't really explain what motivated them. I just smile and know that the Divine Feminine has been at work. The meditation also helps us to ground and collect our thoughts so that we can plan productively and creatively.

During the planning session take time to diagram the layout for the Circle: where you will place the altars, registration/information table, coffee/tea, and projector and screen (if used). Determine who will perform specific roles, such as calling in and releasing the directions, leading the singing or drumming, invocation, presentation, guided visualization, ritual, and don't forget about heating water in advance for the tea, etc. If someone is going to read or present the main information they should commit to practicing the material by reading it out loud at least 2 or 3 times. This will familiarize them with the material and the information will feel less canned when presented.

Once all the roles have been assigned, compile a list of all the items needed and identify who will bring what. Facilitating a circle is a sacred honor.... and it is also a lot of work. Sharing the load with co-facilitators lightens the responsibility and also strengthens the relationship bonds within the Circle.

Day of the Circle

It is important to prepare yourself the day of the Circle to act as facilitator. Remember, as a facilitator you will be functioning as a priestess. It is sacred service. Rushing around at the last minute feeling overwhelmed and anxious creates energetic static that creates imbalance and disharmony not only within you, but within the energy of the circle and the participants. In addition, on a psychic level, participants have their intuitive feelers out sensing the energies. If there is static, they will sense it, hesitate and probably not attend.

Determine what you will wear ahead of time. Women love to adorn themselves, and the goddess loves beauty and beautiful things. If you have special clothes or jewelry or other adornments for sacred events make sure they are clean and ready for you to wear. As we adorn ourselves with special attire, we begin to mentally shift into the role of sacred service.

Schedule time in advance so you have plenty of time to prepare for the Circle. I usually allow three hours which also gives me time to practice the presentation one last time before the circle. Set aside at least 20 minutes to meditate while calling in the Divine Feminine as you reflect on her myths and characteristics to help you ground and center. Be quiet and let her speak, delivering any messages that are important. The messages I have received while meditating have been profound. When I first started leading the Circles I was excited and very nervous. One of Her first messages was gentle but quite clear. "This isn't about you! This is about me, the Divine Feminine—remember!" It was a revelation that helped me realize that I wasn't the center of focus. I wasn't on stage. She was! I was just Her mouthpiece. My anxiety plummeted, and I immediately felt more grounded and calm.

Not everyone grounds and centers in the same way. For me meditation works. Others might find walking in nature, or luxuriating in a bath with special oils, scents or bubbles, or listening to music or gardening while reflecting on the Divine Feminine is a more suitable grounding and calming tool. Employ what works for you; just take time to ground and be with the Divine Feminine so that energetically you prepare yourself for sacred service.

Purification of your body is another way to prepare. If you have time, bathe or shower, and wash your hair. If time is limited at least wash your hands or face while focusing on the task as a ritual to purify your body for service to the Divine Feminine.

Collect the items for the Circle ahead of time. Be sure to do any shopping early so you aren't rushing into a store at the last minute. As you collect and pack the items allow yourself to reflect on the Circle, the Divine Feminine you will be honoring and the destination or outcome you hope to achieve. Scheduling time to prepare will enable you to arrive early feeling centered and calm with plenty of time to set up.

Circle Set Up

Once all the facilitators have arrived clear the space together with sage or incense. Start in the east pausing at each direction point (east, south, west, north, center) while mentally or verbally declaring the space sacred. Shannon and I end in the center and also call in the directions of below and above. This creates a sacred sphere of safety and protection. Then we clear our own personal space by waving the smoke from the incense or sage over each other, beginning at the feet and rising to above the head covering both the front and back of our bodies. As you breathe, imagine that you are inhaling in peace and calm, and exhaling tension, stress and the busyness of life so that you can drop into sacred space. As we cleanse the space for each other we might feel called to utter a blessing or special intention. Shannon has Aquarius Rising and a demanding job so she can get stuck on the mental plane, so I might spend extra time cleansing the area around her head to release mental chatter so she can drop into her body and be fully present.

Once you have cleared both the meeting space and your personal space, join hands and meditate calling in the Divine Feminine. Ask her to bless the space and to offer support and guidance as you gather to celebrate In Her Name. Remember to ask her to call in all the women who will benefit from this circle and who most need to connect with her. After the meditation, complete setting up the space (altars, chairs, projection equipment, etc.) while taking note of the energetic difference. You should notice a greater sense of calm and groundedness. These steps have clarified your intention and helped set the right energies for the Circle. This will facilitate greater harmony and balance and a positive flow of energy during circle.

Gathering the Participants

About 5 or 10 minutes before the Circle is to begin put on some chants that pertain to the Divine Feminine manifestation you are honoring. If you sing or have a singer as one of your facilitators, have them lead the participants in singing. This begins to draw the group together and helps newcomers integrate into the circle with less awkwardness. At about 5 minutes after the start time wind down the chanting and introduce yourself and the Circle, state the vision or intention of your Circle, and briefly summarize the evening's program: i.e., Tonight we will be celebrating Hecate, and discover if she is the wise crone or queen of the witches. Introduce yourself and then ask each participant to check in. Depending on the size of the group the check-in can simply be their name and one word that expresses how they are feeling. If time allows I like to ask what brought them to the Circle and what they hope to gain from it. These two exercises help to gather all the participants into a cohesive group, and invite them to be fully present.

With this process the intention for the Circle has been clarified, the energies have been set, the facilitators are centered and grounded, and the participants have been gathered and are present. Now you may begin the Circle.

CIRCLE FORMAT

Facilitating a circle that celebrates the Divine Feminine is sacred service. It is both an honor and a responsibility. On behalf of the Divine Feminine, you will be guiding the participants on a journey that will expand awareness, shift behaviors and attitudes and help them release that which is no longer serving them. If you are a solitary practitioner, casting a circle and creating sacred space for your private ritual will also lead you on a journey to expanded awareness that can help you release and shift attitudes, behaviors and beliefs. For individual practitioners I encourage you to journal in order to record your experiences, thoughts and emotions.

Shannon and I have put on Circles for over three years and have developed a format that works well for us. We allow two hours for each circle, plus time for a social hour with tea and cookies at the end. In this section I will cover each phase of the Circle. They are:

- ❖ Introduction
- ❖ Casting the Circle
- ❖ Opening
- ❖ Presentation of the Divine Feminine
- ❖ Group Discussion
- ❖ Guided Visualization
- ❖ Ritual
- ❖ Group Share
- ❖ Goddess Cards
- ❖ Closing – Charge of the Star Goddess
- ❖ Releasing the directions
- ❖ Social Hour with Tea and Cookies

Each section on the individual Divine Feminine persona will be complete with all the information necessary to hold your own circle.

Introductions

If a large group is present, have each participant say their name and a word as to how they are feeling. If it is a smaller group and you have the time, have each participant give their name and ask what brought them to the circle and what they hope to gain out of the evening.

As mentioned in the previous section on Circle Energetics, the introductions are used to gather the participants and help them be fully present.

Casting the Circle

We cast a sacred circle by calling in the directions. The text for the different directions may be read by different participants, or one person may read them all. We have experimented with both. Unfamiliarity with the pronunciation of the Goddess names can create an awkwardness that interferes with the calling in of the energies. I prefer that either Shannon or I lead the Casting of the Circle. I encourage you to experiment and see what works best for you. Many thanks to Shannon who fine-tuned "Casting the Circle!"

CASTING THE CIRCLE

(Everyone faces East) Hail and Welcome, powers of the East and of Air! Corner of the rising sun and new beginnings! Ea, Astarte, Aurora, Goddess of all Beginnings! Come and blow negativity from our minds and awaken us to illumination. Hail and Welcome, powers of the East!

(Everyone faces South) Hail and Welcome, powers of the South and of Fire! Corners of the hearth fire, the noonday sun and passion, Goddess Pele, Kali, Sekhmet, Amaterasu, and Hestia! Come and aid us to be catalysts of compassion within our own lives and in others! Hail and Welcome, powers of the South!

(Everyone faces West) Hail and Welcome, powers of the West and of Water! Life-giving Goddess of the Sea, Aphrodite, Yemaya, Tiamat! Come and fill us with inner knowing and self-acceptance! Hail and Welcome, powers of the West!

(Everyone faces North) Hail and Welcome, powers of the North and of Earth! The corner of all power! Great Demeter, Persephone, Kore, Ceres! Earth Mothers and Fates! Come and show us how to be in balance with cycles, forms, and functions! Hail and Welcome, powers of the North!

(Everyone faces the center for Below) Hail and Welcome, powers of below! To the realm of our planet and to all that makes up our planet in this moment! Gaia, Rhea, Shekhinah! Contain and hold this space for us as we honor and celebrate the Goddess (Name of Divine Feminine).

(Everyone faces the center for Above) Hail and Welcome, powers of above! To the realm of the cosmos and celestial spheres. Nuit and Arianrhod. Guard our circle and surround us in divine light as we embrace the Divine Feminine in the form of the Goddess (Name of Divine Feminine).

(Everyone faces Center) - Hail and Welcome Great Mothers of the center and within! Guadalupe, Isis, Tara, Grandmother Spider, Hecate! Open our hearts to the Divine Feminine as we awaken to the Goddess (Name of Divine Feminine) and are receptive to what she has to show us.

Casting the circle is in effect an enacted group meditation. Together as a group we define a space within the boundaries of ordinary time and space. Together we delineate our sacred space for the evening. In Wiccan tradition it is called "between the worlds." We have invoked the Divine Feminine in all her aspects, so that within this Circle her presence may be revealed. Now she can more fully offer guidance, protection, healing and wisdom. Casting a circle can also be very powerful when casted by the individual practitioner. The circle in itself is an energy form, a boundary that contains the movement of subtle forces. This boundary serves both to keep negative forces out, as well as to keep inside the sacred energies of the Divine Feminine. We have virtually created a sacred container within which we reside with the energies of the Sacred Feminine. This intimate connection with the Divine enables us to more fully connect with the Divine spark that is burning bright within each one of us.

The casting of the circle is the formal beginning of the Circle. It is the cue informing us that it's time to transitions into a deeper state, to suspend belief and allow the analytical critical-self to relax so the intuitive receptive feeling-self can be more present, thereby allowing us to fully participate and receive the benefits of the experience.

Opening

The opening poem serves as an invocation. It serves to both invoke the presence of, as well as to direct each participant's focus to, the Divine Feminine persona we are honoring.

Presentation and Slide Show

Each section includes a 20 to 25 minute presentation on a female deity. The presentation material may be read and enjoyed by the individual practitioner, or shared with a group. If shared with a group it may be read, summarized or paraphrased. I encourage the presenter to practice their presentation out loud several times before the actual Circle so that the content can flow easily and sound less canned. Copies of accompanying PowerPoint slides may be found on my website.

The information has been thoughtfully researched. The reference sources are provided if you desire to do further research. Trained in Women's Spirituality, I have attempted to trace each Divine Feminine image back to her pre-patriarchal roots and to point out where the masculine lens may have denigrated or demeaned her stature, or demoted her in relation to newer male deities.

Group Discussion

Thought provoking questions are provided to stimulate discussion. The individual practitioner is encouraged to ponder and reflect on each question, recording her thoughts in the journal pages provided. For group discussions please see the following section on Group Processes. I usually allow 10 minutes for a group discussion.

Guided Visualization

I have found that many women are hungry for deeper connection to the Divine Feminine. I have found the Sacred Feminine also wants to develop a relationship with us and often has a special message that can differ from person to person. Guided Visualizations allow a time when we can close our eyes, embrace silence and go inward to that still place within. By using verbal cues that elicit visual images a journey or experience can be created in which the female deity is invoked. Using a technique called silent process each person is free to experience the Divine Feminine and to hear whatever message or advice She offers. Many women have had very unique and healing experiences. I have included the text for each guided visualization in this book. Audio recordings of the guided visualizations may be purchased on my website. (www.celebratedivinefeminine.com)

If you take time to listen to a guided visualization, please allow yourself time to journal about what might have come up for you. Sometimes important insights emerge during visualizations. If you don't take time to write them down they might slip away. Time is frequently given during circles for participants to draw or journal after I lead a guided visualization.

Ritual

Rituals are an important part of the Circles. When I first started, I just gave talks on the Goddesses. It was very dry and academic. After several years of trial and error, I realized that an experiential piece was needed. Ritual helps participants to process, integrate and internalize the information, making it a more meaningful experience. Each section on the Divine Feminine has a ritual created specifically for that particular female deity. Each ritual has a different focus such as releasing, transformation, compassion, unconditional love, self-acceptance, prosperity, etc. Many of the rituals, however, can be used independently of the Circles for other sacred events. Adaptations for the individual practitioner are noted.

Group Share

Participants are encouraged to share their experiences. This helps to deepen the personal experience as well as expanding awareness and facilitating positive change with others in the Circle. Please see the section on Group Processes.

Goddess Cards

As part of our In Her Name Circle we have a shuffled and spread deck of the *Goddess Guidance Oracle Cards* by Doreen Virtue on our altar. By virtue of being on the altar in the presence of the Divine Feminine, these cards have been energetically charged and are now an informative divination aid. Each participant draws a card to see what Goddess energy they will walk in for the month. We share the cards we draw. As we have just circled together, each card has relevance for each one of us. It has been remarkable to discover how applicable the cards are to what is going on in the lives of the Circle participants.

Closing

We close with the Charge of the Star Goddess by Starhawk

STARHAWK'S CHARGE OF THE STAR GODDESS

I who am the beauty of the green earth
And the white moon among the stars
And the mysteries of the waters,
I call upon your soul to arise and come unto Me.
For I am the soul of nature that gives life to the universe.
From Me all things proceed and unto Me they must return.

Let My worship be in the heart that rejoices, for behold-
All acts of love and pleasure are My rituals.
Let there be beauty and strength, power and compassion,
Honor and humility, mirth and reverence within you.
And you who seek to know Me, know that your
Seeking and yearning will avail you not, unless
You know the Mystery:
For if that which you seek, you find not within yourself,
You will never find it without.
For behold, I have been with you from the beginning,
And I am that which is attained at the end of desire.

From *The Spiral Dance* by Starhawk, pp 102-103.

Releasing the Circle

We release the directions in the reverse order of which they were cast, beginning with the center and ending with the east.

Begin with Center - Hail and farewell, Great Mothers of the center, thank you for your presence and guidance. We release you. Hail and farewell, Great Mothers of the center!

Above - Hail and farewell, powers and Goddess of Above, thank you for your presence and guidance. Hail and farewell, powers of the Above!

Below - Hail and farewell, powers and Goddess of Below, thank you for your presence and guidance. We release you. Hail and farewell, powers of the Below!

North – Hail and farewell, powers and Goddesses of the North, thank you for your presence and guidance. We release you. Hail and farewell, powers of the North!

West – Hail and farewell, powers and Goddesses of the West, thank you for your presence and guidance. We release you. Hail and farewell, powers of the West!

South – Hail and farewell, powers and Goddess of the South, thank you for your presence and guidance. We release you. Hail and farewell, powers of the South!

East – Hail and farewell, powers and Goddesses of the East, thank you for your presence and guidance. We release you. Hail and farewell, powers of the East!

Social Hour with Tea and Cookies

We follow each circle with a social hour and provide tea and cookies or finger food.

GROUP PROCESSES

Women are relational. It is natural for women to gather in small groups for support, comfort and a compassionate ear. Jean Shinoda Bolen, who wrote the classic text on circles, titled *The Millionth Circle: How to Change Ourselves and the World*, goes so far as to say that circles are "an archetypal form that feels familiar to the psyches of women." She goes on to say that circles are personal, egalitarian, enhance collaborative undertaking and bring people emotionally closer in a less hierarchical way.

A lot of excellent books have been written on the art and maintenance of circles and I will refer to them at the end of this section. I want to stress a few points that I feel are important considerations for facilitating successful circles. Each In Her Name Circle offers time for group sharing. I found out early that it was important for circle members to not only ask questions and offer feedback, but also to share their personal experiences and insights. Often in a circle setting the group share offers opportunities for group insights that can't be arrived at individually. In order for members to share, however, they first must feel safe. To feel safe circle members need to know that they can trust the people within the circle to hold confidences and to listen compassionately. Compassionate listening means to listen without trying to fix or give advice. It means to listen with respect and tolerance honoring each person's right to speak as well as their point of view. In 12-Step programs they have a saying that I find is useful to remember in a group setting:

"Take what you like and leave the rest."

Gathering with other women, especially gathering in the name of the Divine Feminine, can facilitate a sense of connection, personal growth, spiritual awareness and transformation. Here are a few suggestions that will help with the success of your circle.

The Art of Circle Maintenance

❖ Encourage people to speak for themselves. Conversely, let others speak for themselves.

❖ Respect each person's right to be silent. Resist the urge to pressure everyone to contribute during a group share. Sometimes people aren't ready, or feel shy, or are intimidated by the process. Let it be.

❖ Remember that there are no absolute right or wrong answers. Everyone has a right to their own opinions.

❖ Create openings for people to share by asking open ended questions like

    ❖ What is your understanding?

❖ What ideas do you have?

❖ How could this be done differently?

❖ Each person is responsible for their own experience. I have had participants who have amazing experiences during guided visualizations; others have found them to be mildly relaxing. It is all OK and perfect for that individual at that moment.

❖ Honor the group's need for safety by reminding them that whatever is said should be kept in strict confidence.

❖ Unless asked, avoid giving advice, no matter how hard this might be! Listen with a compassionate ear. Many times just being heard is the greatest gift.

❖ Be sensitive to the emotional impact some of the material may have. Be positive and gentle. Remember this is a circle for community, support and celebrating the many manifestations of the Goddess. It is not group therapy.

❖ Show consideration for differences in abilities, cultures, religions, ethnic backgrounds, gender preferences, etc. Each person's background and experience is different and unique. Show respect and tolerance.

❖ Avoid judging anyone's behavior or opinion.

❖ If there is a conflict, seek out that person's point of view and sincerely try to work towards a resolution. Generally, if people see that you care and are sincerely trying, they will meet you half-way.

These suggestions were compiled from the resources listed below.

Jean Shinoda Bolen, *The Millionth Circle: How to Change Ourselves and The World--The Essential Guide to Women's Circles.*

Christina Baldwin, *Calling the Circle: the First and Future Culture.*

Robin Deen Carnes and Sally Craig, *Sacred Circles: A Guide to Creating Your Own Women's Spirituality Group.*

CIRCLE LOGISTICS

Frequency

I hold my circles once a month. This is what works for me in terms of time and effort. It also allows member time to work with and integrate the material. If you are trying to develop a more cohesive group you might want to meet every week or every two weeks. Meeting more frequently can help to foster closer relationships where there is more trust and deeper connection. I have found that the time constraints of circle participants are generally a hindrance to meeting more frequently. People today lead very full lives. Even once a month can be a challenge for some.

Location

My Circle meets at the Unitarian Universalist Congregation in San Mateo. I have found that Unitarian and Unity Churches are very open to hosting these kinds of groups. Some may ask a nominal fee which can be covered by asking for a donation or a participation fee from the members. You can also try bookstores, coffee shops, community centers, and the home of members. The important thing is to make sure the place is clean, safe, comfortable and welcoming. It is the love and sincere intent to call in the energies of the Divine Feminine that will draw in her presence. The size, shape or luxury of the environment is secondary.

Number of Participants

The number of participants will vary with your intent. My desire is to reach out to as many women as possible. I would be thrilled to have 20 to 40 attend each Circle. This size, however, makes it hard to manage meaningful sharing and connection. If you want to create close connection and community, then you might want to keep the circles smaller with 8 to 14 people. If your circle is held in the home, then 8 is a very manageable number. I have also had very powerful groups in which only 4 have shown up. It is not the numbers but the intent and the sincerity of working with the energies of the Divine Feminine that are most important. I always ask the Divine Feminine to inspire those who most need to connect with the featured goddess to be drawn to the Circle.

Time

If you are starting a group, set a time that works best with your schedule and see who shows up. If you are working with several others to organize the group, then solicit potential times and select the best option. You might want to play with different times and days of the week to see what works best. Friday nights work best for me because I prefer to hold the circles on a night when I don't have clients the next day. I also see clients in the evenings, and prefer to hold the circles on a night that doesn't conflict with the needs of my clients. Very few clients are interested in seeing a Hypnotherapist on a Friday night! Fridays are not always ideal, however, because people often make personal plans for Friday nights. I would select the best night for you and see how that works.

Male Participants

Generally it will be women who are called to attend In Her Name Circles. Occasionally a man may ask to participate. I have had a few attend. My only request of a male participant is that they come respectfully with the intent to honor the Divine Feminine. The men who have attended my circles have been gentle souls with a strong connection to their own internal feminine. It was a rich experience for all of us. We all, female and male, carry the Divine Feminine within. In my experience, the men will come once, maybe twice, but will not become regular members.

Open or Closed Circles

Circles can either be open or closed. When a circle is closed the membership is static. After the circle is formed new members are added only rarely. A closed circle allows for greater trust and deeper relationships to develop over time. The challenge is that there is no growth, no new blood and limited outside stimulation. The circle tends to die out as members leave.

In an open circle the attendance can vary with each meeting, as new members cycle in and out continuously. It allows for growth and new ideas. Relationships may not deepen sufficiently for the sharing to be insightful because a deep level of trust can't be achieved with the constant change in membership.

My In Her Name Circles are open circles because I am trying to reach out to as many women as possible in order to introduce them to the Divine Feminine. I do not proselytize, however. I trust that the Goddess will bring to me those who can be best served by introducing them to the Sacred Feminine. And generally this is the case. Even when the circle attendance has been small, the sharing and connection has always been powerful.

You have read why the Divine Feminine is important, learned "her-story" and discovered how the Goddess is connected to all of life. You have also been given the tools and information you might need to lead your own circle, if you choose to do so. Hopefully you are now beginning to realize why there is a growing desire among women to gather in circles to share Her story and reclaim the ancient wisdom of the Goddess for self-empowerment in our contemporary times. In the next section, "Earth, the Body of the Goddess," you will have an opportunity to learn and experience the Divine Feminine manifestations that resonate with the element earth: Neolithic Goddess, Grandmother Spider, Demeter and Persephone, Hecate, Lakshmi and Our Lady of Guadalupe. In the three books to follow I will focus on the Divine Feminine archetypes that resonate with the elements air, fire and water.

PART III

EARTH

The Body of the

GODDESS

Neolithic Mother Goddess

Neolithic Goddess
The Great Mother

CHARGE OF THE QUEEN

I am woman of the sky.
I am woman of the grave.
I am mirror of the moon.
I am reflection of the day.

I am song of the wind.
I am river of the rain.
I am pulse of the stars.
I am churn of the deep.

I am child of the daughter.
I am sister of all sisters.
I am woman of the woman
I am mother of myself.

I am defender of the beauty.
I am midwife of the change
I am creator of the vision.
I am lover of it all

by Donna Henes

10. The Neolithic Goddess: The Great Mother

(Visit www.celebratedivinefeminine.com to view the complementary PowerPoint that accompanies this text.)

IN THIS FIRST section on the Neolithic Goddess you will be introduced to the Ancient Mother Goddess and many of the forms in which she was perceived, honored, and worshipped during the Neolithic Era. Old Europeans were dependent on the earth and the cycles of nature. They saw every part of nature and life as sacred. The goddess manifested in the birds, snakes, bear, deer, fish and many other forms that helped to nourish and sustain their culture. Included are pictures, sketches and line drawings to help you conceptualize the many forms representing the goddess to our early ancestors. I draw upon the work of Marija Gimbutas and present the images according to the categories that she identified and coined: Life Giving Images, Life Sustaining Images, Images of Death and Regeneration, and Images Specific to Regeneration. I offer a brief explanation of the fate of the goddess who faded into obscurity with the advance of Indo-Europeans, the Christianizing of the conquered world by Constantine, and the witch burnings of the 1400 to 1600s. Finally I offer some contemporary applications of the Neolithic Mother Goddess.

I believe it is important for us to research our past, because when we know and understand what came before, we have greater knowledge of how to deal with what lies ahead. Reclaiming the goddess enables us to recover our full human history, both the female and the male story, so we can better understand our behaviors and patterns. With this knowledge it is my hope that we can re-establish the balance between humans and the world we live in. Our current tendency to dominate and control without replenishing may be causing unknown damage to the Earth's natural environment that depends on a very delicate ecological balance we don't fully understand or appreciate. Understanding our ancient ancestors' appreciation and connection to the natural world will, hopefully, encourage you to strengthen your own connection to the Earth, the Great Mother.

Marija Gimbutas is a renowned archaeologist, linguist (over twenty languages) and author of twenty books. The Gimbutas website (www.marijagimbutas.com) calls Marija "The Archaeologist of the Goddess." Initially, she didn't intend to do research on the ancient goddess;

she spent the first part of her career studying and excavating the Bronze Age Kurgan culture, which inhabited most of Europe through the Near East. The Kurgan peoples, who are now more commonly referred to as Indo-Europeans, were a patriarchal culture thought to have originated in the eastern steppes of Russia. They were a pastoral and semi-nomadic group of peoples, who had a hierarchical class structure. They were war-like, produced weapons, rode horses, and their religion centered on the male sky gods. Their agriculture was rudimentary and their ceramic art was poorly developed. They buried their dead in pit graves covered with a cairn, or earthen mound (Gimbutas, *The Living Goddesses*, p xv).

Indo-Europeans migrated from north of the Caucasus to the geographic area that includes much of Europe, Turkey, India, Iran, and Chinese Turkistan. This migration occurred in successive waves from 4400 to 2800 BCE. Sometimes the migrations were more peaceful with a melding of the two cultures. Other times large scale destruction and dislocation occurred (Gimbutas, *The Living Goddesses*, p xvi). The more Gimbutas studied the Kurgan people, the more interested she became in the indigenous people who inhabited the area during the Neolithic Era prior to the Indo-European migration. She spent the last twenty years of her life excavating and researching Neolithic sites in Yugoslavia, Greece, and Italy, which were part of an area she came to call the Goddess Civilization of Old Europe. Gimbutas referred to the inhabitants of Neolithic Old Europe as Old Europeans.

1. Venus of Laussel, c. 30,000 - 25,000 BCE, Laussel (Dordogne), France. ©Lydia Ruyle

The roots of Neolithic lie in the Paleolithic Era. It is now believed that Ice Age people were fully evolved human beings, capable of speaking and comprehending symbolically based languages. They lived in established communities and shared common norms and values. Their religion evolved into the belief that the earth was the source of life, and was therefore the sacred mother (Gadon, p 3-4). This picture is of the Venus of Laussel. Carved from limestone, she is about 4 ½ inches tall and was found in Laussel (Dordogne), France. She is believed to date back to 30,000-25,000 BCE. She appears to be in the late stages of pregnancy and is still marked with traces of red ochre (Gadon, p 12). Her generous layers of fat were possibly considered beautiful and were a symbol of abundance in the harsh and unpredictable Paleolithic environment.

These sketches of vulvas were inspired by drawings found in Elinor Gadon's book *The Once and Future Goddess: A Sweeping Visual Chronicle of the Sacred Female and Her Reemergence in the Cult.* The originals date back to 30,000 to 9,000 BCE and were found engraved, scratched, or painted on walls of caves, on stones, or on rock formations. Our Paleolithic ancestors understood sexual fertilization in animals and humans. The vulva is one of oldest markings representing the goddess, and it symbolized

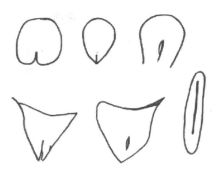

2. Vulvas - Earliest markings representing the Goddess. Originals date back 10,000 to 30,000 years.

fertility and the potential to create, to birth and to give life. It is a pervasive symbol for the goddess spanning time and space. The sacred triangle, a downward pointing triangle, is a natural evolution of the vulva and is a contemporary symbol of divine feminine power (p 14-15).

The Neolithic people of Old Europe were a peace loving agrarian society. The culture was earth based and centered on crops and domesticated animals. They worshiped goddesses, or rather a goddess who appeared in various manifestations throughout the seasons of the year. The Neolithic Mother Goddess was not one, but existed in many forms, though she was always the Mother Goddess. She was present within everyone, and women were her living symbols on earth.

Old Europeans saw themselves as part of nature, not separate. Even their settlements blended with their natural environment. They believed that the earth was the sacred mother. The earth produced plants and crops that supported both animals and humans. When life died and withered, it wasn't the end; instead the decaying matter fertilized the earth for rebirth. This was the great seasonal round. Neolithic culture centered on the wheel of life and its cyclical nature: birth, death and regeneration.

3. Venus of Willendorf ©Lydia Ruyle, 25,000 BCE. Found on Danube near Willendorf, Austria.

Marija Gimbutas pointed out in her book *The Living Goddesses*, that from the Western perspective—which is typically viewed through a masculine lens—the female body is a symbol for sexual arousal or fertility. This perception was projected onto Paleolithic and Neolithic female figurines. To our ancient ancestors, however, nude depictions of the female body were not obscene, but were rather a sophisticated artistic representation of their reverence for the Great Mother. Fertility was important during the Neolithic, but the female body conveyed a much broader symbolism. It represented nourishment, the ability to procreate and was life enhancing. In fact, the concept of the obscene as we understand it probably didn't exist (p 5).

The female force was the pregnant vegetation goddess, but she also personified every phase of life from birth to death and regeneration. She was the Creatrix, the Great Mother, from whom all life arose and to whom everything returned. Figurines were not actual representations, but were abstracted or exaggerated. The accentuated part often pertained to the function that was being venerated, possibly to express gratitude and appreciation, or to make a request. The figurines and pottery paintings or carvings were, therefore, artistic expressions of various manifestations of the goddesses or gods (p 5).

CHARACTERISTICS OF NEOLITHIC ART:

Schematic Forms:

4. Clay Cup as
Breast,
Novi Sad Museum,

Many of the artifacts from the Neolithic Era are schematic representations. They may appear unfinished and strange. Sometimes they portray a single body part such as this single clay cup with an exaggerated breast. Other images used are of buttocks, or a pregnant belly without arms or legs. A breast on a vessel probably represented liquid nourishment. These artifacts were the original modern art and were created to convey a symbolic message much like the Christian cross, a contemporary schematic image, conveys an important religious message. Just because we don't understand the significance of a particular symbol doesn't mean there was no original intent. These early images are not disparaging of the human body, but most likely express a sacred message we just don't understand (p 5-6).

Exaggerated Body Parts

Generative organs, in Neolithic art, were frequently exaggerated, Gimbutas pointed out. This included breasts, vulvas and buttocks. The emphasis is thought to have enhanced the power of that particular body part. The vulva and buttocks were not simply sexual symbols but signified life giving properties and sustenance. For instance, exaggerated buttocks possibly relates to breasts and/or to double eggs, therefore symbolizing the power to increase by doubling. This illustrates the state in which one human being becomes two through pregnancy. We can't know for sure. It is important to think outside our cultural lens which can be limiting when we attempt to understand cultures that are foreign to us. The vulva dominates in both Paleolithic and Neolithic art and is represented as a triangle, an oval, an open circle or as a bud or branch. These symbolize life-giving properties rather than merely symbolizing the erotic or simply fertility (p 7-8).

5. Exaggerated Buttocks
c. 6000-5800 BCE
Novi Sad
Museum, Serbia

The Manifestations of the Goddess

According to Marija Gimbutas in *The Living Goddess*, the Neolithic artistic representations of the goddess fall into four main categories, and reflect the cycle of life.

- Life Giving Images
- Life Sustaining Images
- Images of Death and Regeneration
- Images Specific to Regeneration

LIFE GIVING

The Birth Goddess

The birth goddess is one of the oldest representations of the goddess appearing for more than twenty thousand years. Birth was one of the most sacred events in the Neolithic Era. The famous image on the right is believed to be the mother goddess giving birth. In some locations

6. Mother Goddess of Catal Hoyuk, Museum of Anatolian Civilization, Turkey, c. 6000 - 5000 BCE. ©Lydia Ruyle.

special rooms were constructed for birth, including Catal Hoyuk, Turkey and the island of Malta. In Catal Hoyuk, a Neolithic archaeology site in south central Turkey, there is what is thought to be a birthing room. It is painted red, the color of blood and of life. Stylized figures painted on the walls resemble women giving birth. Also painted on the walls are circular forms and wavy lines thought to be symbols for the cervix, umbilical cord and amniotic fluid. A low plaster platform could have been used for the actual birthing (p 11).

Water Signs

There has been a long connection between moisture, life, and the life-giving goddess. Life on earth began in water, and human life begins in the waters of a woman's womb. Because water is necessary to begin life, as well as to sustain life, it was believed that the Great Mother ruled all water sources including lakes, rivers, springs, wells and even the rain clouds. Throughout history springs and wells have been designated as special centers of healing and were said to be watched over by manifestations of the Divine Feminine. (Our Lady of Lourdes in France and the

7. Clay Seal with
Water Symbols,
Pazardzik, Bulgaria

goddess Brigit, or Saint Bridget of Ireland, are just two examples.) This connection of the goddess to water explains the appearance of water symbols (i.e. nets, streams or wavy lines, and parallel lines (possibly symbolizing rain)) on many Neolithic artifacts (p 12). In more recent historical times Christian churches and cathedrals have been built near or on these sacred springs or wells that were formerly ancient goddess sites.

Mother and Child

The mother and child theme popularized in Christianity is an old theme dating back to the Neolithic. The sketch on the right is the subject on one of Lydia Ruyles' Spirit of the Divine Feminine banners. It is of a terracotta clay sculpture found in Western Romania that is 7000 years old. There are symbols carved on her front and

8. Madonna of
Rast. Sketch
©Lydia *Ruyle*
Terracotta clay
sculpture,
W. Romania,
early 5th
millennium BCE

back which Gimbutas believed were an early form of writing or script. Notice how tenderly the mother is cradling her child, which is very similar to how a mother might hold her child today.

Life Sustaining

Bear and Deer

The bear and deer frequently appear with the birth-giving goddess. Artemis was said to incarnate in these forms by the ancient Greeks. She is also the Greek goddess of childbirth.

Bear Goddess

The bear is connected to the goddess as a mother image because of her legacy as a nurturer, and because she is fiercely protective of her young. The bear also disappears in winter to hibernate (a deathlike sleep) and reappears in the spring with her cubs, which connects her to the birth, death and rebirth cycle (p 13). Mother and child figurines may sometimes have the head of bears or wear other animal masks. Some Eastern European customs still refer to a pregnant woman as "the little bear" (p 12).

9. Pregnant Bear Goddess Pazardzik, Bulgaria

10. Deer Figurine Vase, Karonova I (Muldava, central Bulgaria) c. 5800 BCE.

Deer

The deer and elk were also sacred to the goddess, possibly because deer lose their antlers in the fall, and re-grow them annually in the spring. Antlers were symbolically powerful talisman, and deer antlers, shoulder blades and teeth have been found at Neolithic burial sites. Attractive figurines and pottery dating back to the Neolithic have been found shaped like a deer, or with deer painted on the artifacts or displayed in relief. (p 13).

The Bird Goddess

(The clay figurine to the right was modeled from a sketch in Marija Gimbutas' *Language of the Goddess*, p 8) The bird symbolizes the life sustaining aspect of the goddess. Birds were plentiful during the Neolithic era, and birds and eggs were an important part of the Neolithic food supply. It's not surprising, then, that birds are a popular subject in Neolithic art. Their mysterious seasonal disappearance and re-appearance probably enhanced the association of birds with the goddess. Many ancient myths and folktales still survive today which incorporate eggs, i.e. *Jack and the Beanstalk and the Golden Egg* (*The Living Goddesses*, p 14).

11. Bird Goddess, c. 4500 BCE, Svetozsarevo, Central Yugoslavia

Frequently the bird goddess is depicted with a beaked or duck-billed mask and a human female body. Many figurines combine the human female

12. Cucuteni Venus ©Lydia Ruyle Terracotta, c. 5000 BCE. National Historical Museum. Bucarest. Romania

form with a specific species of bird, such as waterfowl, birds of spring and birds of prey. The bird goddess may have arms placed like wings, like this figurine from Crete, or stumps in place of arms. Some have exaggerated buttocks suggestive of a bird's body. Others have small holes in the shoulders and masks for feathers. Many bird goddess figurines display symbols of the goddess—chevrons, tri-lines, meanders and streams—as is found on this banner by Lydia Ruyle of the Cucuteni Venus, on the left. Some water vessels were also formed in the shape of birds (p 14).

Snake and the Snake Goddess

Snakes were another life sustaining symbol for the goddess. Marija Gimbutas suggests that it's not the body of the snake that was sacred but rather it was the energy of its coiling and spiraling movements which she felt were indicative of the energy found in the functions of life, from walking and running, to sexual activity, to the fertilization and growth of plants and animals. The snake was also a symbol of renewal because it hibernates during the winter and re-appears in the spring, suggesting the continuity of life. Its annual re-emergence coincides with the spring, which led to the belief that the snake actually brought the spring, rather than announcing its arrival (*The Language of the Goddess*, p 121).

13. Snake Coil on vase flanked by zig zag pattern. Cucuteni B Koshilvtsi, c. 3700-3500 BCE

Because snakes make their homes in the ground they were believed to have a deep connection to the goddess and deceased ancestors. This linked the snake to the death aspect of the goddess. We will visit this later in the section on Death and Regeneration.

Symbols of the snake goddess, Gimbutas says in *The Living Goddess*, include snake coils (such as in this artifact from a museum in Bulgaria on the left), spirals, zigzags and wavy lines that imitate the movement of snakes. Snake crawls or zigzags were popular designs on vases and pottery during the Neolithic through the Bronze Age and beyond (p 14-15).

Pregnant Vegetation Goddess

The Neolithic farmers were awed by the annual cycle of germination, growth and harvest. Highly observant of nature, they understood the connection between the germinating seeds in the fields in the field and new life growing in the womb. In Catal Hoyuk a clay female figurine was found with a grain seed pressed into her stomach cavity. She is one of the first representations of a pregnant vegetation goddess, earth goddess, or Mother Earth. Hundreds

14. Pregnant Pazardzik Venus ©Lydia Ruyle, East Balkan Civilization. Pazardzik. Central Bulgaria. c. 4500 BCE

of other pregnant goddess figurines have been excavated from Old European settlements. The pregnant vegetation goddess was associated with food, fertility and harvest. At other times the pregnant goddess was found in graves or tombs, like the Pazardzik Venus by Lydia Ruyle, which suggests she is the goddess of birth, death, and rebirth. The Greek and Roman agrarian rituals and festivals, and the harvest festivals still celebrated around the world, quite possibly have their roots in the Neolithic. Artemis, as the Goddess of Agriculture and Demeter, as the Goddess of the Grain, share similarities with the pregnant vegetation goddess which links them back to the Neolithic.

Vegetation Year God

A male deity appears to have been worshipped during the Neolithic as the consort of the pregnant Vegetation Goddess. He was a divine metaphor for the cyclic growth and decay of the plant world. He may be the

15. Vegetation Year God. Sesklo Culture, Thessaly, c. 5900-5700 BCE.

forerunner of Dumuzi, the consort of the Sumerian goddess Inanna. The male year god of vegetation took several forms mirroring the changing of the seasons. In spring he is a young man embodying the strength and virility needed to awaken the sleeping goddess and revive the earth that has been frozen with snow and dark. At the end of summer, the time of harvest, he is shown as a mature man embodying the harvest, sometimes depicted with a sickle or a crook across his shoulder or attached to his belt.

Figurines of the male god in his old age have been found dating back to 6000 BCE. They portray him seated on a throne with his elbow on his knees and his hands supporting his head as if he is reflective during the quiet of the winter. He is sometimes called the Sorrowful God or Sorrowful Ancient. It was believed that the year god died in the winter only to be reborn again in the spring, according to the great cyclical round of birth death and rebirth as marked by the seasons (p 17).

It is important to note that here we have a compatible joining of the female and male harvest deities, both contributing to the rebirth and revitalization of the land. This is in sharp contrast to the later Indo-European sky gods that dominated and subjugated the female deities, or, as in most monotheistic religions, sought to exclude the Divine Feminine altogether.

Vegetation Goddesses & Gods

It is speculated that Old Europeans believed that male and female coupling was necessary to insure the fertility of the land, plants and animals. The Gumelnita Lovers, c 5000-4750 BCE, from the Karonova Culture in the East Balkans (see right) may be a representation of this. A similar belief existed in the 3rd millennium in Sumer, from which there are documented references to the sacred marriage, or what the ancient

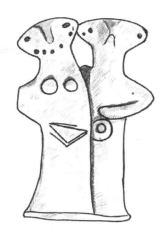

16. Gumelnita Lovers, terracotta statuette, possibly portrays a sacred marriage. C. 5000-4750 BCE, East Balkan Karanovo culture (Gumelnita Tell, lower Danube, Southern Romania).

Greeks called *hieros gamos*. The enactment of a sacred marriage ritual ensured the well-being and fertility of the land. The male god aroused and stimulated the goddess, impregnating her so that she could bring forth new life. Without this coupling, impotency and famine was feared. Beliefs surrounding this ancient ritual appear to be rooted in the Neolithic (p18).

IMAGES OF DEATH AND REGENERATION

Birds of Prey – Vulture

Vulture, raptors and other birds of prey embodied death in Old European imagery. The vulture dwells both in Near East and Europe. There is a wall painting, or vulture shrine, at Catal Hoyuk that shows vultures swooping down on headless bodies. Some, though not all, Neolithic communities practiced excarnation. The dead were not buried immediately, but instead the corpses were exposed on outdoor platforms. The flesh was stripped from the bodies by the birds until only the bones were left. After the removal of the flesh, the bones were buried (p 21).

17. Clay Figurine of Vulture, Konya

Birds of Prey – Owl

18. Owl Goddess
c. 5000 BCE
Linearband-keramik Culture,
Upper Rhein

The Owl, another bird of prey, lives in most of Europe. Its likeness is carved into monuments and tombs of Old Europeans. In southern France the owl appears on Upper Paleolithic cave walls in Les Trois Freres caves. Images of the owl, especially its eyes, were carved on pottery and pieces of bone. Throughout time it has evoked a sense of mystery and awe. The owl is almost supernatural in appearance with its upright perch, focused stare and eerie screams in the dead of night (p 20).

Both history and iconography has connected the owl with important goddesses such as Athena, the Greek goddess of knowledge and wisdom; and Lilith, the Sumerian-Akkadian goddess whose name appears in the Hebrew Old Testament and the Hebrew Midrash, a collection of myths and folktales that didn't make it into the Hebrew bible. Lilith was the first wife of Adam. According to legend she refused to be submissive and fled when Adam insisted that they couple with her beneath. When she refused to return even though God threatened her with isolation and the death of her children, Lilith was demonized. Myths claim she snatches young babies from their cradles at night. Her name is thought to mean screech owl. The goddess of death, as represented by the owl and raptor, also assured rebirth.

The Stiff White Nude

Stiff white goddess figurines, such as this figure to the right which Gimbutas originally referred to as schematized bone figurines, are found mostly in Neolithic graves. Frequently their forearms are folded across their torsos resembling a corpse in their final repose. Frequently a bone color, which associates them with death, they are carved from marble, alabaster or white stone. They have small or almost non-existent breasts which downplay their life-sustaining aspects. It is conjectured

19. Schematized Bone Figurine from Ruse, N. Bulgaria, c. 4500 - 4000 BCE.

that Old Europeans believed that the goddess in this form accompanied them on their journey to the realm of the dead. Believing that regeneration follows death, just as spring follows the frozen lifelessness of winter; they believed the goddess accompanied them through their transition to rebirth. Some stiff white goddesses have exaggerated pubic triangles (as this one has) which links death with regeneration (p 21).

The Gorgon

Because the snake disappeared in the winter to hibernate (a death-like sleep) and lived in the ground where the deceased ancestors were buried, the snake was also linked to death and regeneration. On the left is a replica of a mask excavated from the Varna cemetery in Bulgaria on the Black Sea Coast. It is thought to be the snake goddess of death and has round eyes, a long mouth, and studs representing teeth, which were characteristic of the snake. On the right is a banner by Lydia Ruyle of a modern representation of Medusa, the Gorgon who was the goddess of death. Medusa was believed to be a fierce and wise goddess of great power and energy, as symbolized by the snakes in her hair and belt, and around her body. Old Europeans did not fear death as we do today. Death was part of the cycle of life and lead to rebirth. It was the Indo-Europeans and the rise of the sky gods that sought to control and subjugate nature, and thus life, who split death off from life and made it something frightening. Masks of the snake goddess of death, such as the one above, are thought to be forerunners of the Gorgon, which dates back to 6000 BCE. (p 24-25).

20. Death Mask replica, c. 4500 BCE, found in grave at Varna Cemetery, Bulgaria.

21. Medusa Banner, ©Lydia Ruyle by Lydia Rule

The most famous and frightening depiction or rendition of the Gorgon was Medusa, and dates back to the 7th to 5th centuries BCE. She became the terrifying manifestation of death goddess. Masks and images of her paralyzing face were frequently combined with symbols of dynamic life energy: vines, snakes, spirals and lizards. Greeks texts record that the blood from Medusa's snaky locks contained magic properties that could both create and destroy. This could be a distortion of earlier beliefs and taboos about the power of a woman's moon blood, or menstruation.

22. & 23. Two heads of Medusa that serve as the base for two pillars deep in the city's cistern, Istanbul, Turkey.

The Gorgon was considered so powerful that she was placed on coins, public buildings, temple pediments, and on shields of warriors. She adorned the breastplate of the warrior-goddess Athena. In Istanbul two heads of Medusa still reside deep in the city's cistern as the base for two pillars.

IMAGES OF REGENERATION

Frog and the Frog Goddesses

Frogs live in an aquatic environment with parallels to amniotic fluid. They appear in the spring, are cyclical, and have a close resemblance to the human fetus. The goddess as represented by a frog has a long history. The primordial mother of the Egyptians was the frog goddess, Heket. Her hieroglyphic sign was a frog, and she

24. Sheila na gig, 1200 CE, from Medieval Ireland and England was incorporated and honored in old churches.

was believed to control the potential for fertility, as well as regeneration after death. The Celtic Sheila na gig with her round eyes and large vulva is a more modern version of the frog goddess. As birth giver and regeneratrix she was inherited from the Neolithic. Her image can be found carved on castles, churches and other buildings built between the 12th and 16th centuries in England, France, Ireland and Wales. Sitting naked, her legs stretched out froglike, her hands either point to her genitals or part her labia. Some of the Sheila na gigs have frightening heads or skeleton-like skulls. She is highly revered, but very little is known about her history or mythology (p 28-30).

Fish and the Fish Goddesses

The fish is another regenerative image. It has a strong resemblance to the uterus as well as associations with aquatic symbolism. The fish shape appears in engravings and paintings dating all the way back to the Paleolithic era in Old Europe. The excavation at Lipinski Vir has unearthed many remarkable fish goddess sculptures that date back to 6500-5500 BCE. Net designs were also popular Neolithic images because the net was used to capture the fish (p 30-31). The fish was also a popular sign in Christianity. Fish was *Ichthys* in Greek; the five letters became an acronym for Jesus. They are: *Iesous* **Ch**ristos **Th**eou **Y**ios **S**oter. Or *'Jesus Christ, God's Son, Savior.'* (www.catholic-saints.info)

25. Fish Goddess carved in stone, c. 5500-6500 BCE, Lipinski Vir, Serbia.

26. Fish Goddess, Danube River near Lipinski Vir, Serbia, c. 5000 - 6000 BCE,
© Lydia Rluyle

Fish Goddess

Compare the image on the banner by Lydia Ruyle (left) of a 7 to 8000 year old fish goddess found along the Danube in Serbia at Lipinski Vir, to the Sheila na gig image above. Some images from our ancient ancestors defy logic and span time and space. Though this artifact is identified as a fish goddess, it has a strong resemblance to the Sheila na gig, emphasizing the Sheila na gig's connection to both the Neolithic frog and fish goddess. This image of the fish goddess is especially interesting with her bird-like claws spreading her vulva. Her almost nonexistent breasts, her vulva and her bird of prey claws signify she is an image of the goddess of death and regeneration.

109

The Bucrania

The bucranium—the skull of the bull or cow's head with horns—was also a symbol of regeneration; both early cows and bulls had horns. Bucrania bear a strong resemblance to the female uterus and fallopian tubes. At the archaeological site at Catal Hoyuk, rooms thought to be temples or shrines contained bucrania. In one instance the bucrania were placed below the spread eagled image of the goddess (see right).

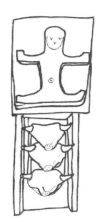

27. Replica of Bucrania Shrine, Catal Hoyuk, Turkey, Museum of Anatolian Civilizations, Ankara, Turkey

Elsewhere, such as in Crete, sculptures of bucrania, or sacred horns, were placed either above or flanking entrances to ancient buildings or tombs. Possibly the life energy that rose from the bull or cow's head represented rebirth, new life, or the goddess herself (p 36).

The Phallus

The phallus represents the male life force and can be compared to the snake, the life column, or the tree of life. Sometimes the phallus is portrayed separately. Other times it is part of a figurine, such as the neck of a female figurine (see right), or an object such as a wine cup stem. Artistic representations of the phallus originated during the Neolithic. It continues to be a sacred icon in contemporary times. There are temples

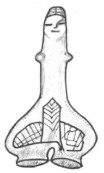

28. Phallic Symbol intensifies regenerative qualities of the goddess. Starcevo culture, SE Hungary. 5000 - 5300 BCE

in India that feature rigid phallus-shaped stones know as lingams. These are not merely sexual symbols or fertility symbols. The lingams and phallus shaped artifacts symbolically connect the male life force energy to the goddess of regeneration(p 37-38)

The Triangle

29. Triangles on pottery, Pazardzik, Bulgaria

The triangle, especially the downward pointing triangle which represents the pubic triangle, is a regenerative symbol of the goddess dating back some 300,000 years (p 38). Modern triangular images would be the Triple Goddess or the Christian Trinity.

In Neolithic art the triangle's regenerative symbolism becomes more apparent when found in association with other regenerative symbols, such as solar rays, sprouts, branches, hair, spirals, hourglass, etc. The triangle's regenerative message is also emphasized when found in conjunction with symbols of death, i.e. raptor or bird's feet. Death to the Neolithic was just part of the cycle of life and was the stage preceding regeneration. The goddess regenerates all plant, animal and human life (p 38-40).

THE FATE OF THE NEOLITHIC MOTHER GODDESS

As long as the Old European civilization survived, the Great Neolithic Mother Goddess lived. If you remember from the "Herstory of the Goddess," around 4400 BCE waves of semi-nomadic Indo-European gradually migrated into Old Europe. Twenty-five hundred years of sometimes aggressive migrations simply overwhelmed the peaceful agrarian Old Europeans. Initially the goddess(es) shared power with the pantheon of sky gods, but eventually the prestige of the goddess diminished, and women and women's values were suppressed. In the Near East she became Lilith, Asherah, Astarte, Cybele, Inanna and others. In Eastern and Southern Europe she became fragmented into the manifestations of Artemis, Demeter, Hera, Hecate, Athena, Aphrodite, and many more.

The final blow to the goddess came with the conversion of the Roman Emperor Constantine in 320 CE. He imposed Christianity as the state religion. Since then Christianity has attempted to convert the rest of the world to the one "true" faith. With the suppression of the goddess, her culture and history were submerged, for history is written by the victors, which in this case were the males of our patriarchal monotheistic Western Culture.

Eventually the goddess religion and those that worshipped her were portrayed as heretical. The witch burnings that began in the 1400s and lasted into the 1600s were another attempt by the religious patriarchs to wipe out the last remnants of the followers of the old ways of the goddess. Many healers, herbalists, and midwives, those who did the most good for the common people, were thought to be frequent victims of the witch burnings. (Gadon xiv) The legacy of our past is that we still fear the archetype of the witch. Pagan traditions -- often synonymous with goddess traditions -- are thought to be primitive, superstitious, and uninformed. However, "pagan" is derived from the Latin word *paganus;* it simply means "rural" or "rustic."

The earth is beginning to reveal the secrets of the past, however. Archaeological evidence, some of which you have had a glimpse of in this section, is beginning to indicate that an ancient goddess civilization existed. Much of this information is coming from Eastern Europe, as information was finally able to be released to the West with the fall of the Iron Curtain. Limited funds and other pressing priorities are hampering this research, however. But every day we are recovering more information about the goddess for she is re-emerging into human consciousness. In our own time, in our own culture, claims Elinor Gadon, the goddess once again is becoming a symbol of empowerment for women. The goddess is becoming:

❖ a metaphor for the earth as a living organism

❖ an archetype for feminine consciousness

❖ a mentor for healers

❖ the emblem of a new political movement

❖ an inspiration for artists

❖ a model for re-sacralizing the female body and the mystery of human sexuality

❖ For some, a catalyst for an emerging spirituality that is earth-centered (p xv)

NEOLITHIC MOTHER GODDESS: CONTEMPORARY APPLICATIONS

The Great Mother of the Neolithic reminds us that she is the creatrix. She is the earth; the source of procreative energy for all life. From her body all life is sustained. She is the mother who nourishes and nurtures all her children without discrimination. She desires that all people enjoy her abundance, celebrate their bodies and be passionately alive. The Great Mother also warns us that when Her body, the earth, is ravaged and plundered, and Her gifts are disrespected, there will be retribution and many innocent will suffer. We see this in the regions of the Sahara where desserts have expanded, in the Gulf where oil spills have spoiled the seas and the coastlines, and globally where melting polar ice threatens to destabilize the earth's climates and ocean currents. Balance is a criterion of our Great Mother's gifts. When balance is honored and maintained, all life flourishes. When there is greed and gluttony, suffering follows. The Great Mother sends out a call to each one of us to take action, to do what we can to restore balance to the earth.

The Great Mother is also the Goddess of Death, for all things must eventually come to an end. The old must be cleared away to make room for the new. Just as the goddess is generous and nurturing, she can also be as ferocious and powerful as thunder and lightning, and as destructive as the hurricane or tornado. These are all aspects of the goddess. In nature, decaying plants and animals fertilize the soil providing nutrients for new growth. Old ideas and behaviors, and the wisdom, love and lessons from those who have passed on, also fertilize the new ideas and behaviors of today. Nothing is truly lost, it is just recycled.

In summary, the Neolithic Goddess has her roots in the Paleolithic and has probably been worshipped for 25-30,000 years. Old Europeans were agrarian, peaceful and lived close to nature. All of life was sacred. To them the earth was the mother, and they saw the goddess in the birds, snakes, deer, bear, fish and other living creatures that nourished and sustained them. She gave life as the birth giving goddess, she sustained life by providing food sources and water, and she was the goddess of death, for the people of the Neolithic saw death as a part of life. The goddess was also regenerative. There are many symbols that represent the goddess' regenerative qualities, including fish, frogs, bucrania, and triangles.

The goddess declined in importance eventually becoming, with the advent of patriarchy, monotheistic religions and the witch burnings, just characters in legends and mythology. Worshipping the goddess became not only unpopular, but dangerous. Times are changing though, and archaeological excavations are indicating that an ancient goddess civilization did exist. Every day more information about this ancient goddess civilization is surfacing. Today there is a growing movement that honors the Divine Feminine, and many are re-claiming the goddess as a symbol of empowerment for women.

QUESTIONS FOR REFLECTION

One of the gifts of the Mother Goddess is the cycle of life. It is Her promise that death is followed by renewal and rebirth. When we truly understand this cycle we are able to live in harmony with ourselves, with others and the world.

Take a moment to reflect on the cycle of nature. What cycle are you in?

- ❖ Are you in a cycle of reflection and gestation?
- ❖ Are you sowing seeds for a new venture?
- ❖ Is there a phase of potentiality, procreation and creativity which lies ahead of you?
- ❖ Is this a time of tending and nurturing your projects or your family?
- ❖ Or is this a time to harvest what you have sowed throughout your life?
- ❖ Is there waste to be discarded?
- ❖ Is there fertilizer for new growth, new ventures, new opportunities?
- ❖ Is there wisdom to share with others?

SOURCES

Elinor W. Gadon, *The Once and Future Goddess: A Sweeping Visual Chronicle of the Sacred Female and Her Reemergence in the Cultural Mythology of Our Time.*

Marija Gimbutas, *The Language of the Goddess.*

Marija Gimbutas and Miriam Robbins Dexter, *The Living Goddesses.*

Marija Gimbutas, www.marijagimbutas.com.

Lydia Ruyle, *Goddess Icons: Spirit Banners of the Divine Feminine.*

"*Ichthus* / Fish Christian Symbol,"http://www.catholic-saints.info/catholic-symbols/ichthus-fish-christian-symbol.htm.

NEOLITHIC VILLAGE GUIDED VISUALIZATION

You might want to have some paper and crayons or markers close by, or even some clay, so that you can capture what you experience during this guided visualization with the Great Mother of the Neolithic.

Now close your eyes and settle back into your chair and as you allow your breath to deepen begin to let go of any stress or tightness you may be carrying in your body..... Now take a deep breath breathing in peace and calm all the way into you diaphragm and hold a second... then exhale slowly letting go of any tension, any holding in your body. Take a second deep breath, breathing in peace and serenity and hold... and as you slowly exhale just let go of the busy-ness of your day as you become calmer, more relaxed. Just feel that tension and anxiousness begin to drain out and away as you become calmer and quieter...... Take a third deep breath filling up with up with the stillness of tranquility... and as you slowly exhale, surrender to deep inner peace and quiet.

Now begin to call back all the pieces of yourself that you may have scattered out and about into the cosmos over the last days and weeks and begin to spiral all those pieces right back into your heart space so that you are totally present right here, right now... Allow yourself to sink even deeper into the stillness within.

As you sink into the calm stillness of your inner landscape feel yourself being drawn downward as if you are descending down through a tunnel, a tunnel through time and space....traveling a long distance over many lands, floating far back into time, through centuries and centuries until you find yourself in old Europe, when all was peaceful and life was simple and dependent on the generosity and abundance of the earth. This was a time when all life came from the mother, the Great Mother, the source of all, and to whom everything returned.

Imagine yourself walking through the streets of your Neolithic village. You recognize and greet the people who are busy at work preparing food, or making pottery, or weaving or making nets. You notice some of the people are missing. Some of the men and boys are missing, probably out hunting, or fishing, or checking the traps for small animals, or tending the heard of animals. Several of the women may be off in the fields with the crops, or gathering the fruits and nuts that are in season. Everyone is content and busy, and you may hear singing, chanting, or the rhythm of drums.

You are walking towards the center of the village to the central building that serves as the community temple where the sacred rites are performed, where the Great Mother, the Goddess is honored. You are going there because there is something you need. Possibly you are in need of healing, either physically, emotionally or spiritually. Or maybe you are seeking some insight or advice regarding a challenge or issue that is troubling you. Take a moment to reflect on your purpose for visiting the sanctuary of the Great Mother.... You know that you will find peace and quiet in the temple and you hope that the Great Mother will come to spend time with you there.

You walk inside and you pause to give your eyes time to adjust to the dim light....In one area there is an altar. On the altar is a collection of figurines that represent the Great Mother in her many manifestations. Take time to look at all the different images. Some are realistic representations... others are symbolic with schematic designs of breasts or vulvas... a few have exaggerated body parts such as large buttocks or elongated necks.... and some are part animal and part human...All were made by members of your clan as part of a devotional practice to honor the Mother Goddess, to symbolize one of Her many aspects, or to request a blessing or a favor from Her, such as good crops, ample hunting, the promise of a much wanted child. All of the goddess figurines were made to invoke the presence of the benevolent Mother to the community.

One of the goddess figurines catches your eye.... You feel drawn to it.... It has the right healing energy for you.... There is something that you need, or that you need help with and this particular goddess figurine is calling to you.... Stoop down and pick it up and gaze at it.... Study it closely.... Look at the markings.... turn it over. How big is it? .... What shape is it? .... How heavy is it? .... What color is it? ....

Listen the Great Mother has a message she wants to convey to you.

The Great Mother of the Neolithic reminds you that she is the creatrix. She is the earth, the source of procreative energy for all of life. From her body she nourishes all her children, each without discrimination. It is her desire that all peoples should enjoy her abundance equally. She insists there is enough for everyone to have shelter, clothes and full bellies. She weeps at how her body, the earth, has been ravaged and plundered, how her gifts have been disrespected. She is filled with deep sorrow that many innocent will now suffer from the wanton carelessness of those few arrogant ones who feel entitled to take without respecting the natural balance of her laws. There is enough for all, when the balance of nature is honored and maintained, all life can flourish, she claims. She invites you to enjoy the abundance of the earth, which is her body. She wants there to be laughter and pleasure and plenty for everyone. In exchange She requests that you respect Her body and that you do what you can to restore balance according to the laws of nature.

Now the Great Mother asks what healing energy you need for your body or for your life. (pause) What knowledge or answers do you seek? (pause) Continue to hold the Goddess figurine and allow a flow of connection or energy to take place.... Be still and allow yourself to receive a vision or a message. (pause)

If you need clarification or more information, take time to ask it now and listen for her response.

When the communication is complete take one last look at the goddess figurine you are holding... Imprint the image in your mind. You will soon have an opportunity to create a replication of what you see and experience. And know that the Neolithic Goddess may continue to reveal information or ideas over the next few days or weeks. This knowledge may come in dreams or as sudden insights, so be sure to be open to receive these epiphanies.

Now it is time to return. Set the goddess figurine back in her place on the altar and bid farewell. Breathe in the energy of this room that is filled with the essence of the Great Neolithic Mother. Then turn and take you leave. Find your way back through the village nodding to the people you know as you pass by. And now slowly begin to feel yourself being drawn back through the tunnel of time to this time and this place remembering everything. Feel the breath in your lungs, the weight of your body in your chair and your feet upon the floor. And when you are ready, open your eyes and stretch.

(An audio recording of this guided visualization may be purchased on my website at www.celebratedivinefeminine.com for a nominal fee.)

RITUAL FOR THE NEOLITHIC GODDESS

Supplies

Clay, tools for working with clay, string for cutting (dental floss works great), plastic table clothes (optional), pictures of Neolithic goddess figurines (optional), willing hearts, creative spirits and permission to get your hands dirty. Candle for the altar and incense with which to bless your clay goddess images.

Set Up

Prior to the circle, set up a separate area in which you can individually or as a group work with clay to make your own clay goddess images. Plastic table cloths taped down over the table or counter tops makes a nice protective surface for working with clay. It is also an easy way to dispose of the mess. Pictures of Neolithic goddess figurines for ideas are helpful. Use the ones in this book, or you can access pictures from the PowerPoint on the Neolithic Goddess that can be found on my website (http://celebratedivinefeminine.com/Neolithic_Goddess.html), or use some of the fabulous pictures and drawings from any of Marija Gimbutas' books. Use your imagination and let your hands guide you. Your goddess image doesn't have to be perfect. Just feel the call of the Neolithic Goddess and let your hands create what comes forth.

After everyone has completed their goddess (approx. 30 min) ask people to gather and place their goddesses on the altar. Light the candle. Invite each woman to share what their goddess image means to them. Then light the incense and invite each woman as they are ready to pass their goddess image through the incense to bless them.

They may say the words below, or they may say what is on their hearts:

I offer the creation of my hands to the Great Mother. May it always remind me of the Goddess, who has been with us since the beginning, and will be with us at the end of all time. She is the creatrix, the source of all life. May I always remember to walk in balance and to respect her body, the earth. I offer gratitude for her benevolence and ask that she bless me and this image I have created in remembrance of Her.

Have fun!

TABLE OF CORRESPONDENCES FOR THE NEOLITHIC GODDESS

Element: Earth

Symbols: Moon, trees, snakes, birds

Color: Greens, browns, earth tones

Animals: Bear, deer, wild boar, cow, birds, frogs, fish

Nature: Earth, rocks, mountains, forests

Mates: The Green Man, the Sun King, the Vegetation God

Season: Winter, harvest

Moon: All phases

Festivals: Earth Day, harvest festivals

Geography: Old Europe - Eastern and Southern Europe, Anatolia, North Africa

Timeframe: Neolithic - 7000 to 3000 BCE

Women's Cycles: All cycles, especially moon times and birthing

Crops: Crops, farmland, vineyards, trees

Children: All humankind

Music

Guided Visualization: "Sanctuary" from *Awakening II* by Kieran DeVerniero, or *Vision Quest* with Hemi-Sync (Metamusic)

Ritual – music options for listening while making clay goddess figurines:

Meg Rayne, *Voices*: Maiden Mother Crone, She Is Moving Through Me

Megan Wagner, *Starlight Stage Live*: We All Come From the Goddess, Ancient Mother

Ruth Barrett, *The Year is a Dancing Woman, Vol. 1*: Invocation, Lady of Three

Ruth Barrett, *The Year is a Dancing Woman, Vol. 2:* Earth Mother, Grandmother Chant

Ruth Barrett, *Garden of Mysteries*: New Crone Rising

(The following is a proposed agenda if you choose to hold a circle to celebrate the Neolithic Mother Goddess)

IN HER NAME CIRCLE
NEOLITHIC GODDESS: THE GREAT MOTHER
CIRCLE PROGRAM

Welcome to In Her Name Circle on the Neolithic Goddess

Introductions: (5 min) Name, city, and a word that expresses how the participant is feeling

Calling in the Directions: (3min)

Opening: (2 min) poem

Neolithic Presentation: (30 min)

Q&A (10 min)

Guided Visualization: (10 min)

Ritual: Making Clay Goddesses: (30 min)

Sharing about process: What came up: (15 min)

Divination (10 min) – Pull Goddess cards to see what Goddess energy you will walk in during the up-coming month

Closing: (3min) – Charge of the Goddess

Releasing the directions – (2min)

Total Time: 2 Hours

Grandmother Spider with Corn Woman & Aliquipiso

Grandmother Spider

THE CREATRIX

IN THE BEGINNING was the Spider. In the center of the universe she sang. In the midst of the waters she sang. In the midst of heaven she sang. In the center she sang. Her singing made all the worlds. The worlds of the spirits. The worlds of the people. The worlds of the creatures. The worlds of the gods. In this way she separated the quarters. Singing, she separated. Upon the face of heaven she placed her song. Upon the face of water she placed her song. Thus she placed her song. Thus she placed her will. Thus wove she her design. Thus sang the spider.

Adapted from: *Rise Up and Call Her Name: A Woman-honoring Journey into Global Earth-based Spiritualities* by Elizabeth Fisher.

11. *Grandmother Spider*

The Creatrix

(Visit www.celebratedivinefeminine.com to view the complementary PowerPoint that accompanies this text.)

GRANDMOTHER SPIDER, OR Spider Woman, appears in the origin stories of many Native American groups. As the specific cultures vary significantly between the numerous Native American groups, you will be introduced in this section to several of the main cultural groupings. You will have a chance to hear several Native American legends, not only those of Grandmother Spider but also of other honored ancestral American Indian mother archetypes. It will be explained why legends and stories were so important in Native American cultures and how they helped American Indians adapt to both the natural and supernatural worlds. Finally you will learn how Native American deities differ from those of Western traditions.

Learning about Native American traditions has value because they can teach us greater respect for the Earth as well as to feel a deeper connection to the Earth, which American Indians believe is the mother. We Westerners can be so caught up in our busy lives as we run from one task to another that many of us have lost our ability to be present in the moment, to appreciate the world around us and to feel gratitude for how much the Earth does provide. Becoming more familiar with Native American beliefs can help us begin to rebuild this connection to the Earth and the Web of Life. The guided visualization "Grandmother Spider Weaves the Web of Life" will help you capture the experience of this connection to the universal Web. The ritual on "Weaving the Web," especially if done in Circle, will provide a wonderful visual experience of just how connected we all are to each other, to our ancestors, to those that will follow and to the Web of Life. As you learn more about Native American culture and the importance of their legends, I hope you will come to realize the wisdom of their ancient ways.

It is generally believed that Native Americans are descendants of waves of migrations that occurred some 12 to 42,000 years ago. They are believed to have migrated over a land bridge that stretched across the Bering Strait connecting Siberia with Alaska. Racially American Indians have ties to Proto-Mongolian groups of Asia. Merlin Stone, art historian, teacher, author of a number of works on goddess history and a source for this section, states in her book, *Ancient Mirrors of Womanhood*, that there are some 550 different native languages and as many tribes who have vastly different cultures (p 284). They range from cave dwellers, to mound builders, to plains tribes, and to the highly organized government of the Iroquois.

One prominent Native American group is the **cave dwellers.** Caves appear in several ancient myths of female deities, especially among the Pueblo tribes of the southwest. The Pueblo believe their ancestors emerged from a hole in the earth referred to as the Place of Emergence, or the Womb of the Mother. The *Kiva,* a round subterranean Pueblo shrine used for rituals and ceremonies, is symbolic of the sacred site from which the Pueblo people believe they too have emerged (p 285).

Anyone who has seen the cliff dwellings at places like Mesa Verde in Colorado can attest that they are amazing feats of structural engineering. Some of these cliff dwellings boast hundreds of rooms built of clay bricks in caves on high rocky cliffs. Other extensive dwellings, like those in Betatakin, Arizona, are set deep in massive caves. The Pueblo cave dwellings were built by the Anasazi or the Ancient Ones, a culture that flourished from 300 to 1300 CE. Stone suggests that many of the contemporary Pueblo tribes, such as the Hopi, the Zuni, and the Keres, have retained beliefs and customs that may have survived from the Anasazi period (p 285).

The Hohokam culture, often referred to as **Those Who have Vanished**, inhabited a large territory from southern Utah and Colorado to northern Mexico. Though the Hohokam people have vanished, they left clues to their culture in the form of a well-developed network of irrigation reservoirs and canals that were built some 2000 years ago. They are thought to be part of a culture that migrated north from Mexico and South American. Linguistic studies of American Indians of both North and South America support this theory. If so, Stone suggests, then the similarity between the Corn Mother of the Hopi and Chicomecoatl of Mexico -- the Aztec goddess of maize, food, and fertility -- may be more than just mere coincidence (p 286).

Ohio, Kentucky, and Wyoming are the home of the Adena and the Hopewell Native American cultures, who were **mound builders**. Some of their earthen mounds rise as high as seventy feet and often stretch for miles. The Hopewell was an extensive culture that spread over a broad territory ranging from Minnesota to New York and as far south as Florida. They were especially skilled at working with copper and quarrying stone and had an extensive trade network for acquiring stone from Wisconsin, mica from the Appalachians and obsidian from as far west as the Rocky

Mountains. Stone claims that the mound builder culture lasted 1500 years, from about 1000 BCE to about 500 CE. Their decline is thought to be the result of a devastating widespread invasion around 500 CE. It is believed that the Cherokee are descendants of the mound builders (p 286).

The **Plains Indians** were comprised of a variety of cultures living both on the Plains and in the Rocky Mountains, including the Blackfeet, the Salish, the Nootsac, the Kutenai, the Nootka, the Lummi, the Flatheads, and many others. As these cultural groups relied to a greater or lesser degree on the buffalo as a primary food source, the buffalo was central to their religious traditions. The Plains Indians were more male centered than other Native American culture groups, and their recorded stories feature mostly male protagonist and deities. Stone points out, however, that some groups had prohibitions against males being told female stories. As white males primarily gathered the stories, this could account for the small number of stories about female deities and protagonists.

Also problematic -- as Vicki Noble, author of *Shakti Woman* and *Double Goddess*, often points out -- is that most anthropologists and archaeologists are primarily male or male identified, and therefore the information gathered tends to be viewed through a male lens. In other words, we are frequently getting only a limited or distorted version of female stories and history. The male bias is such an integral part of our culture that it frequently goes unrecognized as a biased point of view.

The **Iroquois** occupied the territory stretching from the New York area to the Great Lakes Region and into Ontario, Canada. Their language group includes the Seneca, the Mohawk, the Onondaga, the Tuscarora, the Cayuga, the Huron, the Cherokee and the Oneida. They are most famous for their constitutional form of government. The League of Nations formed by the Iroquois of the Great Lakes Region may even have influenced some concepts of U.S. democracy. The governing body of the Iroquois was called the Council of the Sachems and was chosen by women who headed the individual clans. Women retained the authority to remove members of the Council if they performed unsatisfactorily. Also under the control of women was the food supply, even hunting results. This control enabled women to decide whether or not to supply food for war parties. Their refusal canceled many battles (p 286-287).

There is a recent attempt to roll all Native American into a Pan Indian identity. This does not always work, however, because of this wide spectrum of social groups that comprise the highly diverse American Indian cultures. Each tribe has its own origin stories, legends and spiritual beliefs, some thousands of years old. As these traditions are oral, it is difficult to even date them or trace their origin.

NATIVE AMERICAN LEGENDS AND STORIES

According to many American Indian origin stories, creation began in the dark void where only thought existed, and the source of creation was often female. Woman, as the mother or the grandmother, is core to American Indian tradition for they believe they owe their lives to the mother. She is the old woman who tends the fires of life. She is Spider Woman who weaves everything into a fabric of interconnectedness. She is the eldest divinity, the one who remembers and re-members. She is called Corn Woman, or Serpent Woman, or Earth Woman. According to Paula Gunn Allen, an English Professor, Native American literary critic, Laguna Pueblo/Sioux Indian, and the author of several books including *Grandmothers of the Light* and *The Sacred Hoop*, this creative female energy is credited with being at the center of all spirit and creation.

How many of you as women have thought that being a mother was not enough? That you had to be or do something important? Or have a job or career by which to be identified so you could have status? In pre-conquest Native America, claims Allen in *Grandmothers of the Light*, women were valued as the creatrix and were imaged as the vitalizer. It was believed that the female body birthed vital beings, and mothers received respect for being mothers. The power of the mother was not just biological, however, nor was it limited to giving birth. The creative power of woman also manifested through social organization and the material culture such as through hunting, war, healing, communication, rain-making, etc. Native Americans believed that the power of mother informed and created right balance and right harmony which organized all relationships. She also had the power to destroy through wars, hexes and illnesses (p 28-29).

The role of mother was so honored that Native American males were honored by calling them Mother. Male adepts studied for years to acquire these traits. This creative power is the source and model for all energies generated during ritual and sacred ceremony, for the ritual magic of mother was potent (p 29).

There are numerous Native American myths and legends of the archetype of mother as creatrix, as the ancestral mother of tribe or clan, as teacher and as bestower of culture. The myths of Grandmother Spider and Spider Woman emphasize how important this role was. Some Grandmother Spider legends connect her with sound, the void and light. Even the spider's web is mirrored in the pattern of sound waves and is one of her tools. Spider Woman or Grandmother Spider is featured most predominantly in legends of the Pueblo, the Cherokee, the Kiowa, the Dine and the Keres. Holly Iglehart Austen, in her book *Heart of the Goddess*, writes that the Keres, tribes of the Pueblo culture residing in New Mexico, tell a legend of

Spider Woman who existed in the Original Womb Void. At the beginning of time it was Spider Woman who spun her web in the four directions while singing her two daughters into being. Nau Ut Set became the mother of the sun, moon, and stars. She placed them in the heavens to give living creatures light and warmth by day and a silvery glow of light by night. She also created all other substances including iridescent abalone shells, turquoise and brilliantly colored rocks. Ut Set, her second daughter, became the mother of the Pueblo People (p 12).

Both the Cherokee, a tribe belonging to the Iroquois language group who occupied parts of southeastern United States, and the Kiowa, a Plains Indian culture that has more recently settled in Oklahoma, have legends of Grandmother Spider and credit her with bringing fire to the people. According to the legends, early in the beginning of time only the Sun People, or the people in the East, had fire which they jealously guarded and refused to share. Therefore the rest of the world was cold and dark, and all living creatures were quite miserable. A great powwow was called amongst all earth's creatures to decide how to get fire from the Sun People. It was decided that some brave creature must go and steal the fire. Grandmother Spider spoke up, but she was ignored because she was so small. The Possum, Crow and Buzzard were all honored with the challenge of going to the land of the Sun People to bring back Fire. Each one tried, and failed.

Feeling hopeless, the council finally gave Grandmother Spider a chance. She fashioned a pot of clay and attached a strand of web to it. Then she dragged it to the land of the Sun People. She snuck into the camp of the Sun People and rolled a glowing ember into the pot. Then she dragged it back to her people. At first, not seeing the fire because it was hidden in the pot, all the creatures of the earth thought Grandmother Spider had also failed. But she proudly tipped the pot and out rolled the glowing red hot ember. After sharing the fire with everyone, Grandmother Spider tossed the glowing ember into the sky and created the sun. Her courageous act is said to be immortalized in the design of her web, which is like the rays of the sun. Grandmother Spider is also credited with the discovery of pottery making.

Austen mentions another myth in which Grandmother Spider used different colored clay—red, yellow, white and black - to make the people of the four races. Then over all the people she wove with patience a mantle of wisdom and love. It is said that she attaches a strand of her web at the doorway at the top of each of our heads, which is our psychic connection to the universe. (This is also reminiscent of the crown charka, which in Hinduism is each individual's connection to universal consciousness.) Grandmother Spider is said to have cautioned against letting this opening close and forgetting our connection to both her and universal wisdom, least we lose our way. This door, she claimed, can be kept open by chanting and singing (p 12).

Allen, in *The Sacred Hoop*, writes of another variation of a Keres origin story. This legend is of Thought Woman who is the Supreme Spirit and is both mother and father to all. Thought Woman existed in the void before all else along with her dormant sisters. She sang them into life and then has them sing over the contents of their medicine bundles. It is the singing, or sound vibration, which imparts life and vitality to all that lies within the bundles. Everything is dependent on the medicine power of the three great creatrixes: Thought Woman, Uretsete, and Naotsete, who are spiritual sisters connected by powerful medicine. The Keres Pueblo tribe believes that Thought Woman brought corn, agriculture, pottery, weaving, social systems, religion, ceremony, ritual, language, dance, human to animal relations, and more to the Keres (p 15), much like Inanna, the ancient Sumerian goddess, brought the *Me*, or the laws and keys of civilization to the people of Sumer

Corn Woman, or *Iyatiku*, is both an aspect of Thought Woman and an important mother deity who brought corn to the Keres, writes Allen. According to the legend, initially Corn Woman lived with the Keres in a beautiful village. Eventually drought came to the land, and to distract the people from worry Corn Woman provided a gambling game. Soon the men became obsessed with the game and neglected their rituals and ceremonies. The drought worsened and famine followed. Too late men came to their senses. The rains came flooding the village and forcing the people to leave. Angered by their neglect, Corn Woman left the people and returned to *Shipap,* her sacred cave (p 17).

It is believed that Corn Woman still resides in her sacred cave today. She sends counsel and greets the souls who enter the world of the dead. She left *Irriaku*, Mother of the Corn -- which is her heart -- with the Keres and gave them the power to grow crops. Corn Woman left instructions that the people must share the fruits of her body, and remain at peace in both their hearts and in their relationships, for the rains will come only to peaceful people. To this day the Keres abhor violence and hostility and are careful to contain emotions and to smooth over hurt or angry feelings for fear that the rains will stop. Rain is essential, for without rain all life stops (p 17).

Corn Mother, or *Irriaku*, is the Keres' connection to Corn Woman and to the spirit world, claims Allen. It is Corn Mother who authorizes the religious leaders and is the heart of the people. In the image of a perfect ear of corn, Corn Mother must be present at every ceremony. Without her presence the ceremony will fail to produce the energy needed for ritual magic (Allen 17).

White Buffalo Calf Woman is an important deity of great power for the Lakota, a Plains Indian tribe. She brought the sacred pipe, which is sacred to White Buffalo Woman just as the corn is sacred to Corn Woman. The sacred pipe empowers Lakota ceremonies and rituals. Without the pipe their rituals and ceremonies are powerless to produce the required energy for ritual magic. The Lakota invoke the four directions of the winds during their ceremonies. White Buffalo Calf Woman is believed to live in a cave and to preside over the four winds, which are powerful beings that she is able to influence. To this day the sacred pipe resides with the Lakota, and White Buffalo Calf Woman is an integral part of Lakota tradition and ritual ceremony (Allen 16-17). Brooke Medicine Eagle, author of *Buffalo Woman Comes Singing*, is a member of the Lakota Tribe.

Hard Beings Woman, or *Huruing Wuhti*, is the Creatrix of the Hopi, a Native American group of Pueblo descent who constructed large, apartment-style complexes in northern Arizona and New Mexico. According to Allen, Hard Beings Woman lived in the void on an island, the only land in the waters of space. She is identified with all hard substances including beads, coral, and shells. Though she is of the earth, she has also been called a sea goddess. She also resides in the worlds above the earth where she owns, or empowers, the moon and the stars. Her aspects are solidity and hardness. She is similar to Thought Woman in that she does not give birth to creation, but breathes life into male and female effigies that become the parents of the Hopi. She created *Muingwu*, who is the God of the Crops, and his sister-consort, Sand Altar Woman, who is also called Childbirth Water Woman (Allen 14).

A creation myth of the Seneca (who belong to the Iroquois Nation and occupied the territory of New York) tells of Sky Woman, who is married to an angry man who is jealous because she has received unsolicited attention from another. He is so jealous that he decides to do away with her by throwing her into the void, which he creates by uprooting the tree of light. Depending on the version, she is either tricked into jumping or she is pushed into the void by her husband. Her fall is broken by Water Fowl who lives in the void. Rescued, Sky Woman is carried to Grandmother Turtle, and from the hard shell of Grandmother Turtle an Island is formed which becomes the Earth (Allen 15).

Not all legends are of grandmothers or creatrixes, however. The Oneida, one of the five founding nations of the Iroquois Confederacy, tell the legend of the warrior maiden Aliquipiso, who saved her people from their enemy. According to the Manataka American Indian Council, the Mingos -- the enemy of the Oneida -- had invaded their land, destroyed their corn-fields, and set fire to their long-houses. Many of the Oneida escaped to the surrounding mountains and secret caves, but they were not safe for the

Mingos were searching everywhere for them. Soon they were threatened with starvation. The chiefs and warriors held a council to decide what to do. A young girl stepped forward and said that they good spirits had told her how to save the people. They were hiding on top of a high cliff, she explained, with many boulders and heavy sharp rocks. She would descend and lead the Mingos to the place below the cliff. The Oneida could destroy their enemy by throwing rocks and boulders on top of them. She was not afraid to give her life for her people, Aliquipiso claimed. Amazed at her bravery the council honored her and said that she was blessed by the Great Spirit.

That night Aliquipiso bravely wandered down the mountain and allowed herself to be caught by the Mingos. To make her actions believable she allowed herself to be tortured with fire. When she finally pretended to weaken from pain, the Mingos were impressed by her courage and endurance. They tied her hands and told her to lead them to her people threatening her with more torture if she betrayed them.

With the Mingo warriors creeping silently behind her, Aliquipiso lead the way to the area beneath the cliff. She called the warriors to gather close so she could lead them up a secret passage. When they were gathered round she yelled out the signal to her people. The boulders and rocks began to rain upon the Mingos from what seemed like an angry mountain. There was no escape. So many warriors perished that the Mingos left the area and never made war on the Oneidas again. From then on the story of Aliquipiso's courage was told over and over again around the campfires, and has been handed down from one generation to the next.

Adapted from 'The Warrior Maiden (Oneida),' Manataka American Indian Council.

In more contemporary Native American creation myths, Allen states that new versions are beginning to surface in which humans are born from the mating of the sky father with the earth mother. Allen feels this is a patriarchal/Christian revisioning of older stories and traditions. This is part of the on-going process of oral tradition. Stories, myths and legends are changed and altered to reflect the social realities of the times. These alterations facilitate the education and rearing of children who must grow up and adapt to both American as well as Tribal society (*The Sacred Hoop*, p 29).

IMPORTANCE OF NATIVE AMERICAN LEGENDS

Legends and stories are central to American Indian culture. Tribal leaders and medicine people used stories to provide information and guidance for operating in and understanding the universe. They forewarned of different supernatural entities, or of animal or plant entities that might be encountered during the course of their daily lives. These encounters were considered normal. I have a friend who plays cards with a group of women. Periodically, though no one smokes, there is a distinct scent of pipe tobacco. The hostess claims it is her grandfather who has come by for a visit! Have you or anyone you know had this kind of an experience, or something similar? From my experience as a Hypnotherapist I estimate that about seventy per cent of the population has had some form of mystical or metaphysical experience. The mystical or spiritual realm is more real and present than is acknowledged, or acceptable to admit, in our rational culture that requires hard facts and proof.

American Indians are more comfortable with the spirit or metaphysical world because their stories and legends have prepared them for their own experiences in both the natural and supernatural worlds. Native American stories reinforce that humans, animals, plants, spirits, supernaturals, and deities like Spider Woman and Corn Woman are all connected and interconnected. Walking the medicine path is not an academic subject taught in college, says Allen in *Grandmother of the Light*, and it is not as simple as chanting, singing and using herbs. It is a different way of thinking and operating in the world than to what we Westerners are accustomed (p 3-5).

The difference between Western myths and fairy tales and Native American stories and legends is that in Western stories the giants, fairies and talking animals are treated as imaginative characters. Native American stories contain details from ordinary reality woven with the supernatural and non-physical worlds and are treated as factual. Such weaving between the worlds can be confusing for the Western logical mind accustomed to linear thought processes. In Native American stories women or men change into bears or other animals, or they interact with thunderbirds, animal spirits, katsinas, or female and male deities. These figures and stories are real, claims Allen, and contain valuable information. The figures are not just metaphors for instinctual patterns deeply embedded in the human psyche as Jung or other psychotherapists might interpret. Though the stories function on multiple levels, they are factual accounts. For Native Americans they create an awareness of spirits and supernaturals who live within the same environment as humans, and who communicate and interact with them, some more than others (p 8)

MAJOR AMERICAN INDIAN THEMES

Even with the diversity and variations in the culture and beliefs among the over 550 different American Indian tribes there are four major Native

American themes. First and foremost, American Indians are deeply connected to the Land, which is the Mother. The Land is not a place separate from people upon which they act out their dramas. Nor is Land merely a source of survival, nor an inert substance or resource. It is alive and vital. It is a sentient being. Earth is divine and everything about Earth is divine, Allen says. The medicine energy of a plant or animal might talk to you. It might give you a message, or advice, or it might give you healing medicine. Spiritual and energetic properties are not separate from the biochemical properties, or the soil, light, protein and sugars of a plant, claims Allen (*The Sacred Hoop*, p 119).

The experience of a classmate of mine, let's call her Sally, illustrates the potential we humans have to connect with the Land and to receive her gifts. Sally was diagnosed with breast cancer and was facing a mastectomy. She went hiking with friends to distract herself from her worries. While hiking in the dense forest she felt an irresistible urge and was drawn to one particular tree. It was a call of love and a need for connection. She remembers going over to the tree, hugging it and rubbing her body all over it. She stayed with the tree a long time and meditated. Then the tree emitted a sap which Sally felt a strong intuition to eat, though it was very bitter. Eventually her friends returned and they ended their hike. Sally didn't think anything more about her experience.

A week later she returned to the doctor for her pre-surgery prep. The tumor was gone! They did an X-ray and there was no tumor to be found! Mystified Sally consulted a shaman who told her that the tree had given her a healing. Sally was instructed to take the tree an offering of gratitude. There has been no re-occurrence of the cancer. This experience profoundly changed Sally's relationship to the natural world. She grew to understand first hand that the land is not something to dominate and control, like many Westerners believe. It is a sentient being that is alive and vital. It has much to teach us and can offer many gifts that we Westerners fail to understand because we are too busy and to greedy. Mother Earth is now facing threats of partial or total destruction by radiation, pollution, toxic chemicals and the abuse of resources. Viewing earth as the Mother may be a viable and necessary path to our survival.

Secondly, wherever you find Native Americans there are spirits. We have already discussed this at length. Native American understanding of power, or energy, is tied into their understanding of the relationship between the human and the non-human worlds which are linked and in active communication with each other. More than just acknowledging the existence of the supernatural world, this spiritual link contains power or energy which enables magic to happen. This magic can range, Allen claims, from the transformation of objects from one form to another, to teleportation, curing the sick, creating illness, and communication with animals, plants and non-physical beings (spirits guides, katsinas), the compelling of the will of another, and the stealing or storing of souls (*Grandmothers of the Light*, p 22-23). One of the intentions of Native American rituals and ceremonies is to activate this spiritual link to generate power so magic can happen.

In addition Native Indians possess the ability to endure. They have inhabited the Americas for thousands of years. There is no question that the occupation of North America by Euro-Caucasians, and their attempt to control and dominate the land, has had a profound impact on the customs and culture of Native Americans. In spite of this, however, American Indians have endured. Currently there is a revitalization of Native American spirit and pride as witnessed by the Pan-Indian movement, despite conflicts created by vast diversities within Tribal societies. Paula Gunn Allen was a prominent figure of this movement until her death a few years ago. The concept of the Earth as the Mother has also endured. This is evidenced by the concerns about global warming and our recycling and energy conservation efforts.

Finally, traditional tribal lifestyle, though diverse, is generally gynocratic, or woman centered, and almost never patriarchal. According to Allen a gynocratic social system, is characterized by an ease around sexuality and personal preferences and styles in which diversity is appreciated and accepted. Males tend to be more nurturing, pacifistic and passive than as defined by the Western mind. In turn females tend to be more self-defining, assertive and decisive. While personal expression is encouraged there is a focus on social responsibility rather than on privilege. There is a greater acceptance of the individual with all their quirks and frailties, rather than conformity. Goods are distributed more evenly and there is an absence of punitive means of social control. Powerful women are central to social well-being and there is a focus on the welfare of the young. Lastly, there is awareness of and an emphasis on the interconnectedness of all life forms (*The Sacred Hoop*, p 2-6)

WESTERN VERSUS NATIVE AMERICAN DEITIES

The relationship between Native American and the Supernaturals is different than a Westerner's relationship to God who is considered to be all powerful and all knowing. It is even different than the Greek and Roman relationships to their gods and goddesses, states Carol Bodeau, Unitarian Universalist Minister and practitioner of the Lakota tradition. In the Goddess community, Grandmother Spider, or Spider Woman, might be viewed in an archetypal way, as having spider-like qualities: weaving, creating worlds, creating realities, making beautiful things. Spider Woman might be invoked during a ritual, or she might be prayed to asking for some kind of assistance, or she might be sought out to provide answers.

In American Indian spiritual traditions the supernaturals and spirits are not gods in the classical sense. The relationship between a supernatural could range from a divinity to a sister, or a grandmother, or wise woman, or as an ancestor. Native Americans would not invoke a particular deity; that would be presumptuous. Instead they would observe nature to see what kind of answer nature would provide. In a vision quest the participant waits to receive, they don't initiate the exchange, ever! The information received is private and personal. If faced with a challenge, a Native American would think about what animal or insect, such as a spider, had come into their life recently. The spider might mean different things to different people based on tribal legends, their knowledge of the spider, their personal experiences, their personal relationships to spiders, their dreams, their vision quest, etc. The meaning of a spider may be very different for any ten people in a room.

Upon seeing a spider an American Indian might think about all that they have learned about spiders from nature - they can be dangerous, they might bite. They have the power to protect themselves, thus they have a certain power. They are hunters, and they bring about death, but death can be associated with transformation and the birth/death cycle. They lay thousands of eggs at once. They lay traps and are crafty and clever. They are patient. Their webs are invisible but very sticky and resilient. From this compilation of information Native Americans would derive an answer to their problem.

American Indians have a very personal and intimate connection with nature and its interconnectedness. Westerners have lost this connection because we struggle with the mind/body/spirit split. We tend to live in our heads, separate from our bodies, and deny spirit, as a Native American might understand spirit. In the American Indian culture there is a greater connection to their bodies, their community, to nature, to the supernaturals and the spirit world. The Earth is the mother, the animals are their brothers/sisters, and the connection to the spirit world is real. Westerners might benefit from paying more attention to the stories and traditions of our Native American sisters and brothers.

In summary, you have received a snapshot of some of the varied Native American cultural groupings and have been introduced to several legends of Grandmother Spider and other American Indian ancestral mother archetypes. Hopefully you now recognize that in the Native American world view diversity exists as there are numerous cultures, beliefs, stories and legends which vary from one extreme to the other. Yet even among this diversity there are several main themes: American Indians have a close connection to land and to nature, as well as to the world of spirits and the supernatural. Native American culture is resilient and has the ability to endure, and has endured through 500 years of colonization during which there has been an intense and focused attempt to exterminate it. And Native American culture tends to be mostly gynocratic, or woman centered, children are protected, motherhood is honored, and women are valued beyond their procreative abilities.

The Native American relationship to their deities differs from the Western model. The Native American relationship is one of reverence for an esteemed elder or ancestor rather than to a god or gods who are powerful and all knowing, which is more typical of the Western concept of deity. American Indians also have a deep conviction that the Earth is the mother and must be protected and preserved because the Earth is also the people and the people are the Earth. They are one and cannot be separated. Learning from our Native American sisters and brothers can help us reclaim respect for the Earth and reconnect to the universal Web of Life. Together we might find ways to help heal the Earth and ensure our survival.

DISCUSSION QUESTIONS

❖ Most Westerners have been brought up with the concept of a monotheistic God who is the Father and Supreme Being. What thoughts and feelings come up for you about having a connection to a Spirit Guide? What do you think that relationship might be like?

❖ How has our view of the land changed in the past 50 years? Is this change good or harmful?

❖ What might a personal relationship with the land be like, rather than viewing the land as something to own or dominate?

❖ In some Native American origin stories the world was created by thought. How do our thoughts impact our reality on a daily basis today?

❖ How might our culture change if women had veto power over our leaders, our religious leaders, and control over the food supply?

SOURCES

Hallie Iglehart Austen, *The Heart of the Goddess: Art, Myth and Meditations of the World's Sacred Feminine.*

Paula Gunn Allen, *Grandmothers of the Light: A Medicine Woman's Sourcebook.*

Paula Gunn Allen, *The Sacred Hoop: Recovering the Feminine in American Indian Traditions*.

Elizabeth Fisher, *Rise Up and Call Her Name: A Woman-honoring Journey into Global Earth-based Spiritualities*.

Merlin Stone, *Ancient Mirrors of Womanhood: A Treasury of Goddess and Heroine Lore from Around the World*.

The Warrior Maiden (Oneida), Manataka American Indian Council, http://www.manataka.org/page66.html

GRANDMOTHER SPIDER WEAVES THE WEB OF LIFE GUIDED VISUALIZATION

Adapted from *The Web of Life* by Spider Taino Ti

You might want to have some paper and pen and/or crayons or markers close by, so that you can capture your experience during this guided visualization with Grandmother Spider.

Now close your eyes and settle back into your chair as you allow your breath to deepen and begin to let go of any stress or tightness you may be carrying in your body.

Now take a deep breath, breathing in peace and calm all the way into your diaphragm, and hold a second...then exhale slowly, letting go of any tension; any holding in your body. Take a second deep breath breathing in peace and serenity and hold...and as you slowly exhale just let go of the busy-ness of your day as you become calmer, more relaxed. Just feel that tension and anxiousness begin to drain out and away as you become calmer and quieter. Take a third deep breath, filling up with up with the stillness of tranquility...and as you slowly exhale, surrender to deep inner peace and quiet.

Now begin to call back all the pieces of yourself that you may have scattered out and about into the cosmos over the last days and weeks and begin to spiral all those pieces right back into your heart space so that you are totally present right here, right now...Allow yourself to sink even deeper into the deep stillness within.

As you sink into the calm stillness of your inner landscape feel yourself being drawn downward as if you are descending down through a tunnel, a tunnel through time and space...through the eons to the beginning of time when all that existed was a dark void of emptiness.... Nothing can be seen, not even the shadows, but Grandmother Spider sits in her web in the Sky World, watching and waiting, for an eternity she has sat waiting for the mind where all consciousness resides, the Universal Mind, to awaken.

Then from her web Grandmother Spider senses a stirring of activity from within the Universal Mind. Then emanations of light float out from the center of the Great Mind and become magnificent stars twinkling with all the spectrums of light. Their radiance against the empty blackness dances and vibrates with the pulse of potentiality. Her time has finally come! Taking a deep breath Grandmother Spider begins to sing her weaving song as she glides across the void weaving her silvery web around the newly birthed stars connecting them to create a passageway, a yonic doorway through which all the rest of life will emerge...

Seeing that this is all good and beautiful, more frequencies of thought begin to flow from the center of universal consciousness and emerge from the Birth Canal into the Sky World and take their places as stars, suns, planets, comets and meteors...Then more thoughts continue to flow each taking up a specific place in the grand design for cosmic order and harmony....Each thought vibration is the spiritual essence for an animate or inanimate object that is part of the larger dream being thought into manifestation....Grandmother Spider's long rest is over, for it is she who is busy weaving her web around each new energy beings. She is spinning the Universal Web of Life that shimmers with the reflection of the Great Mystery's light.

Grandmother Spider sings her song as she dances and weaves her Web of Life through the Sky World until it is filled with the light and life of her creative process. Soon the stars, suns and planets prepare to give birth. Grandmother Spider works even harder as she spins more cord. All the newly born must be included into the Web of Life that is the grand cosmic blueprint. As the Universe Mind expands, so does the Web of Life, a beautiful crystalline grid that connects everything. Grandmother Spider continues to weave her Web of Life through every cycle and season of creation...

Everyone and everything is connected to the Web of Life, this great Crystalline Grid. Though we each carry our separate awareness in our separate physical bodies, we each share the same energy as all other life and are connected to the Great Mystery. As Grandmother Spider weaves her web around each being she weaves in their specific dream-song, as well as the color and vibration that resonates with their talents and gifts that will help them create their reality for this Walk upon the Earth plane. Each person chooses their challenges and lessons for each incarnation before their spirit essence takes flight from the Universal Mind through the Cosmic Birth Canal and into the Sky World. Every human being has a purpose and a direction upon which they must focus if they are to be happy and fulfilled during their time upon the Earth.

Watch Grandmother Spider as she weaves. As soon as each spiritual body enters the soon-to-be-born babe within the womb of her mother, Grandmother Spider begins to sing her weaving song. She weaves her silvery web from the feet to the head securing the spiritual body to the physical body. When the weaving is done she takes the silvery strand from the crown of the head and connects it to the Web of Life. Each being, each object, is connected to the Web of Life.

From Grandmother Spider we are gifted with our own personal energy web with which we walk, talk and experience all of life. This web enables our spiritual body to experience the senses, emotions, and the pain and pleasure of our time on the Earth plane. Our spiritual body, which is connected to the great cosmic Web through the silvery strand stretching out from our crown, enables our physical body to experience the oneness with all of life and the Great Mystery while enhancing our intuitive abilities. Because we are connected to all beings and objects through the Web of Life, we are never alone for through the Web we share the love of All Our Relations...

Shhh....Hear her song....See it is your spiritual body that has just flown though the Great Yonic Passageway into the Sky World....You are being called by your mother....You are being drawn to her womb....Your spiritual body settles into the physical body nestled within your mother's womb. Hear Grandmother Spider's song. She sings to soothe you helping you to settle into your physical body....As she begins to weave her web of crystalline threads you feel yourself merging with your physical body.... Feel your heart beating, feel your tiny hands and feet, so different from the free flow and vibrations of your spiritual essence...Grandmother Spider's song is comforting and calming. It soothes you as the merging and settling continues...It also urges you to remember your purpose and your promise for this time upon the Earth plane...Remember....

What is your purpose for this walk upon the Earth? (long pause)

What are your challenges and lessons?.... (long pause)

What direction do you need to take in order to be happy and fulfilled in this life time? (long pause)

What have you forgotten that you need to remember?... (long pause)

See the Web of Life as it floats all around you!... It is a crystalline grid, a beautiful intricate braid that holds all of life together...Grandmother Spider has sung and danced and woven her web through the eons of eternity...She will continue indefinitely to weave new patterns as each new life begins its walk upon the Earth plane.

Now take a deep breath and begin to gently and easily float back through time and space to this time and this place....Feel the weight of your body in the chair...the firmness of the ground beneath your feet...the coolness of the air against your skin and begin to come all the way back... When you are ready, take a deep breath and open your eyes.

(An audio recording of this guided visualization can be purchased for a nominal fee at www.celebratedivinefeminine.com)

GRANDMOTHER SPIDER WEAVING THE WEB RITUAL

Items needed for ritual: a large ball of yarn, preferably red, and at least one pair of scissors.

Have the group sit in a circle. Pass or roll the yarn between members in three rounds making sure that each person is included in each round. Crisscrossing the circle between members will make the most interesting web pattern. As each person receives the ball of yarn they should wrap the yarn around their wrist at least once while thinking about and stating as indicated below:

Round One:

Think about and name someone you feel connected to from your past, possibly an ancestor.

Round Two:

Think about and name someone your feel connected to who will come to view you as an ancestor, mentor, teacher or guide – this is your connection to the future.

Round Three:

Name a deity or spirit guide to whom you feel connected.

Once the three rounds are completed, take a moment to pause and encourage participants to look at the Web of Life that connects each of you in the circle.

When it feels right, pick up the scissors. Instruct the participants that when it is their turn to take the scissors they should feel their bodies connected to the floor; take a moment to look at their sisters in the room, and state:

I am (name). I am present, and I am connected to the Web of Life.

Then cut the yarn and pass the scissors to the right while your neighbor to the left helps you tie the yarn around your wrist. **Instruct the**

141

participants to be sure to hold onto the yarn with their free hand so the web stays taught and strong.

When this round has been completed encourage everyone to once again look at the Web of Life that connects each of you in the room. Sit in silence for a few minutes while feeling the connection!

Group Share

When the time feels right open it up for a group share. Encourage the participants to share either what they experienced during the meditation, or during the weaving ritual. Respect a person's right to remain silent.

TABLE OF CORRESPONDENCES FOR GRANDMOTHER SPIDER

Element: Earth

Symbols: Spiders, webs, pottery, clay, weaving, dream catchers

Color: Brown, green, black

Animals: Spider

Companions: Naotsete and Uretsete, pronounced Nau Ut Set and Ut Set

Geography: Pre-Conquest North America

Foods: corn

Music

For both the Ritual and Guided Visualization: "Path with a Heart," *Sacred Drum Visions*, David and Steve Gordon.

(The following is a proposed agenda if you choose to hold a circle to celebrate the Grandmother Spider)

In Her Name Circle, Grandmother Spider Circle Program

Song: We are the Weavers

Welcome to In Her Name Circle, Celebrating Grandmother Spider
Intro: (5 min) Name, city, word-
Casting the Circle: (3min)
Opening: (2 min) poem
Grandmother Spider Presentation (30 min)
Group Discussion (10 min)
Grandmother Spider Visualization (15 min)
Individual Process (5 min)
Weaving the Web Ritual (15 min)
Group Share (10 min)
Goddess Cards (10 min)
Closing: (2 min)
Releasing the directions – (3min)
Total time: 120

Demeter

Persephone

Demeter and Persephone

DEATH AND REBIRTH, THE MYTH OF DEMETER AND PERSEPHONE AND THE ELEUSINIAN MYSTERIES

Invocation to Demeter

Demeter, Lady of fruits and grains,
Of ripening suns and harvest rains,
I call to you, Mother, to hear my plea—
Bestow Your blessings here on me.
Goddess, who searches in places wild,
To bring home safely Her stolen child,
Who changes the Summer's greens to gold,
And causes the cycle of life to unfold,
Beautiful Lady, whose love runs deep,
Who banishes growth during Winter's sleep,
And causes the seeds to stir in Spring,
Attend our circle and blessings bring

*by Autumn Rose ***

Hymn to Persephone (Alternate Closing Option)

Hail Persephone, Lady of darkness
Silent you sit, silent you watch
Now and at the hour of our deaths.
Lady of Shadows, you have the power
To see within, to rip away all illusion
To sacrifice you are no stranger
You know fear, horror, and also danger
You gave away that most dear to you
Your innocence and childhood naiveté
Lady of mysteries, you access transformation
Emblazoned phoenix of darkness, fire within
Maiden of treasures, Crone of wealth
To you Hades is ever generous
As long as you eat his fruit

Queen of the Leap of Faith
You challenge us to reach further, find a new path,
Cut the web, face the wrath
You are both towering mountain and minute pebble
Ever brooding, you seek new ways to penetrate the depths
Lady of Spirit, we ask for your blessing in
Passage through darkness and trials of the soul.

by Rev. Lady Bella Sundancer

12. *Demeter and Persephone*

Death and Rebirth

The Myth of Demeter and Persephone and the Eleusinian Mysteries

(Go to www.celebratedivinefeminine.com to view the complementary PowerPoint that accompanies this text.)

THE OLDEST VERSION of the ancient myth of Demeter and Persephone comes to us from Homer, a classical Greek poet, who wrote down the myth about 650 BCE. This myth, as well as many other ancient legends and myths, have survived because they are teaching stories and still offer value today. In this Greek myth you are introduced to a time in ancient history when the world view was changing and awakening to the importance of agriculture. From this myth ancient Greeks were able to understand that the cycle of the seasons also applied to the human condition of life, death and rebirth, a cycle which promises new life after the old withers and dies. In this section you will be introduced to the transpersonal meaning of this myth that Persephone models for us. Her abduction into the underworld, rather than merely being an experience of victimization, becomes a transformational opportunity for growth. The myth becomes a valuable lesson for all of us as to how we can learn from all the experiences of our lives, even the painful ones.

In the guided visualization at the end of this section you will have an opportunity to travel deep into the womb cave of the earth to reflect and face your feelings and fears, a process which can help you re-connect with your core self. The ritual, "Sitting With Your Feelings," is designed to help you spend time with those uncomfortable feelings from which you would rather escape. Sitting with, rather than fleeing or numbing, will help you learn what lessons they offer so that you can finally release their hold over you. In this way you can truly become freer and stronger.

In Western culture, we think of myth as one-dimensional, a fictional or primitive way to explain the unexplainable. However, I prefer the view that myths are not always of the realm of fiction, but can be genuine relics or traces of historical events and cultural practices. Marguerite Rigoglioso, an author who is doing pioneering research on female deities and women's religious leadership in the ancient Mediterranean world, suggests that myth is a repository for secret, subversive, and often repressed religious beliefs, particularly in regards to women, the feminine, and the substratum. I suggest that the myth of Demeter and Persephone is one such repository.

The story of Demeter and the abduction and return of her daughter Persephone from the underworld is a richly layered myth that becomes the basis for a mystery religion, the Eleusinian Mysteries, that lasted for at least fifteen hundred years—well into the Fourth Century CE. The setting was ancient Greece. Demeter was the benevolent grain goddess, whose gifts were vital to human survival. Her daughter, Persephone, who in the virginal maiden goddess form is called Kore, was abducted by the dreaded god, Hades, Lord of the Underworld. On one level this myth explains the seasons and accounts for agricultural dynamics. On a deeper level it serves a universal human need to come to terms with the terror and dilemma of death, and to provide hope for the future in spite of death's inevitability. Homer wrote of the happiness that men who experienced the Eleusinian Rites felt even in the face of death. These Mysteries were considered so powerful that ancient Greeks believed all life and the world would come undone without their celebration.

Kathie Carlson, psychotherapist, teacher of feminine psychology in the ancient religion of the Goddess and author of *Life's Daughter/Death's Bride*, writes from the perspective of a Jungian psychologist and offers some intriguing insights. From a historical perspective Carlson claims the abduction of Kore/Persephone from the Mother, when viewed through a feminist lens, is a myth that mirrors historical events. Beginning around 3500 BCE the older Mother Goddess religion of southern Europe was gradually over hundreds of years appropriated and incorporated into the newer religion of the Indo-Europeans. These were patriarchal warring sky-god invaders from the north who would change the face of the known world at that time. Hades, the abductor and villain in this myth, is the Lord of the Underworld. He was the brother of the sky god whom the Greeks came to call Zeus. Both were introduced by the advance of patriarchy into Greece. Demeter and her daughter, Persephone, are female deities who have direct links back to the ancient indigenous Mother Goddess religions of southern and Eastern Europe (p 3).

This assimilation of the older indigenous Mother Goddess religion by the new dominant male sky gods appears repeatedly in myths from around the globe, including the Babylonia myth of Tiamat and Marduk. In these myths the ancient goddesses are often depicted as being dismembered, slain, raped, or married off (as in the case of Aphrodite and Hera) and thus subordinated to the more dominate gods. Carlson asserts that the myth of

Persephone and Demeter can be seen as an ancient drama of the convergence of values, tensions and oppositions of these two old religions (p 3).

The most complete and well-known source of the story of Demeter and Persephone comes from the first Homeric "Hymn to Demeter," composed around 650 BCE. According to this myth one day Kore, the maiden version of Persephone, was with her companions picking flowers in a field not far from her mother. Suddenly she spies a flower she had never seen before, the narcissus. Delighted Kore reaches for the blossom, but just as she does so the earth splits open and from the depths emerges Hades, the dreaded Lord of the Underworld, with his chariot and horses. He grabs the girl and carries her back through the chasm into the underworld. Terrified Kore screams for her father, Zeus, but as he was busy accepting offerings he doesn't hear her. Only three people hear her cries. Hecate, deep in her cave, hears Kore's screams. (Hecate, the Goddess of Ghosts, was connected with the night and the moon. In her full powers she was the Goddess of Death and embodied the Crone aspect of the Triple Goddess. By the time of Homer hymns she was no longer an honored goddess but was viewed disparagingly, frequently as a witch (Carlson 23).)

Two others hear Kore's cry: Helios, the Sun God, (who Carlson states represents the patriarchal point of view in this story), and Demeter, Kore's mother, who frantically begins searching for her daughter. If you have ever feared that your child, or the child of someone close to you, was abducted, then you can empathize with the depth of Demeter's horror over the disappearance of her daughter!

For days Demeter searches for her daughter, but to no avail, for no one knows what has become of Kore. Finally Hecate meets up with Demeter and they decide to approach Helios. As the Sun God he is able to see and hear everything as he travels across the sky. Helios tells them that it was Zeus who has given Kore to Hades. Then Helios goes so far as to reprimand Demeter for being so upset. He reminds Demeter that Hades is her brother and that as Lord of the Underworld he is a worthy son-in-law. Far from being reassured, Demeter becomes even more angry and upset at Helios' words.

According to Carlson, Helios takes the patriarchal stance. Because the abductor is Demeter's brother and well positioned, Helios feels she should be relieved, see this as a positive action, and submit. Demeter is furious, however and refuses to buy into the patriarchal views of male supremacy. She rebuffs a system that supports the rights of the "fathers," especially when it brings injustice and creates bitterness, pain and loss! (p 23)

Demeter is furious and turns her back on Olympus, the home of the gods, and goes to dwell among mortals. She disguises herself as an old woman so no one will recognize her as a goddess. Eventually she comes to the town of Eleusis and stops to rest near the Virgin's Well where the townspeople draw their water. Soon the daughters of the local king, Keleos, come for water. Noticing this sad old woman they feel sorry for her. They ask her where she is from and inquire as to whether she is looking for work as a housekeeper and nursemaid.

Demeter responds by telling an interesting cover story. She says her name is Doso, given to her by her mother, and that she has just arrived from Crete. She claims that she was abducted by pirates and was finally able to escape and has been wandering ever since.

According to Carlson, "Doso" means "giver" and was another way of saying Earth. This links the disguised goddess with the oldest of goddesses. She also identified herself only by her mother, which suggested a connection to a matriarchal tradition and the older religion of the goddess. The link to Crete was also interesting as Crete was the last place to hold out against the advance of the patriarchal invaders. Crete preserved the Mother Goddess religion for many years after the rest of southern Europe succumbed to the new order (p 23).

Demeter then asks the young women if they know anyone who might be looking for help as a nurse and housekeeper. Their mother, Metanira, had only recently given birth to a newborn son and was currently looking for someone. So the young women rushed home to tell their mother. Metanira asked that "the old woman" be brought to her.

The maidens return for Demeter and take her to their mother. Demeter veils her face and allows herself be led. The goddess is taller than most women. When she crosses the threshold her head grazes the top of the doorframe, and the doorway is filled with light. This surprises Metanira, but not recognizing the goddess she ignores it and asks 'the old woman' to sit down.

Metanira offers Demeter the position of nursemaid, which the goddess accepts, saying she will take good care of the baby, whose name is Demophoon. He grows strong and healthy without sustenance because at night Demeter holds him in the fire to burn off his mortal parts to make him immortal. One night, however, Metanira catches sight of Demeter holding the baby in the fire. Alarmed she cries out and creates uproar, as any one of us who is a mother would have done. Demeter is furious, however, and lifts the baby out of the fire and throws him on the ground. Revealing herself as the goddess, Demeter rebukes the mother for her 'stupidity' telling her that she would have made the baby immortal. Now, she says, this is impossible! She then instructs Metanira and her husband, King Keleos, to have the people of Eleusis build her a temple. There, she says, she will inaugurate her Mysteries there.

Carlson points out here that it is interesting that Demeter denounces Metanira as foolish, when Metanira was only reacting with the same terror and grief with which Demeter responded when Kore was dragged into the Underworld. Metanira was fearful because she did not realize that Demeter was bestowing the gift of immortality. Instead she believed she was witnessing the death of her son - that, in effect, he was being sent to the Underworld. Metanira's reaction was the human response to death which we have all experienced: grief and terror. To Demeter, the Goddess of the Grain, however, death was only a period of transformation that led to new life. Though Demeter is still furious with Metanira's interference, the act served as a catalyst. It helped the goddess realize that she needed to initiate humans into the Mysteries so they would no longer fear death as the end, but see it as part of the cycle of life; that death was only a transition leading to new life. This is, according to Carlson, the divine dimension of the myth (p 31).

Soon the townspeople complete a temple for Demeter. Established in her new residence Demeter once again sinks deep into inconsolable despair over the loss of her daughter. In her grief she becomes vengeful and decides to withdraw her gift of grain from the land. When the seeds stop germinating both humans and the gods are in peril. Humans are threatened with starvation, and, since there is no harvest, the gods receive no offerings. Now Zeus is distressed! He sends many goddesses and gods to Demeter in an effort to appease her. They offer her gifts and promises, but Demeter will have none of it and becomes even angrier. She asserts that she will not relent, nor will she step foot in Olympus again, until her daughter, Kore, is returned to her.

Zeus is finally forced to relent. He sends Hermes to the underworld to retrieve the maiden who has now matured into the woman and queen, Persephone. Hermes finds Persephone sad and still missing her mother terribly. Hermes tells Hades of Demeter's wrath and the extent of her vengeance. He conveys Zeus' command that Demeter's daughter be returned. Hades knows he cannot disobey, but he turns to his wife and reminds her of all that will be hers if she stays. He asserts that he is a worthy spouse, and she will reign over his kingdom with him as Persephone, the Queen of the Dead. When Hades realizes that Persephone is eager to return to her mother, he slips her a pomegranate seed. Without realizing what she is doing, she eats it. Consequently Persephone will now have to return to the underworld, for anyone who eats the fruits of the underworld cannot escape.

Reluctantly Hades readies his chariot and drives Hermes and Persephone back into the world. Demeter is overjoyed to finally see her daughter again and takes her in her arms and holds her tight. Then with alarm she asks Persephone if she has eaten anything while in the underworld. When Persephone tells her mother about the pomegranate seed, Demeter regrettably tells her daughter that for one-third of each year she must return to the underworld. However, when the world begins to bloom in the spring Persephone can return bringing happiness and new life to the world.

As you can imagine the goddesses spent the rest of the day talking and laughing as their hearts become light and filled with happiness. Hecate joins them and from that time on she precedes and follows Persephone. Demeter allows the grain seeds to germinate and the fields once again become abundant with crops. True to her promise she begins to teach the Mysteries by first teaching her rites and secrets to the sons of Eleusis and Keleos. Triptolemus, the oldest son of King Keleos, is trained in the art of agriculture so that he can in turn train all of Greece to plant and reap crops. It was rumored that the goddesses provided him with a winged chariot so he could fly across Greece teaching and training others. And it is said that those who are initiated in the Mysteries have a different experience at death than the uninitiated. Those who serve the goddesses with true devotion have bestowed upon them Plutous, the Child of Prosperity, who brings abundance and wealth (p 37).

When Hecate, the ancient Goddess of Death, once again becomes the companion of Persephone, the Crone and her darkness are restored to their proper place. In the Mother Goddess religion, life was cyclical – birth, death and rebirth. As winter, which is the time of darkness, both precedes spring and follows the harvest, the Crone was once again re-connected to the Maiden. "The cycle is restored, the Maiden who germinates from the Crone's fertile death, grows into the fruitfulness of the Mother and dies back into the Dark One, only to rise from her ever anew. The cycle of nature was re-established" (Carlson 37).

Carlson points out that the gift of grain liberated humans from living like beasts, which foraged for their food, and from the brutality of war, because peace was needed to grow grain. With the initiation of the Mysteries death was no longer seen as the end, but was viewed on a continuum of rebirth. Those dying, or facing death or the loss of loved ones, could now turn to the goddess Persephone, the Queen of the Underworld, for compassion and support, rather than to the fearsome and terrifying Hades. The Eleusinian mysteries were celebrated for 1500 years beginning sometime in the middle of the second millennium BCE and continuing until the 4th century CE (p 37-39).

There is another transpersonal meaning to this myth. Kore, the maiden, descended into her traumatic ordeal and sat with her grief for weeks which extended into years. She learned the lessons of the underworld and became wiser, more experienced. Her experience transformed her into Persephone, the mature woman and Queen of the Underworld - or the mistress of her own psyche. Demeter was also transformed. She desired the return of her daughter, but when Kore returned transformed as Persephone, the woman and queen, she embraced the person her daughter had become and was prepared to accept her daughter's fate, a path much different than that of the young maiden.

Megan Wagner, M.A., Therapist, Artist, Kabbalah Teacher and Interfaith Minister, states in her book, *The Sapphire Staff: Walking the Western Mystical Way*, that we all experience abductions that take us into the bowels of the Underworld where we confront our own personal Hades. Sometimes this is the death of someone close to us, the divorce of our parents, or our own divorce. Or it might be the loss of a career, a traumatic move, or a serious health crisis. The pain and loss can be excruciating and take many forms: shame, guilt, regret, anger, hatred, betrayal, sadness, grief. Our pain is central to knowing what Wagner calls our "instinctive body" - to being in touch with ourselves, our deepest feeling self (p 55).

In our world of plenty, we have many opportunities to escape our pain, our true feelings. We can numb out with alcohol, drugs, food, cigarettes, shopping, partying, or television. It's so easy to "check-out!" No one wants to hurt. It feels awful! However, Wagner points out, when we numb ourselves rather than letting ourselves sit with our pain, or process our feelings, we distance ourselves from our own instinctive bodies. When we separate from our feelings, we lose the ability to recognize them, and then we begin to doubt our feelings, to doubt our true needs. We begin to doubt our own instincts (p 59).

Several years ago a client came to me who had spent several years caring for several ill family members who all passed on. She had spiraled into a depression which she tried to numb with drugs, food (gaining 50 pounds) and sleep. She was stuck in an abusive dysfunctional relationship which she was terrified to leave - she had become so paralyzed with grief. I worked with her over several months encouraging her to talk about her experience, to remember the good and the bad while helping her to put her experiences into perspective. I didn't try to fix her, but encouraged her to feel her pain and to nurture herself with things that were healthy - to be the good mother to herself. I wove the Great Mother into many of her guided visualizations so that she could experience the feeling of being lovingly held with deep compassion even though she was feeling such incredible pain and loss. Gradually she broke out of the paralysis that had her stuck in depression and began to make plans for her future. She still missed her loved ones, but she was able to move on. The last time I talked to her she had moved, was building a new life for herself, was exploring a new healthier relationship, and had gone back to school to retrain for a new career. What I felt most positive about was that she felt emotionally and physically strong and centered, and was surer of herself and what she wanted for her future. The paralysis and fear was gone.

Our feelings are our internal alert system that lets us know when the environment and people around us are healthy and good, or dysfunctional and unsafe. When we numb out, flee or try to ignore our feelings, then we can get stuck in depressive or dysfunctional behavior that does not help us grow or learn from our life experiences. Remember the myth of Demeter and Persephone ends with the promise of Plutous, the child of plenty. Pluto is another name for Hades. Pluto's name means "bringer of riches." As such, what appears as a death can be transformed into an opportunity to open up to new life. Pluto exposes us to separation, conflict, grief and loss to help us experience the life-death-rebirth cycle. It is a cycle that is almost instinctual because we as humans continually cycle through it. This cycle has the capacity to help us become more consciously aware. What this means is that behind the terror of the open chasm is the larger vision of our potential, our ability to become more whole and complete. We can claim the riches that come from our experience of going through the death and rebirth process. We gain a deeper awareness of who we are with a greater trust of our instincts and our feelings (Wagner, 55)

In order to accomplish this, Wagner claims, Pluto is the initiator. He cracks open the earth (a metaphor for our subconscious), and drags Kore (or our own unsuspecting selves) down into the underworld so that we can experience the depth of our own shadow and learn to process our pain, loss, and suffering. The maiden (the joyful, playful part of us) does not want to feel pain. Yet by numbing out rather than fully sitting with the descent, we deprive ourselves of the opportunity to transform, to become the wise, mature, experienced Queen of the Underworld (p 60-61).

One of the symbols of the great mother is the womb. Some cultures used caves; others dug huge womb-like caverns deep in the earth which for years puzzled archaeologists who were trying to interpret them through a masculine lens. When finally a female perspective was brought to some of these sites, it became clear that the caverns were wombs. They were used as such in ritual and worship of the great earth mother. Our earliest memories, our prenatal memories, are of being contained, held safe and secure within our mother's wombs.

When Persephone descends into the dark underworld, it can be perceived as a tomb, or as a womb, Wagner says. She sits with her emotional pain and trauma for days and weeks, which become months and years. She does not deny her situation, nor numb out, or become bitter; nor does she crack open or go mad. She simply sits with herself and allows the underworld, the womb that surrounds her, to hold her while she feels the loss, the separation from the familiar, the grief and anger (p 60).

By sitting with her emotional pain Persephone models for us how to both survive and heal the trauma to our instinctual selves. She shows us how to be present with ourselves even when we are trapped in our descent to the underworld. By being present and just sitting with our emotional pain, we learn to be present so we can become consciously aware of our feelings and evolve into the queen of our own underworld, or our own subconscious. Being present with our feelings, rather than running from them, helps us mature and become wise. This is how we earn our winkles and gray hair. These are symbols of our courage showing that we have endured and survived the grief, loss, anger, regret, shame or whatever shaped our own personal underworld (p 60).

In summary you learned from this section that the myth of Demeter and Persephone originated during a time of great change and upheaval in Greece, when the new patriarchal ways and sky god religions were becoming more dominant and the older mother goddess traditions were fading away. This myth, which reflects agricultural dynamics, helped the common people understand that the cycle of the seasons also applied to the human condition of birth, death and rebirth bringing reassurance and the promise of new life after the old passes away. For centuries this belief, which was passed on through the Eleusinian Mysteries, brought comfort and peace both to the dying as well as to those losing their loved ones.

This myth also has an important transpersonal application for our contemporary times. I am sure that you would prefer, as I do, to avoid pain, suffering and grief. Yet, as Persephone models for us, it is when we sit with and process these deep painful feelings and experiences that we are able grow, transform, and become wise. We gain more by embracing our pain and our fears than by running from them.

DISCUSSION

Sit for a few moments and reflect on what feeling or feelings you are most likely to numb. Or what life experience you have been suppressing. We all have at least one.

❖ What feeling or life experience do you recognize that you are trying to numb?

❖ What is your favorite way of numbing out? Alcohol, shopping, partying, working, television?

❖ What would happen if instead of numbing out you allowed yourself to sit with your feelings?

❖ What keeps you from sitting with your feelings?

SOURCES

Kathie Carlson, *Life's Daughter/Death's Bride: Inner Transformations through the Goddess Demeter/Persephone.*

Mara Lynn Keller, "The Eleusinian Mysteries of Demeter and Persephone: Fertility, Sexuality and Rebirth," *Journal of Feminist Studies in Religion.*

Marguerite Rigoglioso, *Bearing the Holy Ones*, UMI Dissertation Services.

Megan Wagner, *The Sapphire Staff: Walking the Western Mystical Way.*

PERSEPHONE GUIDED VISUALIZATION

Settle back into you chair and begin to take three deep breathes. With each breath breathe all the way into your abdomen and release slowly....As you exhale let go of all the stress and tension that you have collected during the week....On your next inhalation begin to call back all the pieces of yourself back to you that you may have scattered out and about the world.... Call these pieces back to yourself so that you can be totally present right here...right now...

As you continue to follow your breath allow yourself to sink deeper and deeper into yourself...and begin to enter into your inner landscape.... Imagine that you are following a rocky mountain path that in some ways looks familiar, as if you have walked this path before....It is a sun drenched day and the heat bakes the stones and the dry earth beneath your feet.... You walk with a heavy heart...carrying a heavy load...you know the burden you carry. You have carried it a long time....

Now imagine that you come to the mouth of a cave. You can smell the moist cool smell of clean rich soil....The cave offers relief from the sun and you enter with your burden....you begin to follow the downward path to the center of the cave...You are drawn downward with the descent as you walk deeper and deeper...feeling the weight of your burden on your shoulders.... You have walked a long distance...the bulk of your burden is enormous.... You are bowed over with its magnitude....

Eventually you enter a torch-lit cavern....The sides are dark, smooth, and rounded, like a womb....In the center, seated on a soft pile of furs, blankets, and pillows, is the figure of a woman.... You know her to be the great mother....She radiates compassion and mercy....She knows you are carrying a heavy burden....She knows that this is your burden to carry...that it is profound and somber....She knows you so want to relinquish it, to give it up....She knows she cannot take it from you, yet she invites you to sit a bit with her...to let her hold you...to contain you and steady you while you adjust your burden.... Her lap is large and her arms stretch wide to gather you up....With relief you sink into her bosom and you feel secure as she holds you...and you sit...you sit with your burden....Feeling safe, you allow yourself to feel the pain...the depth of emotion....You allow yourself to stay with your authentic feelings and you sit honoring your feeling... feeling the feelings and letting them be...Like Kore, you sit in the underworld... in the womb of the Great Mother, enduring the loss... the separation from the familiar...the grief or anger...or whatever feelings come up as you sit...and hold... and allow yourself and your feelings to just be (long pause).

Once we allow ourselves to feel the emotional pain we begin to realize that the effort of numbing the pain, of stuffing the pain has caused us to lose some of our vitality, our instinctive energy... It might be passion, joyfulness, or spontaneity, or sexuality, or resiliency, or acceptance, or patience.... What has your effort to numb the pain caused you to lose? (long pause).

Once you have identified what instinctive energy you have lost, try to notice where your body either feels an ache, or it could even be numbness... This is where you might be holding the grief...or anger...or guilt...or whatever emotional pain you might be carrying that has caused you to lose your instinctive energy....Actively begin to call your instinctive energy back to you....Call your power right back into that spot...Invite your lifeblood to return...Call it back with the vibrations of the rattle, and if it feels right, let your own sounds join the vibrations as you re-awaken to sensation and call your vitality and power back. (RATTLE RATTLE RATTLE RATTLE...).

Feel the lifeblood returning...celebrate the return of your instinctive energy....Make a commitment to allow yourself to sit with your feelings, just as you have tonight...If it is hard, just imagine that the Great Mother is holding you...containing you as you sit with the feelings...just as you are doing right now...The Great Mother is always here to gather you up and hold you...to support you....

As you begin to notice what instinctive energy you have lost... continue to call it back to you...it is your lifeblood, your vitality, your passion, your spontaneity, your joy...Each time you reclaim a piece of your vitality, remember to honor it in a sacred way...light a candle to Persephone...plant a flower...take a reflective walk on the beach...In your own way, honor and commemorate each time you have made a transition and reclaimed a part of your vitality and your soul...

And now it is time to come back to this time and this place. Gently become aware of your breath in your lungs...the feel of your body in the chair...the weight of your feet upon the floor...And when you are ready you may open your eyes coming all the way back to this time and this place. Take a deep breath and stretch.

Portions of this guided visualization are taken from *The Sapphire Staff*, p 61, and the meditations "Being Held in the Arms of the Mother" and "Retrieving Your Instinctive Power" by Megan Wagner, Ph.D.

(You may purchase a recording of this guided visualization for a nominal fee at www.celebratedivinefeminine.com)

PERSEPHONE RITUAL – SITTING WITH OUR FEELINGS

Music: Jennifer Berezan, *She Who Hears the Cries of the World.*

Supplies

❖ A bouquet of spring flowers (make sure you have one for each person), plastic cups, garden soil, large bowl to hold the soil, garden spade, seeds (preferable fairly large flower seeds that are easy to pick up), a small bowl to hold the seeds, pitcher of water, small slips of paper and pens.

❖ Arrange attractively on a center or side altar the bouquet of flowers, plastic cups, large bowl of soil, garden spade, small bowl of seeds, and pitcher of water.

❖ Have the slips of paper and pens ready to pass out

Introduction to the Ritual

When Kore sat in the underworld with her emotional pain she was surrounded by earth envisioned as a tomb or womb. Kore sat alone with her feelings, yet she was held, contained in the womb of the Great Mother as she went through her transformation.

When we go through our own emotional pain, it is helpful to remember that we are also held in the arms of the Great Mother. Though we must each go through our own transformation, we need not do it abandoned and alone. For she hears the cries of the world. She is always there to hold and carry us, if we let her.

I would like to give you each an opportunity to begin to sit with one of your feelings or emotional wounds that in the past you may have numbed or ignored. This will give you a chance to come to greater understanding of your deeper self, and, hopefully, to transform.

Instructions for the Ritual

1. Pass out small slips of paper and pens

2. Read the instruction
   "Take a moment to reflect on what feeling or memory you might be numbing. Write it down on your slip of paper."
3. Wait 3 to 5 minutes while people process and write down their thoughts
4. Read the following instructions
   - When you feel ready walk to the altar and take a cup. Place your slip of paper in the cup, cover it with soil, plant a couple of seeds, and water it.
   - If you like, you may name it out loud – by naming it, it loses its power to trigger us, and we gain control over it.
   - This ritual is symbolic of your willingness to sit with whatever has come up for you, possibly daily, or even just once or twice a week when you water the seed. Take 5, 10 or 20 minutes to reflect, perhaps to journal, and let whatever needs to be confronted surface. This is an opportunity to sit with and process your issue to see what new understanding and wisdom can be gained.
   - Take a flower for the altar as a sign of spring, a symbol of rebirth, and of the riches that can be gained by facing our stuff.
5. Begin the ritual playing soft music in the background.
6. After the ritual ask the participants to share their experiences, either from the ritual or the guided visualization. If you are a sole practitioner take time to journal about your experience.

TABLE OF CORRESPONDENCES FOR DEMETER AND PERSEPHONE

Element: Earth

Symbols: Grain for Demeter; Pomegranate for Persephone; Narcissus for Kore

Color: Green, earth tones, red for the pomegranate

Animals: Pig. Pigs were sacrificed to the goddesses and barley cakes formed in the shape of pigs were baked in their honor.

Companions: Hecate

Mates: Zeus was the mate of Demeter and father to Persephone. Hades was the mate of Persephone

Seasons: Spring, Fall and Winter

Festivals: The Lesser Mysteries were held on February 26 for the purification of the initiates. Eleusinian Mysteries were held on the Fall Equinox around September 21. It was a 7 day ritual that included: the Day of Assembly; Initiates to the Sea; Now Come the Pig Victims; Purification; Torch Day; Holy Night; and the Pouring of Plenty.

Plants: Grains and pomegranate

Foods: Roast pig, barley cakes, pomegranate seeds

Children: Persephone was the daughter of Demeter. Persephone had a son, Zagreus, and a daughter, Melaena, fathered by Zeus, her father.

Music Suggestions

Guided Visualization: Turkish Lullaby by Eliana Gilad from the album *Noam-Healing Lullaby Music*, or "Sanctuary" from *Vision Quest* by Kieran De Verniero

Ritual: *She Who Hears the Cries of the World* by Jennifer Berezan

(The following is a proposed agenda if you choose to hold a circle to celebrate Demeter and Persephone)

IN HER NAME CIRCLE
DEMETER AND PERSEPHONE, DEATH AND REBIRTH
CIRCLE PROGRAM

Introductions (5 - 10 min)

Calling in the Directions: (3min)–

Opening: (2 min) poem

Demeter and Persephone Presentation: (25 min)

Q&A (15 min)

Guided Visualization: (15 min)

Ritual: Sitting with Our Feelings (20 min)

Group Share: (15 min**)**

Goddess Cards (10 min) -- Pulling a goddess card to see what goddess energy we will each walk in for the up-coming month

Closing: (3min)

Charge of the Star Goddess, by Starhawk or

"Hymn to Persephone," by Rev. Lady Bella Sundancer

Releasing the directions – (2min)

Total Time: 2 hours

Hecate

Hecate

QUEEN OF THE WITCHES OR WISE CRONE?

Invocation to Hecate

Hecate,
Mistress of the Dark Moon
standing at the crossroads
with howling hound
and blazing torches.

Dark Crone Mother
you light our way
with dreams and prophecies
you guide us
through visions and magic.

In the depths of the underground
we find you
and your priestesses
chanting funerary hymns
and incantations.

Beside the sacred poplar and yew,
we feel your presence
as we move from the darkness
of our unconscious sleep
and are awakened to change
by your call.

From *The Dark Goddess: Dancing with the Shadow*
by Marcia Starck and Gynne Stern

13. Hecate

QUEEN OF THE WITCHES OR WISE CRONE?

(Go to www.celebratedivinefeminine.com to view the complementary PowerPoint that accompanies this text.)

TRIPLE-FACED HECATE is one of the most ancient images of pre-Hellenic mythology. In this section you will learn about Hecate's geographical and historical origins. Even though Hecate has ties to the ancient Mother Goddess you will come to understand how over time she became allied with the archetype of the crone, was relegated of the underworld and came to be associated with death and witch craft. You will also learn how her connection to the underworld also links her to the psychological realm of the subconscious and to transformation and change. Hecate can guide you when you must journey into the depths of your subconscious to reflect and re-evaluate your life. Her transformative powers can help you release what no longer serves you so you can make room for new opportunities and growth.

Hecate reminds us of the value of the crone, the wise elder who offers wisdom and insight. She provides a powerful model to emulate for those of us who have reached their crone hood. On my 60th birthday I threw myself a party and invited my women friends, many who were and still are my sisters in the goddess. We had a joyous celebration of my crone hood. I have had my years of struggle and pain, and felt I needed to celebrate the wisdom I acquired earning those winkles and grey hair! I highly recommend a similar celebration for any of you who have attained this auspicious phase of your life.

In the guided visualization you will have an opportunity to Join Hecate and a group of her devotees around a bubbling cauldron on a moonlit night. You will be invited to join them in releasing what no longer serves you, so you can call in new energies for personal growth and expansion. The ritual is an extension of this visualization as you cycle through three altars to discard the old, call upon Hecate for guidance and breathe life into new ideas and goals.

Hecate's nature and roles have shifted greatly over the centuries and sometimes seem almost contradictory. She has been worshipped as the

Great Mother, as well as the Crone. She has been linked to the moon, is guardian of the crossroad and is said to preside over magic, ritual, prophetic vision, childbirth, death, the underworld, and the secrets of regeneration. During the Middle Ages, Hecate became associated with black magic and was debased as the hag, or Queen of the Witches, who led satanic rites

Hecate is one of the oldest primordial figures and is pre-Olympian. She can be linked back to the ancient frog-headed Egyptian goddess Heket. As mid-wife it was said that Heket help to birth the sun every morning. Heket evolved into Heq, the tribal matriarch of pre-dynastic Egypt.

According to some traditions Hecate's geographic origin was Thrace, a part of present day Greece and Bulgaria. She was an ancient and powerful Thracian divinity, and a Titan, who ruled heaven, earth and the sea. She was said to bestow wealth, victory, wisdom, and good luck on mortals. If, however, she felt a mortal was unworthy, she could also withhold her blessings. It is said that she assisted the gods in the war with the Gigantes, and slew Clytius (Hesiod's Theogeny, 411-452; Apollodius, i. 6. # 2).

When I was in Bulgaria in 2004, I visited a Thracian tomb from around 1200 BCE which contained murals of a king foretelling his life in the afterworld. He would rule as king and be honored by the goddess Hecate, or Bendies as she was sometimes called. The goddess was shown welcoming the king to the underworld with the sacred pomegranate. When the king died, his favorite wife was sacrificed so that she might also accompany him to the underworld. This is not an honor that you or I would appreciate today!

Other sources claim that Hecate was worshipped from Middle Europe to Anatolia dating back 5000 to 6000 years ago, to pre-patriarchal times. Indigenous inhabitants of Old Europe, Anatolia and Northern Africa dating back to the Neolithic some 9000 years ago were matrilineal, matrifocal, agrarian, and peace-loving. They worshipped a mother goddess who presided over the cycles of life – birth, death and rebirth. Along the Danube in Eastern Europe the Frog Goddess was a symbol of fertility, death, rebirth and transformation. Patriarchal influences began to overtake the Neolithic Mother Goddess cultures around approximately 5000 years ago, when sun god worshipping semi-nomadic invaders from the eastern steppes of Russia who were hierarchical and warlike began to appear.

This ancient mother goddess preceded Hecate, and quite possibly evolved into Hecate. As patriarchy took root and male gods became more dominant, the goddesses became more submissive and less powerful. Many of Hecate's attributes were split off and given to other goddesses such as Demeter, Persephone and Artemis. Hecate was relegated to her underworld qualities and lost much of her prominence.

Hecate was worshipped by the Amazons who were mother goddess worshipping matrifocal and matrilineal nomadic tribes that lived in Anatolia and North Africa near the Black Sea. The Amazons were believed to have founded several cities in Anatolia (Turkey) and were the first to tame horses. The most famous princess and priestess of Hecate was the sorceress, Medea, who resided in Colchis which is located on the eastern end of Black Sea in Anatolia and is noted for being Amazon country. There is a statue of Medea in Colchis, and this area, according to a friend of mine who spent several years in the country of Georgia, is still known for its strong women.

Hecate appears in the ancient texts of the Eleusinian Mysteries of pre-Hellenic Greece. If you remember from the previous section on Demeter and Persephone, the Eleusinian Mysteries involve a descent into the underworld that is somewhat similar to the descent mythologies of both Inanna and Dumuzi, and Isis and Osiris. In this myth Persephone, the beloved daughter of Demeter, is abducted by Hades, the dreaded Lord of the Underworld, and carried off to his kingdom. It is Hecate who witnesses Persephone's abduction, and who also greets Persephone upon her return. In pre-Hellenic Greece it was believed that Hecate resided in the underworld as its queen and was the Guardian of the Souls.

In Classical Greek mythology Hecate was the daughter of Titans: Perses, the Titan God of Destruction, and Asteria, a star goddess. Asteria was a sister of Leto, the mother of Apollo and Artemis. Hecate was, therefore, the cousin of Artemis. Hecate was respected by Zeus, and was the only deity aside from Zeus who had the power to grant or withhold anything she wanted from humans.

Hecate was worshiped as a moon goddess - the dark aspect of the moon. She was the mirror image of her cousin, Artemis, who was the light aspect of the moon. Selene was the aspect of the full moon. This dark aspect links Hecate to Isis of Egypt as well as the Black Madonna in Europe. Interestingly it is the dark goddesses who are most strongly connected to healing powers and the dark moon. The shrines of the Black Virgins/Madonnas of Europe are frequently connected to miracles and to healing powers, and they are assigned more powers than those of the Virgins of the white aspects.

Hecate, as the great Triple Goddess -- or Hecate Triformis -- is a form of the original trinity: maiden, mother, and aging wise woman or crone. The Virgin was Kore/Persephone, Ceres or Demeter was the Mother, and the crone, or wise woman, was Hecate. Hecate was also part of the three phases of woman's mating relationships: Hebe as maiden, Hera the wife and Hecate as the widow. In women's agricultural mysteries her trinity took the form of Kore as the green corn; Persephone as the ripe ear; and Hecate as the harvested corn. As the Christian trinity postdates the Triple Goddess, it probably evolved from this original goddess trinity, with the wisdom of the crone, or Hecate, going to the Holy Spirit.

When I visited the Thracian tomb while traveling in Bulgaria, our groups was quite excited to notice that painted on the dome ceiling was a Thracian representation of the seven levels of heaven. There were three charioteers driving the heavens or the cosmos. Upon closer inspection we noticed that not only were the charioteers women, but in fact it was the Triple Goddess as Maiden, Mother, and Crone who was driving the heavens! To reiterate, the tomb predated Christ by over 1200 years.

There is a famous pillar called the Hectaerion which depicts the three aspects of Hecate. The three females represent Hecate's powers over heaven, earth and underworld as well as her control over birth, life and death. Her six arms carry three torches, a key, a rope and a dagger. The key illustrates her role as the guardian of the deep mysteries; only Hecate possesses the key that unlocks them. The rope possibly symbolizes the umbilical cord, or represents her role of bringing souls into the underworld and helping them to be reborn. The dagger symbolizes cutting through illusions to true power. The dagger later becomes the *athame* of Wicca.

The aspect for which Hecate is most honored is that of the crone. As the wise woman Hecate offers words of wisdom and provides valuable counsel as well as protection. An ancient ritual honoring Hecate involved leaving food at crossroads where three paths meet. It was called Hecate's supper. This ritual food was left when important decisions had to be made. The supplicants asked for guidance and the most favorable outcome. In life we often find that the way is not clear and confusion exists. This is especially true in today's troubled times. Hecate is the Goddess of Wisdom and Vision. She sees the past, present and future and can be called upon to help us make wise decisions and good choices.

Hecate's responsibility as Guardian of Souls degenerated over time as patriarchy became more entrenched and the status of goddesses continued to deteriorate. Eventually Hecate became a shadowy haunting hag-like figure that at night sent out demons and phantoms who taught sorcery and witchcraft. These underworld beings were said to dwell where two roads crossed, at tombs, and near the blood of murdered persons. Hecate wandered with the souls of the dead; her approach was announced by the whining and howling of dogs.

The realm of the underworld over which Hecate rules has not always been viewed as a place of punishment. It was the Christians who invented the concept of Hell as a place of unending torture. Originally the underworld was the place of the dead. It was a stopover place while the dead prepared for rebirth. Hecate, as you remember, witnessed both

Persephone's descent into the underworld and her return. By being both behind and in front of Persephone, Hecate is symbolically protecting and guiding her. It also symbolized her role as the Queen of the Underworld. Hecate was viewed by the ancient Greeks as the Mistress of Souls who lighted the way as she conveyed souls to the underworld at death, and who guided them on their return when it was time for them to be reborn. In our Western culture death is a taboo subject, and our elderly citizens are shown little respect and are hidden away.

How are the elders treated in your own family? In your community? Our culture favors youth and has an aversion to aging. Take time to notice the numerous commercials and advertisements on beauty products. Notice how many of the actors and models are young and attractive. Only recently with the aging of the Baby Boomers have mature middle aged women begun to make an appearance on ads, and most of those are for health related products. Hecate is the confident wise Crone who appreciates the knowledge gained from a life of experiences, relationships and lessons. She knows death and does not fear it because death is a transition leading to renewal and rebirth.

The ancients had no concept of an inner or psychological realm. The inner world was the spirit realm where all the spirits dwelt. Even today our inner creative world can seem mysterious and appears to be filled with surprises. Hecate is the guardian of the crossroads of our unconscious, the hidden part of our psyches which is the source of our creativity, growth and healing. Sometimes gaining wisdom requires a descent into the underworld of our subconscious where inspiration and vision, the creative juices of renewal, are often found. Because Western culture emphasizes action and productivity, it frequently devalues those times of deep introspection. We have been conditioned to experience them as being stuck, in limbo, or as being depressed. In reality these spaces of non-activity may be part of the journey to revitalization. Hecate, if invited, acts as our guide in this deep inner work.

In my practice I frequently have clients who exhibit symptoms of depression. Many report that their doctors have almost automatically given them anti-depressants, rather than taking time to delve into the source of their low moods. I agree that for the clinically depressed anti-depressants are often warranted and necessary, and can beneficially change a person's life. However, I have found that for many of my clients what was needed was for someone to listen to them and help them sort through the confusion of their concerns, while providing encouragement and tools to help them shift towards a more positive attitude. Going inward can be a productive time of deep reflection that can result in growth and change. Being too quick to take a pill can deprive a person of a valuable opportunity to arrive at important insights and self-realizations.

Transformation and change often requires releasing what no longer serves us. We humans often fear letting go of old beliefs, relationships, assumptions and perceptions about life, as well as letting go of our physical body. We protest and struggle, trying to hold onto the familiar, even though it might be the source of our pain. I've had clients with 50 pounds or more to lose crying with frustration and shame over their weight. Yet they are reluctant to adhere to a food plan or exercise routine. I've had other clients in painfully dysfunctional and abusive relationships who are desperate for change but terrified to let go. We must face the emptiness and the fear of the unknown if we are to receive Hecate's gift of vision and renewal. We must face the Dark Goddess. We can surrender to Hecate what needs to be released so we can be reborn. Many times, even though we protest, the Crone will claim us and recycle us through her cauldron despite our struggles and cries of resistance. Maybe you have already had this experience!

Hecate was skilled in the arts of divining and foretelling the future. As she looks three ways at once, Hecate gives us an expanded vision whereby we can see the present, or warnings or promises of the future, or recall teachings or learnings from the past. She gives us dreams and prophetic visions, whispers secrets to our inner ears, and enables us to converse with the spirits of the dead and guides. As Queen of Ghosts, Mother of Witches, Mistress of Magic, Hecate bestows magical knowledge. She was said to hold the secrets of magical spells, charms, enchantments, and the medicinal use of both healing and destructive substances. One of Hecate's rituals took place on moonless nights at a three-fold crossroads. In a sacred cauldron special herbs were mixed with wine, milk or blood and boiled while Hecate was invoked. Sacred cauldrons also appear in other mythologies from around the world including Hindu, Norse, Babylonian, Chaldean and Hittite mythology.

Late in the1400 CE, an inquisition was unleashed to hunt, torture and burn witches. It lasted until the 1600's, a period during which nine million witches, 80% women including young girls, were exterminated. This was a period of asceticism in which the church denigrated anything of the flesh and had a misogynistic hatred of all that brought life into the world. Anyone could accuse a witch, and the accused were considered guilty until proven innocent. They were frequently tortured for confessions and to implicate others until a coven of thirteen was identified. It is believed that few of those convicted really belonged to a coven or were truly witches. The victims were the elderly, senile, mentally ill, handicapped, physically unappealing, the village beauties that incited lust, homosexuals or freethinkers. It was the midwives, healers and seers, those who did the most good for the country people, who were identified by the Church as the most dangerous. Instead of valuing and honoring these women for the healers they were, and for the wisdom and knowledge they brought to the community, these women were burned at the stake or hanged as witches and were accused of being inhabited by evil spirits such as Hecate. A video by Starhawk called *Burning Times* is a thought provoking documentary about the witch hunts and trials during this period.

Hecate was demonized by the Catholic authorities. They projected onto her their fears and insecurities of the powerful dark feminine. They distorted her into an ugly Queen of Witches. Many pagan country people persisted in practicing their ancient fertility rites and folk customs. This angered and horrified the Church. Because the patriarchal authorities could not control Hecate; and because they didn't understand the powers of the dark feminine, they demonized her. They taught fear of this goddess envisioned as a twisted old hag, who, like the dark of the moon, was considered to be negative and even hostile to men. It was said that she stalked the crossroads at night with her vicious hounds of hell waiting to snatch unsuspecting wayfarers to her land of the dead. They portrayed her as the moon goddess of ghosts and the dead surrounded by a swarm of female demons. And as Queen of Ghosts she was believed to fly through the night, followed by a dreadful train of ghoulish spirits and baying hounds. She was said to give her priestesses the power to enchant, to turn men into animals, and to smite them with madness.

Realizing how Hecate has been maligned by Western religious authorities, it is important to reclaim her for who she truly is:

❖ The wise crone who is protectress, guardian, and counselor.

❖ Guardian of the Crossroads who offers wisdom, guidance and counsel when important decisions need to be made.

❖ Queen of the Underworld, who offers hope for fertility, renewal, and regeneration.

❖ Light bearer, Guardian of the Souls, who protects and offers guidance as she guides souls to the underworld.

❖ Guardian of the Unconscious, of transitions, who guards the doorways of birth, death and transformation

❖ Mistress of Magic and Divination

In summary, it is important to remember that with the advent of patriarchy the power and prestige of women and the goddess declined, and with that Hecate's status. She was demoted to a shadowy hag-like figure who allied with ghosts and evil spirits. She was further demeaned under the

173

auspices of the Catholic Church who conceptualized the underworld as a hellish place and came to associate Hecate, who was the Queen of the Underworld, as the Queen of Witches.

In reality Hecate, who has links to the ancient Neolithic Mother Goddess, is a revered ancient mother archetype who is also frequently imaged as the archetype of the wise crone. Hecate reminds us that wisdom comes from life's experiences. Our female elders, the crones, are valuable repositories of insight and information that can help us navigate through our own personal challenges. If you are a "crone," then Hecate provides a powerful model of strength and wisdom to emulate. With her ability to see the past, present, and future, she is a symbol of wisdom who can be sought for guidance and assistance when difficult decisions need to be made. Because she sees clearly, Hecate also knows when it is time to remove the debris from our lives so we can make room for new opportunities. Hecate is a goddess who is worthy of honor and respect.

QUESTIONS FOR REFLECTIONS

❖ What season of a women's life do your fall into - Maiden, Mother or Crone. What do you like about this time in your life? What do you dislike?

❖ How does our culture view the crone, the image of the old woman?

❖ If we as a culture honored the expanded version of the crone, how might that change our culture?

❖ Have you experienced the underworld in the form of grief, abandonment, loss, rejection, etc.? Describe what you learned from this experience.

❖ How have you dealt with times of transition, crisis or indecision in the past? How might invoking Hecate as a guide and torch bearer help you light the way?

SOURCES

D. J. Conway, *Maiden, Mother, Crone: the Myth and Reality of the Triple Goddess.*

Elizabeth Fisher, *Rise Up and Call Her Name: A Woman-honoring Journey into Global Earth-based Spiritualities.*

Demetra George, *Mysteries of the Dark Moon: The Healing Power of the Dark Goddess.*

Marija Gimbutas, *The Language of the Goddess.*

Merlin Stone, *Ancient Mirrors of Womanhood: a Treasury of Goddess and Heroine Lore from Around the World.*

Barbara G. Walker, *The Women's Encyclopedia of Myths and Secrets.*

Hekate: http://hekate.timerift.net/roles.htm.

Theoi Greek Mythology, Hecate: http://www.theioi.com/Khthonios/Hecate.html

Hecate: http://en.wikipedia.org/wiki/Hecate.

HECATE GUIDED VISUALIZATION

Music Suggestion: "Transformation"–*Return* by Sophia, Chakra Healing Zone

Pass out pens and slips of paper before the meditation.

Close your eyes and take a nice deep breath and as you slowly exhale begin to release all the tension and stress of the day...Take another deep breath, breathing into your abdomen, and hold...and release slowly, just letting go of all your worries and cares...And now take a third deep breath and as you exhale just surrender to total peace and relaxation...Now that you are cleansed of stress and worry and cares, begin to call back to yourself all the pieces you may have scattered about over the past days and weeks. Just call all those pieces back and let them spiral right back into your heart and feel yourself becoming even more centered and calm....

And now let's count backwards from 10 to 1 and with each number imagine that you are descending a staircase, a staircase that leads through time and space to another place, another era. 10, going deeper now, 9, 8, 7... 6... 5... 4... 3... 2... 1...

Now you find yourself on a moonlit road walking through a forest. There is a full moon shining through the tall pines, throwing moon shadows on the ground. The evening is peaceful, and you feel safe, though you are walking with a heavy burden, a heavy load that you have been carrying for a long time. Maybe it is a decision that weighs heavy on your mind, or a challenge or situation that is tugging at your heart. Or maybe it is a something, a belief, attitude, or behavior that you are struggling to release, but just can't seem to let it go. You know what it is... As you walk you hear the sound: a chanting, of women's voices raised in song. You walk towards the singing until you come to a crossroads where three roads meet. Women are gathered there in a circle chanting and swaying to the music. They have gathered around a bonfire upon which rests a huge cauldron. The cauldron emits the comforting smell of herbs and spices.

The women in the circle hear your approach and turn to greet you. They welcome you into their circle. There is an old woman standing at the cauldron. She gently stirs the bubbling mixture uttering chants as she stirs. She looks up at you and nods a beautiful smile in welcome inviting you to join the circle. This is the cauldron of release and transformation, you are told. The women have gathered to release and transform that which no longer serves them. They are here to release and cleanse and be renewed. A time of change, transition and new potential lies ahead and they are here to regenerate and prepare themselves.

Now the ritual is about to begin. The women, some sitting, some standing, all become quiet and deeply reflective. They are reflecting on what they are wanting to release. One by one the women move up to the cauldron and toss in what they are ready to let go of. For one it is her jealousy that is poisoning her relationships, for another it is the need to control others, for another it is the lack of clarity about an issue she needs to resolve. She is seeking to release doubt and indecision.

Now it is your turn. Get up and approach the cauldron and prepare to release the old so you can make room for the new. What is it that you want to release... (pause)

When every woman is done, Hecate stops stirring the cauldron and utters incantations and makes hand signs, imparting the magic of release and transformation.

Then she begins to move from woman to woman looking deep into each woman's eyes. She asks each woman what it is they need or want from the great wise crone, the dark goddess of transformation, tonight...

Then it is your turn. You look into her face which is a mass of lines and winkles from eons of experience. Her eyes are deep pools of compassion, wisdom, and unconditional love. Her gaze pierces deep into your soul and unlocks that deepest part of you. You begin to feel a swirl of energy as you tell her what you desire—what you need from Hecate tonight... (pause for 30 seconds)

When Hecate finally completes speaking with all the women gathered in the circle, you see that all the requests have become a huge swirl of energy. She walks back to the fire and with more incantations of magic she flings her arms upwards over the fire so the desires and dreams and requests can be carried up to the heavens with the smoke to be manifested. You feel the energies as they swirl upwards to be received by the All That Is.

After a time the energies begin to calm and Hecate turns and smiles at everyone and says that the magic has been set in motion. Now it is time to celebrate the manifestation of intentions and dreams. Someone brings out a flute, another a drum, another a zither, and so on—and the music begins. Then as some women starts to sing to the music...others begin to sway... and then to dance to the familiar chants. Soon all the women are celebrating—dancing under the light of the moon, warmed by the fire and each other's company.

Finally it is time to leave. You take your leave of the new friends you have made and begin walking back through the forest. Though it is late and the forest is quiet, you feel safe and at peace and deeply contented. You feel as if a deep change has taken place and have a sense of quiet expectation for the future.

Now you return to the staircase and begin to climb upward to this time and this place. 1 2 3 4 5 6 7 8 9 10 Feeling the breath in your lungs, the weight of your body in the chair, feel your feet upon the floor, and when you are ready, take a deep breath, stretch and open your eyes.

REFLECTIONS AFTER THE MEDITATION

❖ As you come back, please take a few minutes to write down your experience on the paper provided.

❖ On the smaller slips of paper write down what you were ready to release. This will be used in our ritual tonight.

(An audio recording of this guided visualization may be purchased on my website at www.celebratedivinefeminine.com for a nominal fee.)

HECATE RITUAL

by Shannon Dawn

Music Suggestion: "Hecate" – *The Year is a Dancing Woman*, Vol. 2 by Ruth Barrett

Supplies

Pen and slips of paper (**Pass out before the meditation)

Central altar covered with red or black tablecloth divided into 3 sections.

Cauldron section: Black candle, cauldron or cast iron pot, sterno and cooking tripod, plate or pie dish for under the sterno and tripod, wooden spoon, water, wine or milk, herbs and spices (whatever is on hand and feels right), raisins and/or nuts.

Crossroads section: White taper candle and candle holder (from which the tea lights will be lighted), tea lights, plate to hold the tea lights, one for each participant.

Rebirth section: Vase with a large mouth and neck (as big as a large fist), black cloth, red candle and holder, frogs (optional), small crystal points or crystal beads, one for each participant.

Ritual Preparations - Central Altar

Cauldron section: The water in the cauldron (cast iron pot) should be hot. We usually boil the water first in a tea kettle and then pour it into the cauldron. Set the cauldron on the cooking tripod and light the sterno. Stir in the wine, herbs and spices before the circle starts. Keep the water hot to boiling during the circle. A steaming cauldron is an effective mood enhancer for the ritual. Light the candle. The raisins should be in plain view off to one side so the participants can easily reach them for making their offerings. Keep the wooden spoon handy. Participants like to stir the "brew."

Crossroads section: Light the taper candle and arrange the unlit tea candles on a plate. The participants will light a tea light as part of the ritual.

Rebirth section: Wrap the vase in the black cloth and lay it on its side with the mouth facing the edge of the table. This will be Hecate's "womb." Put the crystal points or beads into the vase for the participants to withdraw as their "dream seed." Light the red candle and arrange the frogs around the womb.

Ritual Introduction:

(read or paraphrase the following)

Tonight's ritual will give you the opportunity to envision and call forth transformation. This can be in the form of something you want to release, or something you want to birth into your life, or a decision you need to make, for even a decision is the death of one possibility and the birth of another.

The central altar is divided into three sections, or smaller altars: The Cauldron, The Crossroads, and the Rebirth altars.

Cauldron Altar: At the Cauldron altar you are first invited to make an offering of gratitude to Hecate by placing some of the raisins into the cauldron while calling upon her to assist you tonight and in the future as she both holds and guides you towards personal growth and transformation.

The cauldron represents the stage of death and endings. You may release into the cauldron that which no longer serves you by placing into the cauldron the slip of paper upon which you have written the symbolic word or phrase that represents that which you are ready to release. Take a moment to envision and feel it being released from your energy body.

Crossroads Altar: Circling to the right you will be at the Crossroads Altar. At this altar you are invited to light a candle to Hecate and call upon Her for guidance on any decisions you need to make, or in formulating what you want to birth into your life.

Rebirth Altar: Circling to the right you will be at the Rebirth Altar. As you envision your rebirth you may withdraw from Hecate's womb a dream seed. Blow into the dream seed impregnating your dream with the breath of life, inspiration and motivation.

There is a sequence to approaching the different altars, but always feel free to take a moment to sit down if you need time to reflect before moving on to the next altar.

Ritual Invocations

(Read or paraphrase as the first person approaches each altar during the ritual)

Altar 1 The Cauldron of Transformation and Rebirth

Goddess Hecate, Wise Woman of the People, Crone of the Mysterious Underworld, Guardian of the Gates, Great One of Magic.

We stand in stillness behind all motion before your ancient cauldron of transformation and rebirth. We give unto you that which limits and weakens us, entangles us, binds us to disorder, blinds us to clarity, disorients us, and that which no longer serves our divine souls.

Receive our burdens into the dark depths of your bubbling cauldron; remove our attachments, purify them from our entanglements, decompose them to their bones, transform them and ready them for rebirth.

Altar 2 The Crossroads:

Goddess Hecate, Hecate Trevia, Lady of the Three Ways, Goddess of the Roads, Protectress of the Journey, the One Who Lights the Way.

We stand before you at the crossroads of the past, present, and future, of the meeting point of heaven, earth, and the underworld. In this place of your domain we light candles in your name. We ask for guidance and clarity of vision for the best possible outcomes for the decisions that lay before us. We ask your help in shaping our dreams into the best possible forms for us at this time.

May your torchlight show us the way.

Altar 3 Rebirth

Goddess Hecate, Heavenly Midwife to the Unborn, Keeper of the Gate Between Life and Death, Ancient Frog Goddess of Regeneration, Bringer of New Life Out of the Cauldron of Rebirth

We stand before the gate of rebirth and transformation where you stir your cauldron of rebirth, spinning out threads of new life. Within the depths of your cauldron lie the fragile whispers of our dream-seeds, of decisions made with the clarity of your guidance, the weavings of a new path.

Smile upon our unborn dream-seeds, impart shape and form to them, give them the breath of life, and send them forth to be born into our lives. May your torch light the way for us. May your torch light the path before us and may you guard us on our new journey.

If we have chosen wrongly, or if you have something better in store for us, send us messages loud and clear that we may re-shape our goals.

Closing Statement of Ritual

(to be read when everyone has completed the ritual)

Goddess Hecate, Guardian of the Unconscious, Bringer of Light from the Darkness, Mistress of Magic, thank you for your presence and blessings tonight and always. Blessed be.

TABLE OF CORRESPONDENCES FOR HECATE

Element: Earth

Symbols: Cauldron, crossroads, torchlight, three-headed statues or animals, trinity

Color: Black, orange, yellow-orange, red-orange

Animals: Frogs, dogs, owls, bats, snakes, boars

Companions: Three headed dog, Cerberus

Moon: Dark of the moon

Geography: Ancient Thrace - present day Greece and Bulgaria

Timeframe: Pre-Hellenic to 3rd or 4th Century CE Greece

Rocks/Crystals: Moonstone, black tourmaline, black onyx, hematite, smoky quartz, silver

Plants: Willow, dark yew, blackthorn, groves of trees, mugwort, myrrh, cinnamon

Foods: Raisin and currant cakes, wine, milk, honey

Music Suggestions

Guided Visualization: "Transformation" – *Return* by Sophia, Chakra Healing Zone

Ritual: "Hecate" – *The Year is a Dancing Woman*, Vol. 2 by Ruth Barrett

(The following is a proposed agenda if you choose to hold a circle to celebrate Hecate)

IN HER NAME CIRCLE, HECATE
CIRCLE PROGRAM

Intro: (10 min) Name, city, word-

Casting the Circle: (3min)–

Opening: (2 min) poem

Talk – Hecate – (25 min)

Q&A (10 min**)**

Guided Visualization: Hecate at the Crossroads - (15 min)

Music Suggestion: "Transformation" – *Return* by Sophia, Chakra Healing Zone

Individual Process – Journaling and/or drawing – writing what they want to release on the slips of paper (5 min)

Group Share 5 to 10 min

Ritual - Release and Rebirth 25min

Music Suggestion: "Hecate" – *The Year is a Dancing Woman*, Vol. 2 by Ruth Barrett

Group Share (10 min)

Goddess Cards (10 min)

Closing: (2 min)

Releasing the Directions – (3min)

Total time: 2 hrs.

Lakshmi

Lakshmi

HINDU GODDESS OF ABUNDANCE AND PROSPERITY

Invocation to Lakshmi,

I am whatever is. Whatever is, I am.
I am whatever is visible. Whatever is visible, I am.
I am whatever is invisible Whatever is invisible, I am.
I am whatever is alive. Whatever is alive, I am.
I am whatever moves and breathes. Whatever moves and breathes, I am.
I am the very spirit of life. The very spirit of life, I am.

Everything that exists in time is part of me. I am everything that exists.
When time ends, I will end. I will vanish, disappear, dissolve.
And with me, everything else will vanish, disappear, dissolve.
I alone can create, and I alone destroy, this universe.
Everything that exists is mine. Everything that exists is me.

India

14. Lakshmi

HINDU GODDESS OF ABUNDANCE AND PROSPERITY

(Go to www.celebratedivinefeminine.com to view the complementary PowerPoint that accompanies this text.)

IN THIS SECTION on Lakshmi, the Hindu Goddess of Prosperity and Abundance, you will learn the meaning of the iconography behind the Goddess, and her connection to the long history of ancient mother goddess worship in India. You will hear the tale of how the Goddess of Good Fortune fled angered by the demons and gods, and how Lakshmi rose from the sea of milk returning prosperity and good fortune to the world. Finally, you will discover how to receive the benevolence of Lakshmi and avoid Alakshmi, the Goddess of Misfortune.

Lakshmi reminds us that though she favors virtuous hardworking people, she also showers her devotees with an abundance of joy, pleasure and all things that make people's hearts glad. She reminds us that we each deserve to be happy, satisfied and fulfilled.

In the ritual on Deservingness you will be guided to release those negative labels and thoughts that often plague each one of us with feelings of unworthiness and un-deservingness. In the guided visualization you will travel the barren road of limitations while you prepare to release your devaluing thoughts. Then Lakshmi will help you embrace your deservingness as she assists you in opening your heart with gratitude, the secret to receiving abundance into your life.

In Hindu religious art, Lakshmi is a beautiful goddess dressed in a flowing red or rose pink sari edged in gold, and adorned with ornate gold jewelry. She is accompanied by her sacred elephants, carries a pot in one hand, is frequently shown scattering gold coins, and is gracefully depicted seated or standing on a lotus.

The lotus when seen in relation to Lakshmi represents purity and spiritual power. The lotus is nourished by the muck and mire found at the bottom of ponds, yet the pastel or white blossoms rise above the water unblemished. For this reason, the lotus represents spiritual perfection and authority, which comes from working on our shadow self. Our shadow self is our egoic nature which keeps us stuck in reactive, frequently unpleasant behaviors triggered by greed, envy, jealousy, resentment, anger, and guilt. Becoming more conscious of our egoic nature leads to awakening. When we can acknowledge our base natures, the muck and mire of our lives, and rise above them, then we become more consciously aware and begin the path towards enlightenment. The lotus, therefore, symbolizes the purity of the enlightened mind, and this is the reason why the lotus seat is a common motif in Hindu iconography.

Lakshmi is celebrated as the goddess of wealth, fortune, abundance, prosperity, beauty, fertility, and good luck. She promises material contentment and fulfillment for those who honor her, are generous to others, and good stewards of their abundance. She is maternal and protective, and desires that everyone live happily in comfort and peace.

As the female counterpart of Lord Vishnu, Lakshmi is also called Shri, the female energy of the supreme beings or gods. Shri is the sacred name of Lakshmi and is also a designation of esteem and good luck. For this reason, the word is frequently written at the top of sacred documents and is spoken to initiate a conversation with a respected individual, such as a holy man or teacher. To the student of Hinduism, the word evokes grace, affluence, abundance, auspiciousness and authority. When the word *shri* is spoken or written it elicits an aura of holiness. It is believed that whatever follows is imbued with divine blessing.

Worship of a mother goddess has been a part of Indian tradition for 5000 years or more. Lakshmi's origins are much older and more primal than the Vedic goddesses and gods, which date back to the first appearance of the Indic texts around 1200 BCE. Lakshmi is a manifestation of an ancient goddess called Shri or Devi or Shakti. She is considered to be one and the same goddess with the primal Mother whose primary color is red, the color of our most sacred bodily fluid. Therefore, Lakshmi is one of the mother goddesses and is addressed as *mata* or mother, instead of just *devi* or goddess.

The Hindu ancient mother goddess, whom Lakshmi embodies, is revered in two personas. As Bhoodevi, she is the Earth Goddess who nurtures life. As Shreedevi, Goddess of Fortune, she bestows power, pleasure, abundance, and prosperity. To be in her good graces, each individual must feel gratitude and reverence for the gift of life, as well as respect the laws of nature.

Enjoy this myth of how the greed and arrogance of the demons and the neglect of the gods caused the Goddess of Fortune to disappear from the earth.

THE ORIGIN OF LAKSHMI

In the beginning, water was everywhere. There was nothing to eat and nowhere to live. The divine patriarch (Prajapati), the father of the gods and demons, saw the plight of his children and invoked the goddess Devi.

The goddess whispered into his ear, "The earth lies trapped under the water. Raise it up."

The Divine Patriarch (Prajapati) took the form of a mighty boar (Emusha) and plunged into the sea. He found the Earth Goddess, Bhoodevi, on the ocean floor. Placing her on his snout, he gently raised her to the surface. As there was no land on which the goddess could rest, the Divine Patriarch (Prajapati) turned into Akupara, a giant turtle, and offered the Earth Goddess (Bhoodevi) the use of his back.

Resting comfortably on the back of the Celestial Turtle the Earth Goddess was able to nurture life. With her bountiful nature she generously provided everyone with food and shelter.

She captivated the gods *(devas)* with her beauty, but the demons *(asuras)* coveted her wealth. They fought many battles over her, until finally, under the leadership of Bali, the demons *(asuras)* were triumphant.

In those early days the goddess was impressed by strength, so she chose Bali, the victor, and came to him as Shreedevi, the Goddess of Fortune. Crowning him the King of the Earth she gave him symbols of royalty: a throne, a footstool, and she even gave him a parasol which she held over his head to shade him from the sun. At her command her sacred white elephants turned into beautiful clouds that showered rain upon the earth. The pastures became green so the cows were well fed and gave plenty of milk. The crops flourished and animals and humans were fertile and multiplied. People were happy and prospered. Bali, the demon-king, swelled with pride. He loved the power and fame that came with being king. He became arrogant and declared, "The earth and everything it grows is mine. I am responsible for the prosperity and abundance everyone is enjoying. I am the one who can distribute the riches of the earth."

The Earth Goddess was very upset when she heard these words. She was not someone's property! She was not a gift that could be given away!

Not everyone benefited under the auspices of the demon-king Bali, however. Indra, the leader of the gods (devas), had been reduced to poverty when the Goddess of Fortune's benevolence was directed to Bali. One day Indra approached Bali and begged for some land so that he could grow crops and raise some animals. Puffed up with importance, Bali looked around for the dwarf Vamana, who frequented his court. Spying the dwarf Bali haughtily pointed at him and said, "I will give you as much land as this dwarf can cover in three steps."

Now this dwarf was not really a dwarf, but was the God Vishnu, the Preserver of the Universe, in disguise. As soon as the demon Bali said this, the god Vishnu smiled. This was his chance! He began to grow until he turned into a great giant. In two steps Vishnu strode across and claimed Bali's entire kingdom. It is rumored that with Vishnu's third step he shoved the demon Bali into the lower realms. This was how Vishnu wrested control of the earth from the demons and gave it to gods.

Shreedevi, the Goddess of Fortune, observed what had transpired between the demons and the gods. She thought "The gods may not be as strong as the demons, but they are shrewd and clever. I think I will favor them instead." So she turned her back on the demons and bestowed her graces upon the gods. She gave them the charisma and power to rule, prosperity and abundance, good health, and physical beauty.

The demons, however, were very unhappy with the decline in their circumstances and complained loudly and angrily. Claiming the Goddess of Fortune was unpredictable and capricious they cried, "First she likes Bali, now she likes Indra. She is unfaithful and has no sense of loyalty."

The goddess was not deterred, however, claiming that she will be forever faithful and dedicated to those who appreciated her gifts and used them wisely and generously.

Vishnu let Indra become king even though he was the one who had wrested control of the earth from the demons. This puzzled the Goddess of Fortune. She asked Vishnu why he didn't want to be king and enjoy the pleasures and glory of the universe.

Vishnu replied with unassuming humility. "I just did what was right. Bali was not a good king and needed to be defeated. Doing what is right is reward enough. I don't want anything else."

The Goddess of Fortune was pleased with Vishnu's response and filed it away in her mind.

The goddess then turned to Indra and said, "I will bestow the benevolence of the Goddess of Fortune on the one who will be a good steward of the Earth Goddess (Bhoodevi). He I will make King of the Cosmos."

Indra eagerly accepted. However, he must not have been paying attention. Soon after being crowned king he became intoxicated with all the pleasures available to the King of the Cosmos. He spent all of his time in the pleasure gardens, where he drank wine and enjoyed song and dance and women. He neglected his duties of ruling the universe and ignored his stewardship responsibilities. The earth was left unmanaged, ungoverned and unprotected. The Earth Goddess (Bhoodevi) begged and cried for help, but her pleas were ignored. The Goddess of Fortune (Shreedevi) was incensed by the neglect and became very angry with Indra.

The goddess was now displeased and disheartened with both the demon-king and the god-king. The demon-king became arrogant and corrupted with wealth and power. The god-king was too easily seduced by pleasure and comforts. Neither were responsible stewards of the benevolence and grace she bestowed on them. The goddess turned her back on both the demons and gods and dissolved herself in the ocean of milk.

With her departure a dense depressive grayness descended upon the universe. An eerie silence replaced the sounds of song and dance and the hustle and bustle of prosperity. The fields became barren, cows stopped giving milk, and trees dropped their fruit before it ripened. Warriors lost their will to fight or protect the people, men became impotent, animals stopped multiplying, and women lost their beauty and youthful figures. Joy and laughter became scarce in this bleak and harsh universe.

The desolation and barrenness of the three worlds and the disappearance of the goddess created panic. The gods and demons argued for many years about what to do. They had to bring the goddess back. But how? They came up with and discarded many ideas, feeling more and more discouraged. Then Vishnu came up with the idea of raising the goddess to the surface by churning the ocean of milk.

Vishnu went to Mandara, the King of Mountains, and asked if he would serve as the spindle. Then he approached the King of Turtles (Akupara) asking if he would serve as the base. Then the gods (*devas*) and the demons (*asuras*) joined forces to power a great cosmic churn. The King of Serpents, Vasuki, volunteered to be the churning rope, and soon the gods and demons began churning the ocean of milk.

Eons passed while the churn twisted and turned. Great waves rose and crested, spewing froth and foam all around the churn. It seemed an eternity and still nothing happened. The gods and demons refused to stop, however. Their only hope was to bring the goddess back. Year after year they continued to churn the great ocean.

Finally the goddess decided they had done enough penance and proved their dedication. She emerged as Lakshmi, the goddess of Abundance and Prosperity. She rose from the ocean of milk seated on large Lotus flower. She was draped in red silk and wore ornate gold jewelry. She embodied affluence and abundance. From her body emanated a life-giving essence as delicate as the most aromatic of perfumes. As the earth was bathed in this essence it began to pulse once again with life. The sounds of joy, laughter and happy voices were once again carried on the wind.

The gods welcomed her back with salutations and praises. The demons raised their voices in songs of devotion to her glory. The sacred elephants once again lifted their trunks and sprinkled the earth with life-giving waters.

This time, however, the goddess decided there must be balance. So along with Lakshmi she also sent Alakshmi, the Goddess of Barrenness and Misfortune. She is the forlorn and ugly hag with matted hair, sunken cheeks, shriveled breasts and coarse limbs.

The goddess announced, "Lakshmi will shower her benevolence wherever there is integrity and right action, cleanliness and beauty, compassion and generosity. Alakshmi will scatter scarcity and despair wherever there is filth and laziness, jealousy and greed, envy and conceit."

Those who wish to avoid the misfortunes of Alakshmi must keep their hearts and homes clean, their minds pure, and take pride in the care of their bodies and appearances.

Lakshmi brought with her many gifts of prosperity. She brought a sacred cow (Kamadhenu) who gave an abundant and endless supply of milk, a magical gem (Chantamani) that granted wishes and a miraculous tree known as Kalpataru that bore a multitude of flowers and fruits so that all were satisfied. Lakshmi carried the bottomless basket (Akshaya Patra) which overflowed with grain and gold so that everyone had enough.

Lakshmi also brought from the ocean of milk gifts of pleasure including the delightful God of Pleasure (Kama). This handsome god entered riding in on his parrot surrounded by bees and butterflies. With his bow he shot arrows dripping with desire into the heart of every being, inspiring acts of love as he roused the senses and excited the mind. The Goddesses of Love and Longing (Priti and Rati) accompanied the God of Pleasure as everyone was revitalized with the spark of love. With them came the Lord of Spring (Vasanta). The gods and goddesses were welcomed by the flowers and bees who offered their nectar and pollen.

Walking behind Lakshmi came Rambha, the beautiful nymph who knows 64 different ways to pleasure the senses. To soothe away stress and worry and to sweeten dreams Lakshmi brought Sura, the Goddess of Intoxicants, as well.

In addition the goddess brought forth the symbols of kingship: a throne, a crown, a footstool, a parasol, a fly-swatter, a cushion, a fan, a bow and a conch. She announced, "These will go to whoever has the strength of character to use their powers wisely to preserve and manage the universe and protect life."

Indra and Bali both spoke up clamoring for the goddess to give them the kingship.

Lakshmi adamantly refused them both, "No!" she said, "Wealth corrupts the demon king and makes him arrogant, and the god-king is too obsessed with pleasure. Neither shall enjoy my benevolence and grace."

The goddess wanted someone who wouldn't be seduced by the appeal of power, pleasure and prosperity. She sought someone who was strong, wise and honorable, who would be capable of using their power, authority and charisma with discretion to maintain order and to uphold the laws of life. She turned to Vishnu, the Preserver of the Universe, and placed a fragrant garland of victory (Vaijayanati) around his neck; she made him her consort. He became known as the Beloved of Fortune. Vishnu pledged to honor Lakshmi by placing Shreevasta, the symbol of Lakshmi, on his chest. They made their home in Heaven (Vaikuntha), which is the center of the universe.

Vishnu diligently performed his duties by battling the forces of chaos and corruption. Lakshmi was pleased with Vishnu and gave him her love and devotion. Together they work to uphold the laws of the universe and to bring love, joy and prosperity to all who are willing to be good stewards and generous with their abundance.

The moral of this myth of the Origin of Lakshmi is that if you receive abundance, you must use it wisely and generously. You must be a wise steward with the abundance that is bestowed upon you in life.

(This myth was adapted from *Introduction to Lakshmi, The Goddess of Wealth and Fortune* by Devdutt Pattanaik, which can be found at http://www.lotussculpture.com/lakshmi1.htm)

Lakshmi is seen as the embodiment of Love. This is the pure love that comes from a heart that overflows with good will and gratitude. It is from this love that devotion to the divine (Bhakti) flows. It is believed that it is through this Love or through Lakshmi, that the soul (atma) is able to reach God or Vishnu, the personification of higher consciousness or spiritual awakening. In Hinduism, male divine qualities are inert and lifeless until they are infused with divine feminine energy. Lakshmi is the personification of Kundalini: the divine feminine spiritual energy that is present in the Universe and is within each one of us. When people have a Kundalini awakening, they often feel a powerful jolt of energy that rapidly rises from the base of the spine upwards and out the crown. It can be a powerful energetic experience of bliss, one that brings a person closer to spiritual awareness and enlightenment.

Lakshmi also embodies the spiritual world, or Heaven (referred to as Vaikuntha in Hindu), which is the home of Lakshmi and Vishnu. Lakshmi is said to embody the divine qualities of God and the soul. She is the embodiment of God's superior spiritual feminine energy (Param Prakriti) which has the potential to purify, empower, and uplift the individual. For these reasons Lakshmi is called the Goddess of Fortune.

Lakshmi's special festival is Diwali, the Festival of Lights. It is a joyous celebration, much like the way Christmas is a joyous holiday for Christians. It occurs in autumn when the moon is full, the brightest night of the year.

The people put small oil lamps outside their homes in hope that Lakshmi will come to bless them. It is believed that Lakshmi showers wealth on this night. She is said to ride in on her great white owl and descends to earth to take away the darkness of poverty, stagnation, anger and laziness from our lives.

The goddess Lakshmi is worshiped by those who wish to acquire and preserve wealth. However it is believed that Lakshmi, or wealth and prosperity, is benevolent only to those places which are kept clean and whose inhabitants are virtuous and hardworking. She is said to overlook those places that are unclean or dirty and withholds her blessings from those who are lazy.

The prosperity of Lakshmi carries with it responsibility. It must be used wisely. She requires that you be a good steward of your wealth and that you are generous. Lakshmi rewards those who are generous with the abundance she bestows.

In summary, Lakshmi can easily be identified because she is frequently depicted standing or sitting on a lotus flower flanked by elephants. She arose from the sea of milk churned by the gods and demons, who were doing penance for their greed and arrogance. Lakshmi brought prosperity and good fortune back to the world. In addition to material comforts she also brought those things that would bring pleasure, ease and joyfulness. Though Lakshmi favors those who are responsible and diligent, she also teaches us that life is to be joyfully abundant!

Lakshmi chose Vishnu, the Preserver of the Universe, to be the King of the Earth because he had proven his humility, resourcefulness and good stewardship. Together Lakshmi and Vishnu rule the world upholding the laws of the universe and bringing love, joy and prosperity to all who honorable, industrious, good stewards of their wealth, and who share their abundance with others.

DISCUSSION QUESTIONS

(The discussion questions in this section are incorporated into the ritual. Please see Lakshmi Deservingness Discussion and Ritual if you intend to do the ritual either individually or as a group.)

❖ Lakshmi is generous. But abundance carries responsibility. What I've noticed in my work with people, especially women, is that most of us block abundance, not because we aren't willing to be good stewards, but because we feel we don't deserve it. Somewhere along the way many of us have picked up messages that we are unworthy. Does this strike a chord with you? Take a moment to reflect and write down your feelings of being undeserving or unworthy.

❖ Take a moment to reflect on your positive qualities. Write them down.

❖ Each one of us brings value to the lives of others. Take a moment to reflect on the ways that you bring value to others and the world. Write them down.

❖ What is it that you deserve and desire in your life?

You have many positive qualities. You bring value to others and the world. You deserve to be abundant. Embrace your deservingness!

SOURCES

Devdutt Pattanaik, *Introduction to Lakshmi - The Goddess of Wealth and Fortune*, http://www.lotussculpture.com/lakshmi1.htm.

Goddess Lakshmi, Kashmir, Hindu Deities, http://www.koausa.org/Gods/God6.html.

Lakshmi, Wikipedia, http://en.wikipedia.org/wiki/Lakshmi.

Lakshmi Magick, by Hermeticusnath, http://www.horusmaat.com/silverstar/silverstar8-pg19.htm.

LAKSHMI GUIDED VISUALIZATION

Take a deep breath and begin to call back to yourself all the pieces of yourself that have been scattered out and about over the past month. Call yourself back and allow all the parts of you to spiral right back down into your heart space so that you are totally present, right here, right now.

Take a deep breath breathing all the way into you abdomen and hold, and then exhale slowly, letting go of all the tension and stress of the day. Take another deep breath all the way into your abdomen and hold and as you release, let go of any negativity that might be disturbing your serenity. Take a third deep breath and now as you slowly exhale, surrender to inner peace and calm as you drift and float, drift and float... until you become aware that you are climbing a coastal trail. It is a warm sunny day and you are feeling the heat of the sun upon your face. You know that in the distance lies the vast expanse of the ocean. This is your destination. Sometimes your journey has taken you through beautiful valleys, lush meadows and by beautiful streams and lakes. Other times your path has been blocked with obstacles, or you have traveled barren lands of sun-baked heat or frozen wilderness. You feel the strain of your journey, and the weight of your burden. You have carried your load for a long time.

People that you have encountered have added to your load. Some have given you bread or fruits for nourishment; others have slipped in rocks or thorny branches that have weighed you down or caused pain when you reached out for comfort or sustenance. For some your past experiences have impeded your growth by hampering you with negative message about not being good enough, about not deserving good things in your life, or about having to work really hard to earn prosperity and abundance. Possibly there are other messages of how you might be unworthy or undeserving. You know those message...You feel the weight of your backpack; the names and labels and messages that you have carried for a long time.

The last trek to the ocean lies before you. It is late afternoon. You see that the full moon is rising and has just appeared above the last hill before you. The path up the hill is leading you to the edge of a cliff - the lookout that you have heard about from which you can finally gaze out over the wide expanse of the ocean. As you make this last climb the weight of your pack becomes even more noticeable. You are tired of carrying this weight. You are annoyed with all the labels and names and messages that you have been forced to endure.

At the top you swing off the backpack with a thud, and as you take a deep breath you look out over the ocean. The site is breathtaking. The sky is so blue as it dips to meet the deep aquamarine sea. You hear the waves crash below and you see the white foam spray the dark grey and brown rocks. You feel the power of the waves, the strength of the rocky cliffs beneath your feet, the warmth of the sun and you feel at one with the cosmos.

You now realize that you are done, done with carrying the burdens in your backpack. You decide that from now on you will choose what you will carry. From now on you will carry only that which serves you. What is burdensome and demeaning you now decide to toss over the ledge into the sea below. You reach down and begin to rummage through your pack pulling out those names and labels and negative messages. One by one you toss them over the side of the cliff into the ocean.... Call them out in your mind as you toss them one by one. Hear them crash and disintegrate as they fall onto the rocks below or splash into the ocean... Feel yourself growing lighter. Notice you can breathe more easily. Feel the relief! You are finally free of those burdens. Close your eyes and breathe in the fresh cleansing breathe of the sea.

Now you are ready to receive... Now you can fully embrace what you desire and deserve.

As you open your eyes a beautiful vision materializes before you. It is the lovely Hindu goddess, Lakshmi, standing on a Lotus flower floating on the sea. She is draped in a red sari, bedecked with pearls and gems, lustrous as fire, radiant as gold; resplendent as the sun, calm as the moon... she is flanked by white elephants, with lotus blossoms floating all around. The bright watercolors of the sunset begin to paint the sky behind her in brilliant oranges, yellows, magenta and lavender. Lakshmi smiles benevolently at you. She sees your positive qualities... She knows the value that you bring to the lives of others... She believes in your deservingness. Lakshmi is here to bestow upon you what you desire and deserve. From her hands and heart and crown rivulets of gold begin to flow... Lakshmi becomes a fountain of abundance and wealth. ...... The rivulet of gold flow towards you bringing you what you desire and deserve. Open up and receive...See, sense or feel yourself receiving or experiencing what it is you desire and deserve. I am going to give you a few minutes to envision yourself receiving. Know that you deserve to receive.

Pause

As you receive from Lakshmi allow you heart to be filled with gratitude.... Remember the abundance that has graced your life in the past; express your gratitude to Lakshmi for what you have received and for what you are about to receive.... Resolve to continue feeling gratitude and deservingness, for you are worthy.... Promise Lakshmi that you will be generous with the abundance she bestows upon you.... Promise to share Her generosity with others....

The sun has set and the sky is now becoming dark. And the vision of Lakshmi begins to fade into the ocean. As she leaves she puts her hands in the prayer position before her face, bowing and saying, "*Namaste.*" Return her parting gesture and reply, "*Namaste.*"

Know that whenever you wish you may return to the ocean to envision Lakshmi in her radiance, to receive her blessings, to feel her benevolence and to thank her for her abundance with deep gratitude.

Now it is time to return to this time and this place. Feel the weight of your body in your chair, your feet upon the floor, take a deep breath and feel your lungs fill up with air and then slowly exhale. And when you are ready you may open your eyes.

(A recording of this guided visualization may be purchased on my website at www.celebratedivinefeminine.com for a nominal fee.)

LAKSHMI DESERVINGNESS DISCUSSION AND RITUAL

Supplies:

Slips of paper for negative messages (1/8 sheet), pieces of paper for Deservingness Ritual (1/4 to 1/2 sheet), pens

Altar supplies needed for the ritual:

Picture or statue of Lakshmi, picture or statue of Ganesh, uncooked rice, grapes or raisins, incense (sandalwood), matches or lighter, anointing oil (sandalwood if possible), large bowl, packaged garden soil

Pre-Ritual Discussion

1. Pass out slips of paper for writing down negative messages about deserving. Also pass out separate pieces of paper for the Deservingness Ritual.

2. Introduction (read or paraphrase):

   The message from the myth is that Lakshmi is abundant, but her generosity carries responsibility, a willingness to be a good steward. For many people -- especially with women -- their flow of abundance is blocked not because they aren't willing to be good stewards, but because they feel undeserving. Somewhere along the way, many of us have picked up negative messages or beliefs that somehow we just don't deserve to have an abundant life, or that in some way we are unworthy.

3. Discussion about negative messages (say or paraphrase the following):

   ❖ Do any of you carry negative messages that somehow you are undeserving?

   ❖ Take a minute to reflect and jot them down of the smaller slips of paper. They will be part of our ritual.

   Invite the participants to share any of their negative messages about not deserving, or being unworthy, or not good enough?

4. Discussion about deservingness (say or paraphrase the following):

   ❖ I know each of you has many positive qualities. Take a moment to write down your positive qualities.
   Invite the participants to share

   ❖ I know each of you deserves, because you bring value to the lives of others. Take a moment to write down at least one way in with you bring value.

198

Invite the participants to share

❖ Because you have many positive qualities and because you bring value, you deserve to have what you desire. Write down what you deserve and desire.

Invite the participants to share.

Ritual

1. Review instructions *(see below for the instructions for a group ritual)

2. Put on the music: "Shree Ram Jai Ram" from *Embrace* by Deva Premal

3. Walk to the altar and light incense stick (sandalwood)

4. Make an offering of rice to Ganesh: *Om Gam Ganipataye Namah* (Please, Ganesh, remove all obstacles from my life).

5. Make an offering of grapes or raisins to Lakshmi

6. Shred and bury the negative messages of not deserving while thinking or saying:

   "Please remove these negative thoughts and beliefs from my consciousness."

7. Pass your affirmations of deservingness through the incense while stating silently or out loud your positive qualities, your value and what specific things you deserve and desire.

8. Prepare to anoint the circle participants (sandalwood oil). If performing an individual ritual then anoint yourself and feel the blessings of Lakshmi while expressing gratitude and promising to be generous and a good steward.

*Participants

1. Bring both papers with you

2. Offer rice to Ganesh, asking that he remove any obstacles to you receiving what you deserve.

3. Make an offering of grapes to Lakshmi

4. Shred and bury your negative messages, thoughts and beliefs in the dirt while thinking or saying:

   "Please remove these negative messages, thoughts and beliefs from my consciousness."

5. Pass your deservingness affirmations through the incense smoke

6. State silently or out loud your positive qualities, the value you bring to others, and the abundance that you desire and deserve.

7. Approach the Priestess for anointing and blessing.

8. Return to your seat and meditate on your positive qualities, your value and what you have requested. See yourself receiving what you deserve and desire and give thanks to Lakshmi and the universe for its generosity.

Table of Correspondences for Lakshmi

Goddesses Names: Lakshmi, also known as Lakshmi Ma, Maha Lakshmi, Devi, Shri, Gauri, Ma, Shakti

Element: Earth

Symbols: Lotus flower, elephant, gold coins, red kumkum paste or powder, Sea of Milk, Shri Yantra* (see below)

Color: Red, white, gold and green

Animals: Elephant, owl

Nature: Crops and all growing things

Companions: Ganesh

Mates: Lord Vishnu, the Preserver of the Universe

Season: Autumn, harvest time

Moon: Full

Festivals: Diwali, the Festival of Lights held in autumn on the full moon

Geography: India

Timeframe: Lakshmi's origins date back to Pre-Dravidian mythology (3000 BCE) and have links to the ancient primal goddess called Shri or Devi.

Plants: Sandalwood, flowers

Foods: Fruit, sweets, milk, ghee, yoghurt and honey

*Shri Yantra

Music

Ritual: "Shree Ram Jai Ram" from *Embrace* by Deva Premal
Visualization: "Return" by Sophia

(The following is a proposed agenda if you choose to hold a circle to celebrate Lakshmi)

In Her Name Circle, Lakshmi Circle Program

Welcome to the In Her Name Circle Celebrating Lakshmi: Self Intros: (5 - 10 min) Name, city, each participant says a word as to how they are feeling

Casting the Circle: (3min)

Opening poem: (2 min)

Intro and Myth of Lakshmi: (20 min)

Deservingness Discussion: (15 min)

Lakshmi Ritual: (20 min)

Lakshmi Visualization: (10 min)

Reflections and Circle Share: (15 min)

Divination: (10 min) - Pulling a goddess card to see what goddess energy each one will walk in for the up-coming month

Closing: (3 min) Charge of the Goddess

Releasing the Directions: (2 min)

Tea and Cookies and Socializing

Total Time: 110 Minutes

Our Lady of Guadalupe

Our Lady of Guadalupe
Mother of the People

MARY, VIRGIN OF GUADALUPE

Dark lady, you smile at me across the mountains
The secret smile of ancient people.
What thoughts do you send me, dark beautiful lady?
Will you someday tell me when I come with great armfuls of roses
Over the mysterious mountains to your feet?
Dear, dark queen will you give me too
Lovely roses in December?

By Anne B. Quinn

15. Our Lady of Guadalupe Mother of the People

(Visit www.celebratedivinefeminine.com to view the PowerPoint that accompanies this text.)

THIS SECTION ON Our Lady of Guadalupe is divided into two parts. Part one tells the story of the apparitions of Our Lady to a poor Indian named Juan Diego. It will take several miracles, including the appearance of the famous image of Our Lady of Guadalupe on Juan Diego's shawl, before the bishop of Mexico will believe him and agree to Our Lady's request. Part Two provides historical background and explains the implication of the apparition of Our Lady of Guadalupe.

The value of Our Lady of Guadalupe is her capacity for unconditional love. She appeared to Juan Diego to bring compassion and comfort to a conquered people, and to bring healing between two cultures where there had been conflict, and the domination of one culture over another. She came without judgment, just with a heart full of love and a desire that the people should once again feel the embrace of the merciful Mother. We learn from Our Lady of Guadalupe the healing power of love and compassion.

The discussion, ritual, and guided visualization are interwoven to help you, with the assistance of Our Lady of Guadalupe, in opening your heart to greater compassion and love, even for those people or things that are hard for you to love.

PART ONE: THE STORY OF JUAN DIEGO

Ten years after the seizure of Mexico by the Spaniards, a semblance of peace had finally come to the land. In early December of 1531 there lived a poor Indian named Juan Diego who was a devout convert to Christianity. On Saturdays he would make the long trek into the city of Tlatelolco to receive religious instruction. It was early dawn on this particular Saturday when he reached the hill known as Tepeyac. This was the site of an ancient shrine to a pre-Hispanic earth mother goddess known as Tonantzin. He heard singing, like beautiful birds, coming from the top of the hill. Then he heard a voice calling him, "Juanito, Juan Dieguito." He climbed the hill to see who calling him. He found a Lady who beckoned to him. Her garments were radiant like the sun; the cliff where she rested her feet was pierced with glitter, resembling an anklet of precious stones; and the earth was bright with the colors of the rainbow. The mesquites, *nopales*, and other weeds sparkled like emeralds; their foliage was like turquoise and their branches and thorns glistened like gold. He bowed before The Lady, and she spoke to him in a very tender and courteous manner.

The Lady informed Juan Diego that she was the Virgin Holy Mary, Mother of the True God. She desired a temple to be erected on the hill so the people could receive love, compassion, help, and protection from her, their merciful mother. She promised to listen to their lamentations and alleviate their miseries, afflictions, and sorrows. Then she instructed him to go to the bishop of Mexico and tell him what she desired. For this service Juan Diego would be rewarded.

Juan Diego protested, saying he was unworthy to carry such a message, but the Lady was insistent. So he proceeded to the city and upon arriving at the bishop's palace he petitioned for an audience. After much difficulty he was ushered in to see the bishop who suspiciously listened to Juan's story. The bishop said he would review Juan's claims and dismissed him, telling him to return at a later date.

On Juan's return home he went directly to the top of the hill where he met with the Lady. Crestfallen, he reported that he was unsuccessful and reiterated that he was not worthy to carry such a divine message. He begged her to find someone more worthy.

The Blessed Virgin reassured Juan Diego: she agreed that she had many servants and messengers, but it was Juan Diego that she had chosen to be her messenger. She commanded him to return and meet with the bishop the next day and repeat her request.

The next day Juan Diego returned to the city of Tlatelolco, for he made the journey every Saturday and Sunday to the city for religious instruction. After attending mass he went to the bishop's palace. After considerable difficulty he received an audience. Once again the bishop questioned Juan Diego, who repeated the same message from the Lady. The bishop sent him away again, saying he must return with a sign that the Lady was the Holy Mother of the Savior, the Lord Jesus Christ. When Juan Diego left, the bishop ordered several servants to follow Juan and report back on his actions.

The spies attempted to follow Juan Diego, but near the bridge to Tepeyac they lost sight of him. Though they searched everywhere, they could not find him. They returned, angrily claiming that Juan Diego was lying and deceiving the bishop.

In the meantime Juan Diego was with the Blessed Virgin, relating the bishop's answer. The Virgin, far from being displeased, was satisfied and said that Juan should return the next morning. She would give him a sign to take to the bishop.

When Juan Diego arrived home he found that his uncle, Juan Bernardino was seriously ill. By Monday a doctor was summoned, but it was too late. By Monday evening Juan's uncle requested that a priest be summoned to hear his confession. Early on Tuesday Juan Diego set out for Tlatelolco to summon a priest. As he approached the intersection leading to Tepeyac's hilltop, he decided to take the longer way around the hill. He was concerned that if he went up the hill the Lady was sure to detain him. He needed to hurry to summon a priest for his uncle.

Well, we can't avoid the Great Mother that easily when we've been chosen for a mission! The Lady descended the hill and approached Juan. She asked "What is happening? Where are you going?" Embarrassed and contrite, Juan Diego explained that he was sorry to displease her but his uncle was gravely ill. He was hurrying to the city to summon a priest to hear his uncle's confession so the man could die in peace. Juan Diego promised that as soon as he talked to the priest he would return and take her sign to the bishop.

The Lady told him not to worry saying, "Am I not Her, who is your Mother? Are you not under my protection? Do not grieve or be disturbed, your uncle will not die. Be at peace for he is now cured."

Upon hearing her words Juan Diego was relieved. He begged to take the sign to the bishop. The Lady told Juan to climb to the top of the hill where he would find flowers. He was to gather them and bring them to her. When Juan reached the summit, he was amazed at the exquisite roses he found blooming there. This was a miracle because the ground was cold with the winter chill. The hilltop had many crags, thistles, thorns, *nopales*, and mesquites; it was an inhospitable place for any flowers. Even the weeds were killed by the freezing December weather.

Juan Diego cut and gathered the flowers and took them down the hill to the Lady. When she saw them, the Lady took them and placed them in his tilma or shawl. She told Juan Diego to take the roses to the bishop as the sign he had requested, and instructed Juan Diego not to show the roses to anyone but the bishop. Once again Juan Diego returned to the bishop's palace, and again he had difficulty getting in to see the bishop. The servants were angry that Juan had evaded them and made him wait a long time. Eventually the servants demanded to see what he carried in his tilma. Finally he uncovered his tilma to display the roses. The servants were amazed and tried three times to seize the flowers, but each time they reached for the roses they were unable to see real flowers. Instead, the roses appeared to be painted, stamped, or sewn on the cloth. Finally they went to get the bishop.

Upon admission, Juan Diego repeated his Lady's request and presented the flowers as proof. Untying his white tilma, the roses scattered to the floor along with Juan Diego's tilma. On the tilma there appeared an image of the Holy Virgin Mary, Mother of God, in the manner as she is kept in the Basilica at Tepeyac today, which is called the Basilica of Our Lady of Guadalupe. Upon seeing the image the bishop fell to his knees and was ashamed that he had not believed Juan Diego. He took the tilma with the image of Our Lady and placed it in the chapel.

The following day, which was Wednesday, Juan Diego led the bishop to the spot where the Lady wanted her temple built. Then he asked to return home to see his uncle, and the bishop sent servants to accompany him. They found Juan Bernardino very much alive and happy, as if nothing ailed him. The uncle claimed he had also seen a vision of Our Lady. She told Juan Bernardino that she had sent Juan Diego to the city to see the bishop. Juan Bernardino was instructed to reveal his vision of Our Lady and of his miraculous healing to the bishop.

Both Juan Bernardino and Juan Diego became guests of the bishop until the temple dedicated to the Queen of Tepeyac was erected. The tilma with the sacred image of the Lady was transferred to the temple where all the people could admire her image.

   Story adapted from "The Apparitions and the Miracle," found at http://www.sancta.org/nical.html.

Juan Diego's tilma portraying the image of Our Lady of Guadalupe still maintains its structural integrity after nearly 500 years. I am sure you must question, as I do, how it could be possible for the tilma to exist in good shape after all this time. Continuing miracles and the miraculous manifestation of the image have continued to surprise and confound researchers and investigators. Replicas made with the same type of materials have only lasted 15 years before disintegrating. The tilma recovered from an ammonia spill in 1791 which resulted in a large hole: it self-repaired in two weeks with no external help! In 1921 an anarchist secreted a bomb, which exploded and destroyed the shrine. However, the image of Our Lady of Guadalupe escaped damage. Efforts have been made to analyze the tint on the fabric, including one attempt from Richard Kuhn, who received the 1938 Nobel Prize for Chemistry. He claimed the tint was not from any known mineral, vegetable, or animal source! In 1979 Philip Serna Callahan studied the icon with infrared light and stated that portions of the face, hands, robe, and mantle appeared to have been painted in one step, without sketches or corrections and with no apparent brush strokes (Wikipedia). In addition, there are reports that images are reflected in the eyes of the Virgin. Both in 1929 and 1951 photographers found a figure or figures reflected in the Virgin's eyes, very similar to how images are reflected in the human eye.

The image of Our Lady of Guadalupe is often read as a coded image. Christian writer Miguel Sanchez describes the Virgin's image as the Woman of the Apocalypse from the New Testament's Revelation 12:1: "arrayed with the sun and the moon under her feet, and upon her head a crown of twelve stars." Mateo de la Cruz argues that the image of Guadalupe possessed the iconographical attributes of Mary in her Immaculate Conception. Patricia Harrington and Virgilio Elizondo describe the image as containing coded messages for the indigenous people of Mexico. The Aztecs had an extensive and coherent symbolic system for making sense of their lives. Guadalupe's blue-green mantle was described as the color once reserved for the divine couple Ometecuhtle and Omecihuatl; her belt was seen as a sign of pregnancy, fertility, or potentiality.
(http://en.wikipedia.org/wiki/Our_Lady_of_Guadalupe)

Elizabeth Barton, an astrologer whom we are fortunate to have in our Circle, shared with us her astrological interpretation of the symbolism in the image of Our Lady of Guadalupe. Elizabeth believes that the reason the moon is dark, or eclipsed, is because Our Lady represents the Earth, and Her shadow is falling on the Moon. Thus Our Lady is blocking the rays of the sun, which explains the rays of light emanating from behind her, creating the shadow that falls on the moon. The sun is an astrological symbol that often represents the Male, Elizabeth claims. In this image, therefore, Our Lady is blocking the negative aspects of patriarchy. She holds dominion over the subconscious; i.e., the Moon, which is also an astrological symbol that is frequently used to represent the People. Elizabeth's astrological interpretation of the symbolism is that Our Lady is blocking the advancement of the negative aspects of patriarchy. She came to give the people hope, and still does today.

The new Basilica of Guadalupe, the holiest and most frequented shrine in Mexico, was opened in 1987. Behind it is a museum and older churches that formerly displayed the holy relic. Moving walkways carry the masses past the shrine so they may view the image of Our Lady of Guadalupe which is still on display today.

Before reading the next section take a few minutes to reflect on the questions below. Then do the meditation on Easy to Love. (The meditation can be purchased on my website www.celebratedivinefeminine.com for a nominal fee.)

If you are leading a circle, then first lead the discussion and ritual for Easy to Love. Then lead your circle in the meditation on Easy to Love. When you have done this, move on to the Part Two.

QUESTIONS FOR REFLECTION: EASY TO LOVE

❖ What are some of the things in the world that you find easy to love?

❖ What fills you heart with warmth and good feelings so that you feel open and loving?

PART TWO: HISTORICAL BACKGROUND AT THE TIME OF THE APPARITION OF OUR LADY OF GUADALUPE

Our Lady of Guadalupe appeared to Juan Diego at a time of great strife for the native people of Mexico. In 1521, ten years before the appearance of our Lady of Guadalupe, the capital city of the Aztecs had fallen to the Spanish. During that time the Aztec way of life drastically changed.

The ancient inhabitants of Mexico, which include the Olmec, Toltec, Maya, and Aztec, left behind impressive sacred sites suggesting a rich heritage and a more advanced civilization than originally thought. They were a sophisticated people who had a strong grasp of mathematics, astrology, and architecture and who excelled in deciphering some of the mysteries of the cosmos. The Aztecs, the civilization which was dominant when the Spanish arrived, were destroyed by the Spanish along with many volumes of accordion-style books written in a glyph form on bark-like paper. The Franciscan friars traveling with the conquering Spaniards saw Aztec writing, their beliefs, and religious and historical artifacts as idolatrous, superstitions, and offensive to the one true God. The Aztec priests and teachers were persecuted, the temples and statues of the old goddesses and gods were destroyed, and the books of writings were burned.

The Aztec education system was abolished and replaced by a very limited church education. Eventually, the Indians were not only forbidden to learn about their old culture, but were often denied the opportunity to learn to read and write in Spanish. This made them dependent on the Spaniards in order to operate within a system they were prevented from fully integrating into. The Spanish Crown established a trusteeship labor system called *encomienda*. It was similar to feudalism in that soldiers were given land and a specific number of natives for whom they were responsible, which included instruction in Spanish and the Catholic faith. In exchange, they could exact tribute from the natives in the form of labor, etc. It became a system of oppression and exploitation of the natives.

What evidence that remains of the Aztecs speaks of cruelty, human sacrifices, and blood rites, which serves to justify the Spanish actions. It repulses and upset people like you and I to hear about human sacrifices, and serves to disparage and almost demonize those cultures or cults who participate in these blood-letting rites. The result is that for centuries the Spaniards were viewed as the more sophisticated culture who rescued an idolatrous and savage people by converting them to Christ, thus minimizing the Spaniard's abuse of the indigenous peoples. This is another example of politics and personal greed cloaked in morality. We still see this today in some of our recent wars, except now we have exchanged gold for black gold -- oil!

There survives, however, evidence of the ancient goddesses and gods. Even among the patriarchal Aztecs, there was a strong Divine Feminine presence. In fact the Toltec, ancestors of the Aztecs, may have been matrilineal. Recent Olmec artifacts imply a supreme being who exhibited both male and female characteristics. Other finds suggest the existence of a jaguar cult of priestesses. The Maya worshiped Lady Beastie, a creatrix deity who was both Mother of the ancient Maya and of the goddesses and gods. They were also devoted to Ix Chel, Goddess of the Moon, Childbirth, Weaving, and Healing.

The Aztecs honored the feminine in the symbol of the serpent, or Snake Woman, also called Terrible Mother, who was said to rule alongside the king. She represented both the dark and light aspects, representing the possible dual nature of a deity of darkness, who also brought light and wisdom, much like Hecate, an ancient Greek goddess. The Aztec creatrix deity Coatlique, "Lady of the Serpent Skirt," was later associated with Tonantzin, who was an earth mother goddess. Our Lady of Guadalupe appeared to Juan Diego on Tepeyac Hill, which was a site where there had long been an Aztec shrine to Tonantzin (Tate, p 303-305). It was on this site that the Holy Virgin insisted a temple be built so the people could receive love, compassion, help, and protection from her, their merciful mother. Why would Our Lady chose this particular site if not to link herself with the Aztec earth mother goddess, Tonantzin?

For hundreds, maybe thousands of years, the indigenous people of Mexico had worshipped goddesses, most recently the earth mother goddess, Tonantzin. The old goddesses and gods died along with the old ways, under the brutal conquest of the Spaniards, however. A bridge was needed to help the people make sense of the New Spain, their new way of life, and the new religion. They also needed their mother goddess. The image of Our Lady served to unite the two cultures: by appearing at Tepeyac, Our Lady of Guadalupe united the Christian Mother Mary with the ancient Aztec earth mother, Tonantzin. Prior to the appearance of Our Lady of Guadalupe, only a few hundred of the Indians had converted. After Our Lady's apparition, an estimated nine million Indians converted to Christianity (http://www.sancta.org/table.html).

Some might claim the story of the Virgin of Guadalupe was a "Christianized" Tonantzin used by clergymen to convert the Aztecs to Christianity. Alternatively, the evolution of Tonantzin into Our Lady of Guadalupe gave the Aztec Indians a hidden means to continue worshipping their own earth mother goddess in a Christianized form. This would not be the first time Christians built their churches on the rubble of ancient pagan temples. Indeed, Christians and other religious traditions have often borrowed what were considered pagan customs and images for their own cult purposes. This unspoken agreement served the purposes of both factions, leading to acceptance and eventual peace so the people could once again experience the compassion, love, and protection of the Great Mother.

Take a moment to reflect on what it might have been like for the indigenous Mexican people to come under the domination of their harsh and intolerant Spanish conquerors. It must have been hard. The Spaniards cruelly subjugated the indigenous people: their culture, history, and religion were obliterated, and their freedom and autonomy were stolen.

The apparition of Our Lady of Guadalupe helped heal those wounds. She was a bridge between the two cultures that over time brought healing, reconciliation, acceptance, and compassion.

This is similar to what I envision is important about the return of the Divine Feminine in our culture today. The resurgence of the Sacred Feminine is very much a grass roots movement that is moving gradually into the establishment. Her message is one of love for fellow beings, cooperation, compassion, care for the young, and respect and care for the planet, which is Her body. There exists, however, so much negativity, which is so heavy and dense that we are polarized, blotting out love and compassion. Yet it was Our Lady of Guadalupe's desire to be present and available to the common people, to hear their lamentations, to alleviate their miseries, to offer her protection, love and compassion that finally brought reconciliation. The Virgin Holy Mother wants her people to live in peace, to be able to live, love and enjoy life. When there is anger, hostility, resentment and blaming there is polarization that blocks the channel to love and peace. Haven't you noticed when you are angry and resentful how hard it is to be considerate, polite and caring? Anger, hostility, and resentment are powerful emotions; they tend to overwhelm and smother the gentler and kinder ones.

In our world today there are so many situations and people with which to be angry and resentful. Some things are hard to love and to feel compassion for. Yet Our Lady of Guadalupe challenges us to be loving and compassionate to all, even when we feel justified in our anger, bitterness and resentment. This is not a call to be passive and not take action. Many times action is necessary and needed. Many more Jews might have escaped the concentrations camps if more people had taken action. What Our Lady challenges us to is to take action, but to do it without giving in to the anger, bitterness and resentment. Our Lady of Guadalupe is the power of love, and she asks us to open our hearts to love, for this is the power that will transform the world.

In summary, in this section on Our Lady of Guadalupe you heard the moving story of Our Lady's apparition to Juan Diego, a humble Indian. You heard his struggles in getting the bishop to believe his story and acquiesce to Our Lady's requests. It took the miraculous appearance of roses in December and the manifestation of her image on Juan Diego's tilma to convince the bishop. Our Lady's temple was finally built where the people could come to receive her love, compassion, and protection. A great basilica stands on that same hill today with Juan Diego's tilma still on display with the image of Our Lady of Guadalupe.

Though the historical climate was one of oppression for the indigenous Indians of Mexico, Our Lady of Guadalupe appeared to provide a bridge between the two cultures so that there might be healing and reconciliation. Our Lady appeared on Tepeyac Hill, the site of an Aztec shrine to Tonantzin, an earth mother goddess. Whether the Spaniards appropriated Tonantzin and her sacred site to convert the Aztecs, or whether the appearance of Our Lady provided a hidden means for the Indians to continue worshipping in the old ways, the results were the same. The Aztecs were brought back into the fold of the Mother and there was growing acceptance and eventual peace. This is what Our Lady of Guadalupe wants. She asks us to open our hearts to love, for this is the power that will transform the world so everyone can live in peace.

If you are an individual practitioner take time to reflect and journal on the following questions. Then do the meditation on Hard to Love. (This meditation can be purchased for a nominal fee on my website www.celebratedivinefeminine.com.)

Take time to record your thoughts after the meditation.

If you are leading a circle, then first lead the discussion and ritual for Hard to Love. Then lead your circle in the meditation on Hard to Love. After the meditation lead a group discussion on what came up for your participants during the rituals and meditations.

QUESTIONS FOR REFLECTION

❖ What do you experience in your life, or in your world today, that is hard for you to love or to feel compassion for?

- ❖ Reflect on those major events that have transformed the world.
  - ○ What is the legacy of war? Is there ever a justification for war, for violence?
  - ○ What is the legacy of non-violent protests? Gandhi in India, Martin Luther King in the US, Nelson Mandela in South Africa.
  - ○ Are peaceful methods of protest and change effective?
- ❖ What method of change and transformation do you want to put your energy, time and money into?

SOURCES

The Apparitions and the Miracle, http://www.sancta.org/nical.html.

Chronology of Events related to the Miracle, http://www.sancta.org/table.html.

Our Lady of Guadalupe, http://en.wikipedia.org/wiki/Our_Lady_of_Gudadlupe.

Karen Tate, *Sacred Places of Goddess: 108 Destinations.*

GUADALUPE GUIDED VISUALIZATION

Easy to Love

Take a nice deep breath and begin to call back all the pieces of yourself that you have scattered out and about. Spiral all those parts of yourself right back into your heartspace and feel yourself become very centered and calm...Then take another deep breath and hold for a second, and as you release just let go of any tension and stress that you might be carrying from the week...Then take a third deep breath, again breathing all the way into your abdomen and holding, and as you slowly release, surrender to total peace and relaxation...And as you continue to relax, feel yourself becoming lighter and lighter until you feel like you are floating, so light, so relaxed, so very much at peace...Then feel yourself floating back through time and space to that hill that you know to be Tepeyac Hill, where Juan Diego met Our Lady of Guadalupe. You land at the foot of the hill and hear the sound of birds singing a beautiful melody in the frosty early morning air. Then you hear your name being called from the top of the hill, a sweet loving sound. You climb to the top of the hill where you find a circle of women, some whom you might recognize. In the center of the circle is Our Lady of Guadalupe. Her garments are shining like the sun and rays of light emanate from behind her. The cliff where she rests her feet is pierced with glitter resembling an anklet of precious stones. The earth glows with the colors of the rainbow. The mesquites, *nopales*, and other weeds sparkle like emeralds; their foliage is like turquoise and their branches and thorns glisten like gold.

Our Lady of Guadalupe has the sweetest smile on her face and she looks at you with such love and compassion...Radiating from her is the most beautiful energy. You feel total acceptance. Whatever you have done or not done in your life, whatever regrets, remorse, guilt or pain you feel, you know that she understands. She recognizes your human journey. She understands your struggles and challenges. And she loves you and has compassion for you in spite of everything. She knows that you are doing the best that you can with the information you have. And she knows that as you come to a greater knowing of love and compassion and to feel it within, then you will be able to transform in many ways. She tells you that you have the potential to send out great waves of love, compassion and mercy into the world. When we hold love in our hearts and send it out to the world it creates a shift, a positive planetary shift that can help transform the world, bringing greater love, compassion and peace to everyone.

Our Lady of Guadalupe asks you to join with her to send love out into the world. She invites you to bask in the love that she is radiating and to feel it in your heart. If you have difficulty feeling such great love, then think of someone whom you love very much...It might be a child, your child or a grandchild...It might be a pet that is very dear to you...Or it might be another loved one that brings up wonderful feelings of unconditional love... As soon as you have this heart opening of love then begin to gather up this love as if it is a great ball of light and energy at your heart space...Keep pouring love and compassion into this ball of light...Once you have poured as much love into this ball of light and energy, then send it into the center of the circle as we join all of our light with Guadalupe's, creating a great pillar of light and love before Our Lady right in the middle of the circle. We add our light and love to Hers, magnifying the strength of Her love even more.

Now let's take a few moments to put into this central pillar of light and love those who are very dear to us so that we may bless them...As we place each individual in the pillar of light they may even gently spiral as they receive their blessing...Then let's place ourselves in the center and feel our selves spiral in the light as we receive a blessing...Now let's place the Mother Earth in the center...I always see her as a woman with a great pregnant belly, and within her belly is the earth. She needs our love and our blessings. She is in so much pain; we humans have wounded her with our greed and ignorance. Let's send Mother Earth as much love and light and compassion and blessings as we can... Now let's send this love and light out into the world blessing all the animals... The plant life... the children everywhere... blessing every mother's son and daughter. See this blessing of love and light radiate out like illuminated sparkles of stardust scattering throughout the entire globe...

Now the energy begins to wind down... Guadalupe smiles and thanks us for joining with her to send out this blessing of light and love to the world. She asks that you do it often, for when you send out this energy of light and love into the world, the world is blessed. And the world so needs all of our blessings.

And now Guadalupe begins to fade and the singing of the birds falls silent. And now begin to feel your breath in your lungs. Feel the weight of your body in your chair. Feel your feet upon the floor. And when you are ready you may open your eyes.

GUADALUPE GUIDED VISUALIZATION

Hard to Love

Take a nice deep breath and begin to call back all the pieces of yourself that you have scattered out and about. Spiral all those parts of yourself right back into your heartspace and feel yourself become very centered and calm...Then take another deep breath and hold for a second, and as you release just let go of any tension and stress that you might be carrying from the week...Then take a third deep breath, again breathing all the way into your abdomen and holding, and as you slowly release, surrender to total peace and relaxation...And as you continue to relax, feel yourself becoming lighter and lighter until you feel like you are floating, so light, so relaxed, so very much at peace...Then feel yourself floating through time and space back to Tepeyac Hill, where Juan Diego met Our Lady of Guadalupe. You land at the foot of the hill and hear the sound of birds singing a beautiful melody in the frosty early morning air. Then once again you hear your name being called from the top of the hill. You climb to the top and join the now familiar circle of women. In the center is Our Lady, her garments are shining like the sun, and everything around her is sparkling and radiating light.

You can fell the energy of compassion and love emanating from her... You feel total acceptance...She reminds you that you have the capacity to send love, compassion and mercy rippling out into the world. When we hold love in our hearts and send it out to the world, it creates a shift, a positive planetary shift that can help transform the world, bringing greater love, compassion and peace.

Our Lady of Guadalupe asks you to join with her to send love out into the world. She invites you to bask in the love that she is sending out, to open up your heart and feel the depth of her love for you and all things. If you are having a difficulty feeling this love, then once again think of someone whom you love very much. It might be a child, or a pet, or a loved one that brings up great feelings of unconditional love. As soon as you have this heart opening of love, begin to gather up this love as if were a great ball of light and energy at your heart space. Once you have poured as much love as you can into this ball of light and energy, send it into the center of the circle as we all join our light with the light of Our Lady, creating a great pillar of light and love right before Our Lady of Guadalupe. By adding our light and love to hers, we multiply the strength of her love. Let's just take a moment to feel the strength of our combined love and compassion...

Now let's put into this central pillar of light and love those things or individuals that are hard to love...Just keep opening up your heart and sending love...Imagine that you are sending light to whatever it is...Imagine that whatever you are focusing on is surrounded by a dense cloud that almost obscures it...Imagine that our love and compassion is a powerful ray of light that is burning off the gray denseness, just like sunlight burns off the early morning mist...Just keep beaming your light...

If it is hard to send love and compassion, just notice that it is hard, and have love and compassion for yourself. Allow this love and compassion to keep your heart open so that you can continue to join your heart energy with the love and compassion of Our Lady of Guadalupe. Ask her for help in transforming your emotions so that you can find it easier to have compassion for yourself, and for what is hard to love. Just keep your heart open and allow as much light and love and compassion to flow to the denseness and negativity as you can today...Just imagine that dense cloud of negativity is dissolving...

Our pillar of light is beginning to wind down now. Our Lady of Guadalupe smiles and thanks you for joining with her to send out this blessing of light and love to the world to dissolve denseness and negativity. She knows that it can sometimes be difficult. She asks that you do it often, for when you send out this energy of light and love into the world to dissolve the negative, the world is blessed. And the world so needs all of our blessings.

And now Our Lady of Guadalupe begins to fade, and the singing of the birds falls silent. Now begin to feel your breath in your lungs. Feel the weight of your body in your chair. Feel your feet upon the floor. And when you are ready you may open your eyes.

GUADALUPE RITUAL

Music: "Fourth Chakra, Heart of the Earth," *Chakra Healing Chants* by Sophia

Supplies

Small slips of paper (1/8 to 1/16 of a sheet of paper is sufficient. You will need to ritually dispose of the paper and water (i.e. burying them in the ground) so volume needs to be considered), small bowl for the papers, pens, large bowl for the water, water energized with rose quartz crystal (place a rose quartz crystal in a glass jar of water and let it sit out overnight), red food dye, rose oil or rose water.

First Ritual – Easy to Love (music:)

1. Pass papers and pens and write down those things that are easy to love

2. Discussion: Easy to Love

Introduction (read of paraphrase):

The energy of Our Lady of Guadalupe is one of great love and compassion for her people. She wants the world to be at peace so that everyone may feel the joy and security of love and compassion. Tonight our discussion and our ritual and meditation have two parts. In the first part you are invited to focus on those things that for which you feel love and/or compassion. Let's take a few moments to share about those individuals or things for which we feel love or compassion.

3. Read or paraphrase the following
In this ritual we will strengthen our connection to the feelings of love and compassion so that we can have a Heart Opening and become more aware of, and be in touch with, the feelings of love and compassion. Of course, we may not always want to go around with our heart chakras open, but in a circle of like minds and hearts it is safe to open our hearts.

The central altar contains a bowl of water that tinted red and enhanced with rose oil (or rose water), the essence that is sacred to Our Lady. The water has been energized with rose quartz crystal, which carries the vibrations of love and healing. The water symbolizes emotions and the red tint symbolizes the heart and love. The bowl holds and contains the water just like the womb of

220

our mothers held and contained us. Therefore the bowl of water is symbolic of the heart and love of the Great Mother.

4. Writing exercise (music)

(read of paraphrase) As part of this ritual, you are invited to write on your paper those individuals or things for which you feel love or compassion. When you are ready, you may place your slip of paper in the bowl symbolizing the love of the Mother. This container of love will become our focal point during the meditation.

Easy to Love Meditation (Music) (see above for the text to the meditation or you may purchase it on my website for a nominal fee www.celebratedivinefeminine.com)

Second Ritual – Hard to Love

Music: "Fourth Chakra, Heart of the Earth," *Chakra Healing Chants* by Sophia

1. Pass papers and pens
2. Hard to Love Discussion (cover as many questions as you have time for or as feels appropriate)
   - ❖ What do you experience in your life, or in your world today, that is hard for you to love or to feel compassion for?
   - ❖ Reflect on those major events that have transformed the world.
     - o What is the legacy of war? Is there ever a justification for war, for violence?
     - o What is the legacy of non-violent protests? Gandhi in India, Martin Luther King in the US, Nelson Mandela in South Africa.
     - o Are peaceful methods of protest and change effective?
   - ❖ What method of change and transformation do you want to put your energy, time and money into?
3. Read or paraphrase the following

There are many things that are hard to love. These energies can be dense and negative. People who are caught in these negative energies are stuck in a polarized way of thinking and viewing of the world that is damaging. Resentment and anger magnifies the polarization and keeps us locked in our opposing positions so there is little chance for change.

Our Lady brought harmony and cohesiveness to the people of Mexico through her love and compassion. She was able to dissolve the polarization, even though it must have been hard. By sending compassion and goodwill we can also dissolve the denseness of negativity and polarization in the world **in our time** so that a shift to the light and the positive energies of love and compassion can occur.

4. Writing exercise (Music)

   Introduction: (read or paraphrase):

   Take a moment to write those things for which it is hard for you to feel love and compassion. These are the very things we want to dissolve the negativity around so that we can all move towards greater love and compassion. A shift in just 20% of human consciousness is needed in order to bring about a shift in planetary consciousness. This is one of the purposes of the Divine Feminine. She desires a world of peace, compassion and harmony and seeks to dissolve dissonance and negativity. She needs each one of us to join with her in order to be successful.

   Avoid feeling compelled to control the outcome because what we might envision from our perspective is narrow and limited. The Divine knows what is best for the world. All that is required is for us to join our energies of love and compassion for the purpose of shining light on denser negative energies so that we can help the world move into the light.

   When you feel called, place the paper slips into the symbolic heart of the Mother.

5. Hard to Love Meditation (Music)(see above for the text to the meditation or you may purchase it on my website for a nominal fee)

   Intro to meditation: (read or paraphrase):

   During the meditation, if it is hard to send love and compassion, just notice that it is hard, and have love and compassion for yourself. Allow this love and compassion to keep you heart open so that you can join your heart energy with the heart energy of Our Lady of Guadalupe. Ask Her for help in transforming your emotions so that you can find it easier to have compassion for yourself, and for what is hard to love.

TABLE OF CORRESPONDENCES FOR OUR LADY OF GUADALUPE

Element: Earth

Symbols: Roses, Sun radiating behind her, crescent moon or dark of the moon, cape of stars

Color: Blue-green, rose red

Animals: Snake

Season: Winter

Moon: Crescent, or dark of the moon

Festivals: Our Lady of Guadalupe's Feast Day, December 12

Geography: Mexico

Timeframe: 1600's to contemporary

Women's Cycles: Virgin Mother, possibly pregnant

Plants: Roses

Music

For both the meditation and the ritual: "Fourth Chakra, Heart of the Earth," *Chakra Healing Chants* by Sophia

(The following is a proposed agenda if you choose to hold a circle to celebrate Our Lady of Guadalupe)

IN HER NAME CIRCLE, OUR LADY OF GUADALUPE CIRCLE PROGRAM

Welcome to In Her Name Circle Celebrating Guadalupe

Intro: (5 min) Name, city, and a word as to how each participant is feeling

Casting the Circle: (3min)

Opening: (2 min) poem

Story of the Apparition of Guadalupe to Juan Diego – (10 min)

Discussion of what we love and for which we have compassion (10 min)

Easy to Love Ritual (10 min)

Easy to Love Meditation –sending out love and compassion (10 min)

Spanish Conquest of the Americas: (10 min)Discussion on what is Hard to Love (15 min)

Hard to Love Ritual - (10 min)

Hard to Love Meditation – sending love to what is hard to love (10 min)

Group Share – each person given chance to talk (15 min)

Goddess Cards (10 min)

Closing: (2 min)

Releasing the directions – (3min)

Total time: 125

I hope you have enjoyed the information and insights on the Divine Feminine that I have provided. The creation of each Circle, and subsequently this book and the three to follow (Air, the Breath of the Goddess; Fire, the Bright Spirit of the Goddess; and Water, the Living Womb of the Goddess) have truly been a labor of love. It is my hope that this book will be an inspiration and a guide so that you might create your own circles to celebrate In Her Name.

Glossary of Names and Places

Alakshmi
Hindu goddess of misfortune. She is described as having a dry and shriveled up body, sunken cheeks, thick lips, and beady eyes.

Anatolia
This term is used to denote both geographically and historically the westernmost protrusion of Asia and comprises most of the Republic of Turkey. This region lies south of the Black Sea, north of the Mediterranean Sea, east of the Aegean Sea, and the ancient country of Mesopotamia was to the southeast.

Aphrodisias
A small city on the southwest coast of what is the Republic of Turkey today. The ruins of this city are about 230 km south of Izmir. Aphrodisias was named after Aphrodite, the Greek goddess of love.

Aphrodite
She is the Greek goddess of love. beauty, pleasure and procreation. Historically she has ties to the cult of Astarte in Phoenicia. Hesiod in *Theogony* claims that Aphrodite was born when Cronus cut off Uranus' genitals and threw them into the sea. She is said to have risen from the sea foam or *aphros* which is her root. She washed onto the shores of Paphos on Cyprus, which became a major center of her cult. The gods feared that her great beauty would cause jealousy and strife that might lead to war, so Zeus married her to Hephaestus, the ugly misshapen smith god. Her Roman counterpart is Venus.

Artemis
Artemis is one of the virgin Greek goddesses. She is the goddess of the hunt, animals wild and domestic, the moon, childbirth and agriculture. Her Mother was the nature deity, Leto. Zeus was her father and her twin brother was Apollo. She carries a bow and arrows, her companions are the nymphs, and she is known for coming to the defense of the weak and vulnerable. In contemporary times she has become a symbol of the women's movement. Her Roman counterpart is Diana.

Asherah
The Semitic name for goddess. In the Old Testament Asherah means grove, During the time when the

	Hebrews worshipped a goddess she was worshipped in sacred groves.
Bali	The King of the Demons in Hinduism.
Brigit or Brigid	A Celtic Triple Goddess of ancient Brigantia, which incorporated the British Isles, France, and parts of Spain. She is said to be descended from the Tuatha de Danann, the ancient faery folk who retreated into the hollow hills of Ireland when Christianity overcame the old ways. She is a mother goddess archetype and is the goddess of poetry, healing and smith-craft. Brigit was so revered by the people that the Catholic Church appropriated her as a saint. There are many legends of her as a saint.
Catal Hoyuk	A Neolithic site in central Turkey that dates back to the 6th or 7th millennium BCE. It was first discovered in the late 1950s and was excavated by James Mellaart between 1961 and 1965. A famous statue called the Mother Goddess of Catal Hoyuk, which features a woman seated on a throne flanked by two lionesses, was found in a grain bin at the site.
Demeter	The Greek Goddess of the Grain. She is the mother of Kore/Persephone. When Kore was abducted by Hades she withheld the crops until Zeus was forced to demand that Hades return her daughter who had matured into Persephone, the Queen of the Underworld.
Dumuzi	The Sumerian shepherd god who was the consort of Inanna. He was banished to the Underworld when he took over Inanna's rule when she descended into the Underworld. Inanna later relented and allowed his sister to replace him for the spring and summer months so he could return bringing potent fertilizing energy with him.
Eleusis	A town and municipality in West Attica, Greece, that is 18 km northwest from the center of Athens. It is where Demeter had a temple erected to her so she could institute her Mysteries.
Enheduanna	A daughter of Sargon, the ruler of Sumer, who lived approximately 2285-2250 BCE. She was a High Priestess of Inanna, Sumerian Queen of Heaven and Earth. She is known for her hymns and poetry in praise of Inanna.
Ereshkigal	Inanna's sister, Sumerian Queen of the Underworld. Inanna descends into the underworld to console her sister upon hearing of the death of Ereshkigal's husband. Ereshkigal turns Inanna into a corpse, but Inanna is later

rescued with the help of the god Enki. Ereshkigal is believed to be the mirror image of Inanna, the raw primal shadow side that has gone underground.

Gorgon
The Gorgon was the Goddess of Death in the ancient world. The most famous Gorgon was Medusa who was believed to be a fierce and wise goddess of great power and energy as symbolized by the snakes in her hair and around her body.

Grandmother Spider
In Native American legends and myths of the Pueblo and Navajo/Dineh peoples she is the creatrix of the world. According to mythology, she was responsible for the stars in the sky. She took a web she had spun, laced it with dew, threw it into the sky and the dew became the stars. Then she went on to weave the Web of Life connecting everyone and everything in the universe together.

Hades
The Greek Lord of the Underworld. He was the brother of Demeter and Zeus who abducted Kore/Persephone and dragged her into the underworld. The Roman equivalent for Hades is Pluto.

Hecate
Hecate was a Pre-Hellenic Mother Goddess who was originally powerful and respected. Under the Greek pantheon her traits were split off and distributed to Demeter, Artemis, Persephone and others. She came to embody the Crone archetype and was part of the first original trinity. She retained the death aspect of the Mother Goddess and eventually became the Goddess of Ghosts and the Queen of Witches. She was later diabolized by the Catholic Church.

Herodotus
An ancient Greek historian who lived in the 5th century BC (c.484 BC – c.425 BC). He has been called the "Father of "History" because he was the first to collect his materials systematically and test their accuracy. He arranged his facts in a well-constructed and vivid narrative. Notice that that the word "history" can be broken up to say "his story." This is why many Goddess scholars like to use the word "herstory" when talking about the legends and myths of female deities.

Inanna
The Sumerian Goddess of Heaven and Earth. Her consort was Dumuzi, the Shepherd god. Her most famous High Priestess, Enheduanna, lived during the middle of the 3rd millennium BCE. Enheduanna wrote hymns and poetry in

praise of Inanna; the most popular poem is titled
"Descent of Inanna." This tells th[...] Inanna's
[...] comfort
[...] ey to the
[...] mbols of
[...] stripped
[...] of death,
[...] a meat
[...] to send
[...] s much

Indra
Juan Diego
[...] vert to
[...] e same
Kali
[...] vision.
[...] duism.
[...] and is
[...] sions,
[...] assists
[...] them so
t[...] be open and receptive to more positive forces.

Karl Jung
A Swiss psychiatrist who lived from 1875 to 1961. He
was an influential thinker and the founder of Analytical
Psychology. He is the first psychiatrist to view the human
psyche as religious by nature and to make it the focus of
exploration. He is one of the best known researchers in
the field of dream analysis and symbolization. He
developed the theories of the collective unconscious and
archetypes.

King Keleos
The King of Eleusis who ordered the building of the
Temple to Demeter.

Kore
The maiden daughter of Demeter who is abducted by
Hades and taken into the underworld. According to myth
she matures into Persephone and is finally freed by Zeus
when her mother withholds the gift of grain from
humans and the gods.

Kuan Yin
The Chinese Buddhist Bodhisattva who was the
personification of compassion and mercy. Some sources
hold that she is the feminized version of the Indian
Bodhisattva Avalokitesvara, who embodies the
compassion of all Buddhas. Buddhism found its way into
China during a time when women were suppressed and

needed a compassionate female deity to console them. For this reason it was believed that the Lord of Compassion became feminized.

Lakshmi The Hindu Goddess of Prosperity and Abundance. She is the consort of Vishnu. Together they uphold the laws of the universe and bring prosperity and joy to all who are hardworking and virtuous.

Lilith According to Hebrew legend she was Adam's first wife who refused to submit lying beneath Adam during intercourse. This is probably a reference that she was simply not submissive by nature. Lilith fled to the Red Sea and refused to return even when threatened with exile by God.

Marija Gimbutas A Lithuanian-American archaeologist who lived from 1921 to 1994. She is known for her research of both Neolithic and Bronze Age cultures mostly in Eastern and Southern Europe. She came to call this area Old Europe. She published a series of books combining linguistics and mythological interpretations. She concluded that Lithuania and much of Europe were inhabited during the Neolithic Era by stable egalitarian societies with women placed at the center both materially and spiritually. Her views received a mixed reception among scholars but became the cornerstones of the matriarchal studies and goddess movements.

Mary Magdalene She was a follower of Jesus who is thought by some, especially by the Gnostics tradition, to be a favorite disciple of Jesus and quite possibly his wife. The Gnostics refer to her as the Holy Bride. There is confusion as to who she really is based on the Bible. Some say that she is the woman from which Jesus cast out 7 demons, or that she was Mary of Bethany, or the sister of Lazarus, or the woman who anointed Jesus with the ointment from the alabaster jar, or all of the above. We do know that she was the woman, or one of the women, to whom Jesus appeared to outside his tomb on the day of his resurrection. Some sources claim that Mary was pregnant with Jesus' child and fled after Jesus' death sailing to the south of France where there exist many stories of Mary Magdalene.

Medusa Medusa, according to Greek mythology was a Gorgon, a monster that dwelt in the earth, as in caves or caverns. It was believed that anyone looking into her face would be turned to stone. Perseus, a Greek hero, beheaded her and then used her head as a weapon. Eventually he passed the head onto Athena who put it on her shield. The head of Medusa was believed to be powerful and protective and could ward of danger. Some buildings in antiquity had a Medusa head as one of their cornerstones. Two heads of Medusa lie at the bottom of a cistern in Turkey as the base for two pillars.

Metanira
The wife of King Keleos, the king of Eleusis. She hired Demeter to be the nursemaid for her son, when Demeter was estranged from the gods after Hades abducted her daughter, Kore.

Mother Mary
The mother of Jesus who was believed to be a virgin. She became a saint in the Catholic Church and at one time was given the title of Queen of Heaven. In the 1960s during the Vatican II the title was removed and her status diminished.

Our Lady of Guadalupe
An apparition of the Virgin Mother Mary who appeared to Juan Diego, a poor Aztec Indian, on Tepeyac Hill in Mexico during the 1600s after the conquest of Mexico. A basilica now stands on the site. On display is the *tilma*, or shawl, with the miraculous image of Our Lady of Guadalupe.

Persephone
The daughter of Demeter who in her maiden aspect, Kore, was abducted by Hades and dragged to the underworld. Demeter later withholds the gift of grain from both humans and the gods until Zeus forces Hades to release her daughter who has matured into Persephone, the Queen of the Underworld.

Saint Bridget
Saint Bridget is thought to be a Catholic appropriation of an older Celtic Mother Goddess Brigit or Brigid, who was so revered that the people would not deny her. Brigit was a Triple Goddess and the goddess of poetry, healing and smith-craft. There are many legends and stories of St. Bridget. She was the first nun in Ireland and founded a nunnery in Kildare. St. Bridget was associated with the perpetual flame, or sacred flames, such as the one that was maintained by 19 nuns in Kildare, Ireland.

Sekhmet
An Egyptian Lioness Goddess, originally the warrior goddess as well as the healing goddess of Upper Egypt. She was believed to be so fierce that she was seen as the

	protector of the pharaohs and led them in warfare. She is a fiery goddess of transformation and change.
Shekhinah	In Biblical Hebrew the word means literally *to settle, inhabit,* or *dwell,* and is used frequently in the Hebrew Bible. The term is used to refer to the feminine face or aspect of God, that gentler, caring compassionate aspect that dwells with and has concern for the common people.
Thrace	Thrace is a historical and geographic area in southeast Europe. It comprises the area of southeastern Bulgaria (Northern Thrace), northeastern Greece (Western Thrace), and the European part of Turkey (Eastern Thrace). The biggest part of Thrace is part of present-day Bulgaria.
Tonantzin	An Aztec earth mother goddess who was also called "Goddess of Sustenance", "Honored Grandmother", "Snake", "Bringer of Maize" and "Mother of Corn." Our Lady of Guadalupe appeared at the site of one of her shrines which has led to the speculation that Our Lady of Guadalupe is a Christianized Tonantzin.
Vishnu	The Preserver of the Universe in Hinduism. He is the consort of Lakshmi.

Glossary of Terms

Amazons

Goddess-worshiping tribes in north Africa, Anatolia and the Black Sea Area. They were said to be the first to tame horses, and Herodotus called them warlike. They fought against the Greeks in several battles including the Battle of Troy. They Greeks considered them serious adversaries. There are many ancient artifacts of Amazons, and they are featured prominently in many myths. In Turkey they are believed to have founded several cities including Ephesus and Troy.

Anima

Latin for the "soul." A term used by Karl Jung to refer to the unconscious, feminine side of a man's personality. Jung believed the anima was personified in dreams by images of women ranging from prostitute and seductress to spiritual guide (Wisdom).

Animus

Latin for "spirit." A term used by Karl Jung to refer to the unconscious, masculine side of a woman's personality. Jung believed that over-identification with the animus can cause a woman to become rigid, opinionated, and argumentative. More positively, the animus is the inner masculine who acts as a bridge between the woman's ego and her own creative resources in the unconscious.

Archetype

These are collective universal patterns or motifs which come from the collective unconscious and are the basic content of religions, mythologies, legends, and fairytales. They emerge in individuals through dreams and visions. Examples would be the queen or king, the woman warrior or warrior, the bride or bridegroom, etc. Each archetype possesses a positive and unhelpful aspect.

Aztec

They were an indigenous ethnic group that inhabited central Mexico, and who dominated large parts of Mesoamerica in the 14th, 15th and 16th centuries. The Aztecs were the predominant culture when the Spaniards arrived.

BCE (Before the Common Era)	Alternative, non-religious calendar designation, which corresponds to the Christian BC or Before Christ. Dates after Year 1 BCE are referred to as CE, or Common Era.
Chakra	The concept of the Chakra systems appears to originate in Hindu texts and is featured in tantric and yogic traditions of both Hinduism and Buddhism. The Chakras are said to be "force centers" or energy centers located at seven points on the body: the base of the spine, the abdomen, the solar plexus, the heart, the throat, the third eye center and the Crown.
CE (Common Era)	Alternative, non-religious calendar designation, which corresponds to the Christian AD or Anno Domini. Dates before Year 1 CE are referred to as BCE, or Before the Common Era.
Civilization of the Goddess	See Goddess Civilization
Collective unconscious	A subtle universal ordering of collective reality that incorporates and organizes symbols and archetypes in the subconscious. Karl Jung believed that the collective unconscious has been subject to the essential biological process of evolution. Each human brain has the capacity to access it much in the same way that an individual can tune into a radio station.
Crown Chakra	This chakra is generally considered to be the chakra of pure consciousness. It is stimulated when the female kundalini or Shakti energy rises from the base of the spine to the crown, where it unites with the male or Shiva energy, and a state of liberation or conscious awakening is attained.
Divine Feminine	Sometimes referred to as the Sacred Feminine. The Divine Feminine can be personified by any of the many female deity images from around the globe and can range from Gaia, Mother Earth, to Mother Mary as Queen of Heaven and Mary Magdalene, who is revered by the Gnostics as the Sacred Bride. This concept also includes the valuing of all things woman, and represents women reclaiming themselves, their bodies, and their lives. Sometimes this requires that a woman confront her illusions and the cultural roles and conditionings that have kept her confined in traditional roles that limit her from fully embracing herself as woman.

Divine Masculine	Sometimes referred to as the Sacred Masculine. The Divine Masculine can be personified by any of the male deities and avatars from around the world including, but not limited to, the Christian God, Jesus, Buddha, Vishnu Mohammed and St John the Baptist.
Goddess Civilization	Marija Gimbutas conducted research and archaeological excavations of Neolithic sites in Lithuania and across Europe and her conclusions pointed to long-term stable egalitarian societies with women at the center materially and spiritually and who worshipped a Mother Goddess or Goddesses. Her theories have received a mixed reception by other scholars, but became a keystone of the Goddess and Women's Spirituality movements. Her final book, *The Civilization of the Goddess* (1991), presented theories about Neolithic cultures across Europe, and included her speculations on housing patterns, social structure, art, religion, and the nature of literacy. Gimbutas pointed out some significant differences between the Old European system, which she considered goddess and woman-centered, and the Bronze Age Indo-European patriarchal culture which supplanted it. According to her interpretations the Old European gynocentric or woman-centered societies were peaceful and less hierarchical, with materials and goods shared equally between the inhabitants, and there was more equality between genders. On the other hand the androcratic or male-dominated Kurgan peoples (more frequently referred to as Indo-Europeans today) were more hierarchal and war-like, and worshipped sky-gods.
Hierodule	Commonly referred as sacred sexual priestess, or sacred prostitute. For the most part she has been quite misunderstood and her role demeaned. She is not a prostitute who sells sexual favors. Her role is sacred, and during sacred ritual she represents the Goddess. Her sexuality was key to generating the energy of life that stimulated fertility and potentiality. In ancient times her union with the king was deemed necessary to insure prosperity and abundance for the land and animals, and for the people.
Hieros Gamos	The term means "Sacred Marriage" in Greek and refers to the union of a king, a divine king, or a surrogate for

the divine king, with his goddess, or a priestess-queen who is impersonating the goddess. This annual sacred union was deemed necessary in ancient times to insure prosperity and abundance for the land and animals, and for the people. It legitimized the right of the king to rule.

In Her Name Circles
Circles that gather for the purpose of celebrating the many manifestations of the Divine Feminine. In Her Name Circles were founded by Joy Reichard.

Indo-Europeans
According to Marija Gimbutas it is a family of languages characterized by basic vocabularies that have many correspondences of inflection, grammatical number, gender, and ablaut, including Indo-Iranian, Slavic, Baltic, Germanic, Celtic, Romance, Greek, Albanian, Armenian branches, and a number of dead languages.

Instinctive Body
The part of human nature that pertains to our instinctual rhythms and needs. This can include sexuality, pleasure, play, sensual awareness, creativity, communication, nourishment, rest, need connection and love, etc. Megan Wagner, in *The Sapphire Staff*, claims that being in touch with our instinctive bodies and rhythms is important for our psychological stability. If we ignore them or try to "rise above them," we can push them down into our subconscious from where they might emerge spontaneously in nightmares or in times of stress or fatigue, or they might even result in emotional or psychological breakdowns.

Kabbalah
In Hebrew the word Kabbalah/Kaballah literally means "receiving." It is a discipline and school of thought concerned with the esoteric aspect of Rabbinic Judaism. Its esoteric teachings are an attempt to explain the relationship between an infinite and transcendent Creator and his creation, which is a finite universe occupied by mortal plant, animal, and human life. Its mystical teaching is what Megan Wagner calls a practical road map of self-discovery using the Tree of Life. The Tree of Life provides a step by step process through seven initiations that lead towards both spiritual and psychological health. For more information refer to Wagner's book, *The Sapphire Staff*.

Kurgan Hypothesis or Theory
The Kurgan hypothesis / theory is one of several proposals about the early origins of Indo-Europeans. It suggests the people of an archaeological "Kurgan

culture" migrated from the steppes of Russian into Southern and Eastern Europe, Anatolia, and North Africa. They most likely were speakers of the Proto-Indo-European language. The Kurgan model is the most widely accepted scenario of Indo-European origins and was first formulated in the 1950s by Marija Gimbutas. The Kurgan peoples were a pastoral, semi-nomadic culture who were war-like, hierarchal, patriarchal equestrians who worshiped sky gods. The term *kurgan* is derived from a Turkic loanword in Russian for "burial mound." Today the Kurgan peoples are more commonly referred to as Indo-Europeans.

Matrifocal

A sociological group, as a household, tribe, or family unit where the focus is centered more on the mother, and values female traits. The grouping may be headed by the mother, and may be lacking in a father figure either permanently or for extended periods.

Matrilineal

The descent of offspring in traced through the female line.

Metaformic
Consciousness

Metaformic Consciousness is a theory conceived by Judy Grahn, which she explains and supports in her book, *Blood, Bread and Roses*. Grahn states that human ancestral females recognized their menstrual cycles synchronized with the lunar cycle, giving them a means of identifying when their cycles would start: from observation of this external pattern.

The awareness of this synchronized pattern raised human consciousness above that of other primates. Recognition of the synchronized cycles, combined with the danger posed by blood flow on the open plains, led to practices of seclusion when females were menstruating, which evolved into rituals. (The core of the word ritual is *r'tu*, a Sanskrit word meaning menstruation.) Males in families synchronized themselves to female rites through parallel blood rites, and reflected their own versions of Metaforms; this inter-relationship between the two genders drives human culture in ever evolving cycles.

Human knowledge derived from rituals is constructed and held in forms which Grahn calls Metaforms, meaning embodied forms of knowledge with menstrual roots or components. Therefore a Metaform is any object or gesture containing an idea and having menstruation as a component of its existence. Grahn gives the example that if a pot is understood as the womb of the goddess, and red rice is understood as menstrual blood of the goddess, the act of boiling red rice in ritual context is meaningful and complex far beyond the product "rice porridge." Grahn contends, and expounds upon eloquently in her book, that virtually all the elements of culture can be traced to traditional menstrual rites or related blood rites.

Mother Goddess Civilization
See Goddess Civilization

Neolithic
Refers to the era that is the last phase of the Stone Age, beginning around 9000 - 8000 BCE in the Middle East.

Old Europe
A term coined by Marija Gimbutas, archaeologist, to describe a pre-Indo-European Neolithic culture in Europe that was widespread and relatively homogeneous, particularly in Southern and Eastern Europe. "Old Europe" refers to the time frame from around 7000 BCE to approximately 1700 BCE, or the beginning of the Bronze Age in Northwest Europe.

Old Europeans
The inhabitants of Europe who lived during the Neolithic Era, from approximately 7000 BCE to 1700 BCE.

Paleolithic
A term that designates the early phase of the Stone Age. It is generally divided into 3 phases: Lower Paleolithic from about 200,000 to 150,000 BCE; Middle Paleolithic from approximately 150,000 to 40,000 BCE; and Upper Paleolithic from about 40,000 to 10,000 BCE.

Patriarchy
A social organization that concentrates power with males and acknowledges male norms and values as accepted standards for the entire culture.

Patrilineal
Tracing the descent of offspring through the male line.

Persona (Latin for actor's mask)
A social role derived from the expectations of society and early training. It is the role or image presented to the public. Used in this context to represent the manifestation and characteristics of a particular goddess.

Sacred Feminine
A concept that includes the valuing of all things woman, and represents women reclaiming themselves, their bodies and their lives. Can be personified by any of the many goddess manifestations from around the globe,

	including Gaia, mother earth. See Divine Feminine
Sacred Marriage	See Hieros Gamas
Sacred Prostitute	See Hierodule
Schematic	A diagram, design or structure that is a reduction, organizational pattern or arrangement based on a particular theme. It may be part of an idea or object that is used to represent the whole, such as a cross is a schematic representation for Christ and Christianity.
Unitarian Universalist	A religion that has not adopted a shared creed but rather supports the individual's right to a free and responsible search for truth and meaning. Unitarian Universalists are unified by their shared search for spiritual growth and by the understanding that an individual's theology is a result of that search and not obedience to an authoritarian requirement. Unitarian Universalists draw on many different theological sources and have a wide range of beliefs and practices.

Historically, both Unitarianism and Universalism have roots in the Christian faith. Contemporary Unitarian Universalists advocate a pluralist approach to religion, whereby the followers may be atheist, theist, polytheist, or have no label at all. The Unitarian Universalist Association (UUA) was formed in 1961, a consolidation of the American Unitarian Association (established in 1825) and the Universalist Church of America, which was established in 1866.

Catalog of Illustrations and Art Work

See bibliography for full titles of publications.

1. Venus of Laussel, sketch by Lydia Ruyle, *Goddess Icons: Spirit Banners of the Divine Feminine*. For best viewing of Lydia's images please visit her website at www.lydiaruyle.com.

2. Vulvas, inspired by drawings found in Elinor Gadon's book *Once and Future Goddess*, p14. Author's sketch.

3. Venus of Willendorf, sketch by Lydia Ruyle. For best viewing of Lydia's images please visit her website at www.lydiaruyle.com.

4. Clay Cup as a schematic representation of a breast, Museum of Vojvodina, Novi Sad, Serbia. Author's sketch.

5. Female Figurine with exaggerated buttocks, Museum of Vojvodina, Novi Sad, Serbia. Author's sketch.

6. Mother Goddess of Catal Hoyuk, Museum of Anatolian Civilization, Ankara, Turkey, sketch by Lydia Ruyle. For best viewing of Lydia's images please visit her website at www.lydiaruyle.com.

7. Clay Seal with water symbols, Regional Historical Museum of Pazardzhik, Pazardzhik, Bulgaria. Author's sketch.

8. Madonna of Rast, terracotta clay sculpture, W. Romania, sketch by Lydia Ruyle. For best viewing of Lydia's images please visit her website at www.lydiaruyle.com.

9. Pregnant Bear Goddess, Regional Historical Museum of Pazardzhik, Pazardzhik, Bulgaria. Author's sketch.

10. Deer Figurine Vase, Detev, 1968, draftsperson: James Bennett. After Gimbutas, 2007, p 116. Author's sketch.

11. Bird Goddess clay replication, after Gimbutas, 2007, p 8, courtesy Svetozrevo Museum, Yugoslavia, draftsperson: Patricia Rice. Author's art work.

12. Cucuteni Venus, National Historical Museum, Bucarest, Romania, Goddess Banner by Lydia Ruyle, *Goddess Icons: Spirit Banners of the*

Divine Feminine. For best viewing of Lydia's images please visit her website at www.lydiaruyle.com.

13. Isolated Snake Coils, after Gimbutas, 1989, p124 (1) Kalicz and Makkay 1977, draftsperson: Samir Twair; (2) Hadaczek, 1914. Author's sketch.

14. Pazardzik Venus, Nation Historical Museum, Bucarest, Romania, Goddess Banner by Lydia Ruyle, *Goddess Icons; Spirit Banners of the Divine Feminine.* For best viewing of Lydia's images please visit her website at www.lydiaruyle.com.

15. Sorrowful Ancient, after Gimbutas, 1989, p181, courtesy Volos Archaeological Museum, Greece, photo K. Konya, 1971. Publ. Theocharis 1973 and Gimbutas 1974. Author's sketch.

16. The Gumelnita Lovers, after Gimbutas, 2001, p 18. Author's sketch.

17. Vulture Figurine, Archaeological Museum, Konya, Turkey. Author's sketch.

18. Owl Goddess, *Linienbandkeramik* Culture, Upper Rhein, after Gimbutas, 1989, p 20. Author's sketch.

19. Flat figurines of bone from the settlement of Ruse on the lower Danube, northern Bulgaria, after Gimbutas, 1974, 1982, p 159. Excavation of 1950-53 by Ruse Georgiev-Angelov. Author's sketch.

20. Death Mask replica, Karanova VI culture, found in grave at Varna Cemetery, Bulgaria, Varna Museum, Bulgaria. Author's sketch.

21. Medusa, Relief sculpture, 600 BCE, Temple of Artemis, Corfu. Goddess Banner by Lydia Ruyle, *Goddess Icons: Spirit Banners of the Divine Feminine.* For best viewing of Lydia's images please visit her website at www.lydiaruyle.com.

22 & 23. Medusa Heads as pillar bases, Basilica Cistern, Istanbul, Turkey. Author's photos.

24. Sheila na gig, St. Mary's and St. David's Church, Kilpeck, Herefordshire, England, after Gimbutas, 2001, p 29. Author's sketch.

25. "Founder," Lepenski Vir, quartz sandstone figurine, Nation Museum, Belgrad, Serbia. Author's sketch.

26. Fish Goddess, Stone sculpture, Lepenski Vir, Serbia. Background: Stone architectural shape, Lepenski Vir. Goddess Banner by Lydia Ruyle, *Goddess Icons: Spirit Banners of the Divine Feminine.* For best viewing of Lydia's images please visit her website at www.lydiaruyle.com.

27. Replica of Bucrania Shrine, Catal Hoyuk, Turkey, Museum of Anatolian Civilizations, Ankara, Turkey. Author's sketch

28. Phallus-shaped goddess, Starcevo culture, Endrod-Szujoskereszt, Koros Valley, southeastern Hungary, after Gimbutas, 2001, p 37. Author's sketch.

29. Triangles on Pottery, Regional Historical Museum of Pazardzhik, Pazardzhik, Bulgaria. Author's sketch.

Catalog of Graphic Art

Demeter: photo of Demeter © Kellydbrown | Dreamstime.com, background © Mike Sangiovanni | Dreamstime.com, graphic design by Kristal Jensen kristalmagic.com.

Grandmother Spider: Statue © Cris Palamino, statue made by Sacred Source, background © Mike Sangiovanni | Dreamstime.com, author's photo, graphic design by Kristal Jensen kristalmagic.com.

Hecate: statue © Maxine Miller, photo © http://www.celticjackalope.com, background © Mike Sangiovanni | Dreamstime.com, graphic design by Kristal Jensen kristalmagic.com.

Lakshmi: statue © YTC Summit, background © Mike Sangiovanni | Dreamstime.com, author's photo, graphic design by Kristal Jensen kristalmagic.com.

Neolithic Goddess: Statue by Joy Reichard, background © Mike Sangiovanni | Dreamstime.com, author's photo, graphic design by Kristal Jensen kristalmagic.com.

Our Lady of Guadalupe: © estudiostevelynchsadecv/istockphoto.com, http://www.celticjackalope.com/, background © Mike Sangiovanni | Dreamstime.com, graphic design by Kristal Jensen kristalmagic.com.

Persephone: courtesy of YTC Summit, background © Mike Sangiovanni | Dreamstime.com, author's photo, graphic design by Kristal Jensen kristalmagic.com.

Bibliography

Allen, Paula Gunn. *Grandmothers of the Light: A Medicine Woman's Sourcebook*. Boston: Beacon Press, 1992.

____. *The Sacred Hoop: Recovering the Feminine in American Indian Traditions*. Boston: Beacon Press, 1986.

Austen, Hallie Iglehart. *The Heart of the Goddess: Art, Myth and Meditations of the World's Sacred Feminine*. Oakland CA: Wingbow Press, 1991.

Baldwin, Christina. *Calling the Circle: The First and Future Culture*. New York: Bantam Books, 1998.

Baring, Anne, and Jules Cashford. *The Myth of the Goddess: Evolution of An Image*. London: Penguin Books, 1993.

Barrett, Ruth. *Women's Rites, Women's Mysteries: Intuitive Ritual Creation*. 2nd ed. St. Paul, MN: Llewellyn Publications, 2007.

Bolen, Jean Shinoda. *Crossing to Avalon: A Woman's Midlife Quest for the Sacred Feminine*. San Francisco: HarperSanFrancisco, 1995.

____. *Goddesses in Everywoman: A New Psychology of Women*. New York: Harper and Row, 1984.

____. *The Millionth Circle: How to Change Ourselves and The World -- The Essential Guide to Women's Circles*. San Francisco: Conari Press, 1999.

Carlson, Kathie. *Life's Daughter/Death's Bride: Inner Transformations through the Goddess Demeter/Persephone*. Boston: Shambhala Publications, 1997.

Carnes, Robin Deen, and Sally Craig. *Sacred Circles: A Guide To Creating Your Own Women's Spirituality Group*. New York: HarperOne, 1998.

Conway, D. J. *Maiden, Mother, Crone: the Myth and Reality of the Triple Goddess*. St. Paul, MN: Llewellyn Publications, 1994.

Davis-Kimball, Jeannine, and Mona Behan. *Warrior Women: An Archaeologist's Search for History's Hidden Heroines*. Boston: Warner Books, 2003.

Detev, P. *Praistoricheskoto selischte pri selo Muldava*. Godishnik, Plovdiv, VI.9-48, 1968. Quoted in Marija Gimbutas, *The Gods and Goddesses of Old Europe: Myths and Cult Images* (Berkeley: University of California Press, 2007), 249, 292.

Fisher, Elizabeth. *Rise Up and Call Her Name: A Woman-honoring Journey into Global Earth-based Spiritualities*. Boston, MA: Unitarian Universalist Women's Federation, 1994.

Gadon, Elinor W. *The Once and Future Goddess: A Sweeping Visual Chronicle of the Sacred Female and Her Reemergence in the Cultural Mythology of Our Time*. New York: HarperOne, 1989.

George, Demetra. *Mysteries of the Dark Moon: The Healing Power of the Dark Goddess*. New York: HarperOne, 1992.

Gimbutas, Marija. *The Civilization of the Goddess: The World Of Old Europe*. San Francisco: HarperCollins, 1994.

____. *The Gods and Goddesses of Old Europe: Myths and Cult Images*. 2nd ed. Berkeley: University of California Press, 2007.

____. *The Language of the Goddess*. New York: Thames and Hudson, 1989.

Gimbutas, Marija, and Miriam Robbins Dexter. *The Living Goddesses*. Berkeley: University of California Press, 2001.

Gottlieb, Lynn. *She Who Dwells Within: A Feminist Vision of A Renewed Judaism*. New York: HarperOne, 1995.

Grenn-Scott, Deborah. *Lilith's Fire: Reclaiming Our Sacred Lifeforce*. Boca Raton, FL: Universal Publishers, 2000.

Hadaczek, Karol. "*La colonie industrielle de Koszylowce de l'époque énéolithique*." Gazette of Léopol, 1912.

Kalicz, N., and J. Makkay. *Die Linienbandkeramik in der grossen ungarisschen Tiefebene*. Budapest: Akademiai Kiado, 1977.

Keller, Mara Lynn. "The Eleusinian Mysteries of Demeter and Persephone: Fertility, Sexuality and Rebirth," *Journal of Feminist Studies in Religion* Spring 1988, vol. 4, no. 1.

Kynes, Sandra. *A Year of Ritual: Sabbats and Esbats for Solitaries and Covens*. St Paul, MN: Llewellyn Publications, 2004.

Lerner, Gerda. *The Creation of Patriarchy*. New York: Oxford University Press, 1987.

Meador, Betty De Shong. *Inanna, Lady of Largest Heart: Poems of the Sumerian High Priestess Enheduanna.* Austin, TX: University of Texas Press, 2001.

Monaghan, Patricia. *The Goddess Companion: Daily Meditations on the Feminine Spirit.* St Paul, MN: Llewellyn Publications, 1999.

____. *The Goddess Path: Myths, Invocations, and Rituals.* St. Paul, MN: Llewellyn Publications, 1999.

____. *The New Book of Goddesses and Heroines.* 3rd ed. St. Paul, MN: Llewellyn Publications, 2002.

Murdock, Maureen. *The Heroine's Journey: Woman's Quest for Wholeness.* Boston: Shambhala, 1990.

Noble, Vicki. *The Double Goddess: Women Sharing Power.* Rochester, VT: Bear & Company, 2003.

Phillips, John A. *Eve: The History of an Idea.* New York: HarperCollins, 1985.

Qualls-Corbett, Nancy. *The Sacred Prostitute: Eternal Aspect of the Feminine.* Toronto, Ontario, Canada: Inner City Books, 1988.

Rigoglioso, Marguerite. "Bearing the Holy Ones." PhD diss., New College of California, 2008. UMI Dissertation Services.

Ruyle, Lydia. *Goddess Icons: Spirit Banners of the Divine Feminine.* Boulder, CO: Wovenword Press, 2002.

Sjoo, Monica, and Barbara Mor. *The Great Cosmic Mother: Rediscovering the Religion of the Earth.* New York: Harper & Row, 1987.

Starck, Marcia, and Gynne Stern. *The Dark Goddess: Dancing With the Shadow.* Berkeley: Crossing Press, 1993.

Starhawk. *The Spiral Dance: A Rebirth of the Ancient Religion of the Great Goddess: 20th Anniversary Edition.* New York: HarperOne. 1999.

____. *Truth or Dare: Encounters with Power, Authority, and Mystery.* New York: HarperOne, 1989.

Stone, Merlin. *Ancient Mirrors of Womanhood: A Treasury of Goddess and Heroine Lore from Around the World.* Boston: Beacon Press, 1991.

____. *When God Was a Woman.* New York: Mariner Books, 1978.

Tate, Karen. *Sacred Places of Goddess: 108 Destinations.* San Francisco: Consortium of Collective Consciousness Publishing, 2006.

Theocharis, Demetrios R. *Neolithic Greece*. Athens: National Bank of Greece Cultural Foundation, 1973.

Wagner, Megan. *The Sapphire Staff: Walking the Western Mystical Way*. Redwood City, CA: Veriditas Publishing, 2004.

Walker, Barbara. *The Woman's Encyclopedia of Myths and Secrets*. San Francisco: HarperSanFrancisco, 1983.

Internet Sources

"Aphrodite." Wikipedia. http://en.wikipedia.org/wiki/Aphrodite.

"The Apparitions and the Miracle." http://www.sancta.org/nical.html.

"Chronology of Events related to the Miracle." http://www.sancta.org/table.html.

"Goddess Lakshmi, Kashmir, Hindu Deities." http://www.koausa.org/Gods/God6.html.

"Hecate." Wikipedia. http://en.wikipedia.org/wiki/Hecate.

"Hecate, Theoi Greek Mythology." http://www.theioi.com/Khthonios/Hecate.html.

Hermeticusnath. "Lakshmi Magick." http://www.horusmaat.com/silverstar/silverstar8-pg19.htm.

"Ichthus / Fish Christian Symbol." catholic-saints.info. http://www.catholic-saints.info/catholic-symbols/ichthus-fish-christian-symbol.htm.

"Lakshmi." Wikipedia. http://en.wikipedia.org/wiki/Lakshmi.

"Our Lady of Guadalupe." Wikipedia. http://en.wikipedia.org/wiki/Our_Lady_of_Guadalupe.

Pattanaik, Devdutt. "Introduction to Lakshmi - The Goddess of Wealth and Fortune." Lakshmi the Hindu Goddess of Wealth. http://www.lotussculpture.com/lakshmi1.htm.

"The Warrior Maiden (Oneida)." Manataka American Indian Council. http://www.manataka.org/page66.html.

About the Author

JOY REICHARD IS the founder of Celebrate the Divine Feminine, which hosts classes, workshops and events, including "In Her Name Circles" that celebrate the many manifestations of the Divine Feminine. In her sacred women's circles, Joy uses the art, legends, myths, and "herstory" of the Goddess that have come down to us through the ages to promote female empowerment. She has a master's in Women's Spirituality and is a minister with the United Church of the Masters. Joy is also a Reiki Master, a Lightbody graduate, and has training in Spiritual Psychological.

Joy Reichard is a Certified Clinical Alchemical Hypnotherapist. She has an active Hypnotherapy practice in San Mateo, where she helps her clients make positive change by helping them develop core strengths, reinforce desired behaviors, and access inner resources. Joy also offers Reiki sessions and attunements. Joy is a member of the American Counsel of Hypnotherapy Examiners, the National Guild of Hypnotherapists, and the Alchemy Institute of Healing Arts.